Cougars of Any Color

Wilbert,
I've greatly enjoyed
getting to know such
a kindred utt spirit.
i hope this brings back
good memories!
Katy

COUGARS OF ANY COLOR

*The Integration of
University of Houston Athletics,
1964–1968*

Katherine Lopez

McFarland & Company, Inc., Publishers
Jefferson, North Carolina, and London

All photographs courtesy of *The Houstonian*

LIBRARY OF CONGRESS CATALOGUING-IN-PUBLICATION DATA

Lopez, Katherine E.
  Cougars of any color : the integration of University of Houston
athletics, 1964–1968 / Katherine Lopez.
      p.   cm.
  Includes bibliographical references and index.

  ISBN 978-0-7864-3721-4
  softcover : 50# alkaline paper ∞

    1. University of Houston — Sports — History.   2. Sports — Texas —
Houston — History.   3. Discrimination in sports — Texas — History.
4. African American athletes — History.   5. African American
athletes — Social conditions.   6. Discrimination in sports — United
States — History.   7. Sports — United States — History. [1. University
of Houston — History.] I. Title.
  GV691.U535L67   2008
  796.04'3097641411 — dc22   2008001646

British Library cataloguing data are available

Cover image: On the cover: University of Houston ballcarrier Warren McVea
in a 1966 football game against Tulsa

Manufactured in the United States of America

*McFarland & Company, Inc., Publishers
  Box 611, Jefferson, North Carolina 28640
  www.mcfarlandpub.com*

Acknowledgments

First, I wish to thank my family who stood behind me every step of the way and constantly encouraged me to keep moving forward. Secondly, a thank you to Elvin Hayes, Warren McVea, Guy V. and Dena Lewis, Bill Yeoman, and all the former athletes, coaches, and administrators who took an interest in this project and so willingly shared their memories and granted me the privilege of recounting their stories.

Table of Contents

Preface

Supporting the Cougars is not always an easy charge. They have their good days when they shine brightly and make even the most reluctant fans beam with pride; then there are the days that make the staunchest supporters wonder if their heartstrings can take the agony any longer. But that love-hate relationship is true of every team and its followers across the nation. Those are the perils of being a true sports fan. It was that unbreakable emotional connection that first led me to examine the historical significance of the University of Houston athletic program.

As a graduate student seeking a new research concentration, I decided to intertwine my doctoral training with the pastime I was most passionate about. It was a decision that brought scoffs from some but one that I knew would pay off in the long run. If I could take the fervor I had for the Cougars and apply it to the researching and writing process, I knew the result would be a work which could satisfy the academic crowd and pique the interest of the general reader at the same time. More important, it was a topic worth the three-year investment required to finish the work. Once Houston's landmark integration distinguished itself from the rest of the topics, the researching process began in earnest.

I began my research with the most obvious source — books. The limited number of works dealing with the Houston situation confirmed my suspicions that the field was wide open for new research. No serious monographs existed and the few scattered pieces of information, I could find constituted little more than an outline of the years' events. Newspapers and magazines from the local, state, regional, and national levels offered up a wealth of information about the Cougars' integration. The records on file at the University of Houston athletic department also contained interesting primary documents including student-athlete surveys, inter-office memos, and personal communications. The Special Collections department at the M.D. Anderson Library on the University of Houston campus contained many more records related to the school's integration and the racial events surrounding the athletic program's integration. The Office of the President records, along with the Board of Regents minutes, helped construct a solid picture of the administrative atmosphere during the 1960s and the attitudes toward athletic goings on.

The strongest asset would be the personal interviews and written responses from the coaches, athletes, and staff that lived through these days and events. So many of them graciously took the time to record their perspectives of the athletic program's integration and the perceptions they had as young men in a turbulent situation. Many of them went above and beyond simple interviews, keeping up with the status of the project and always leaving the lines of communication open if further questions begged to be answered. These individuals gave me no reason to doubt their sincerity or believe them to be anything but truthful. Furthermore, their recollections could be corroborated by printed sources. These men and women gave this history a first-person perspective crucial to a solid recounting of the Cougars' integration.

Once all the information had been collected and processed the project begin taking shape. Graduate seminar papers and an article in *The Houston Review* helped refine the work as colleagues and professors weighed in on the topic. They identified the holes and weak spots that needed additional attention or consideration and made certain the work never lost its historical accuracy. Although this history of the integration of athletics at UH was always intended as a public history, my readers constantly pointed out that a flowing narrative still required the highest level of research.

And thus, the work took form. It quickly grew into a dissertation and shortly thereafter into this book. The transition between the two was not too laborious and with the help of my mother's set of eyes the manuscript transformed into this final state. The process was long, but the end result provides a historically accurate recounting of the Houston Cougars' integration, which, until now, has not been covered in its entirety.

Introduction

The University of Houston has always been a fiercely independent institution. From its earliest days as a community college to its current position as one of the most diverse campuses in the nation, the school has forged its own path and made its own history. That pioneering spirit led to the creation of the athletic department in 1946 and instilled in Cougar fans and alumni an unyielding desire for national prominence. Constantly striving to overcome their underdog reputation, the Houston Cougars tried every legal means possible to win games and eventually turned toward what was considered a radical alternative: integration. Although located in the South and surrounded by the perceptions and attitudes of the pre–Civil Rights Movement era, UH charged ahead with its racial experiment, refusing to turn back regardless of the reaction. Three black athletes would be brought in during the fall of 1964 and alongside their progressive-minded teammates and coaches would change the face of southern sports. Don Chaney, Elvin Hayes, and Warren McVea signed on with Houston and made history not only on the court, but off the court.

Sadly, it is a story largely forgotten and ignored. Few in the sports world have chosen to remember the three black athletes who came to Houston that semester, pointing instead to other athletes and other programs as the impetus for racial change. Even *Sports Illustrated*, known for its dedication to athletes and their history, ignored the pioneering Cougars.[1] This book gives to those men, both black and white, the recognition long denied them. It outlines the athletic department's handling of integration, the reaction and interaction of the first black athletes, and the impact Houston's integration had on other programs in the South. The athletic program, despite the University's record of racial discrimination,

3

overcame the existing problems and developed into a dominant program which demonstrated that interracial teams were the future of college athletics. Although only one example of athletic integration, the Cougars show that through athletics, the city of Houston and its university made significant strides and forced others to recognize that integration could occur peacefully and provide benefits to all involved. The University of Houston did what other schools could not. It changed people's attitudes and mindsets, leading to racial acceptance by most people involved.

Before we jump into the account of the integration of the University of Houston's athletic program, we must take a step back to look at the history of integration. It is marked with sports legends such as Jackie Robinson, Chuck Cooper, and Jesse Owens, who stepped forward to break down racial barriers and changed many perceptions in the process. But not everyone sees in these men and others like them true racial pioneers. Not everyone believes that sports have the ability to truly transform the racial perspective of a nation. The field of history remains very much divided on the topic, disagreeing over whether athletics actually assisted integration and facilitated racial acceptance, or whether it did little more than mask the entrenchment of racism and prejudices. While the musings of ivory tower scholars may not seem relevant to the Cougars, they are essential to our bigger picture. We need to understand how historians have classified other sports teams and other athletes to know how to interpret Houston's integration.

On one side of the discussion are those historians who observe a series of changes in society as a result of athletic integration. They point first of all to the ambassador role sports played in the integration process by demonstrating the ability of black and white athletes to peacefully co-exist. E.B. Henderson, an African American sports writer during the height of athletic integration, was one of the earliest commentators on the role of sports in the struggle for racial equality. He believed and argued, as many others would, that the integration of sports would serve as the gateway for widespread racial improvement. Acknowledging that "the athletic page [was] a good advertising method for news of more serious import [than simply sport]," he used his newspaper articles to communicate the racial importance inherent in sports.[2]

When Jackie Robinson joined the Dodgers in 1947, Henderson saw the man who would bring down the existing racial tradition and prophesied that the young baseball player, if athletically successful and a model citizen even in the face of intense opposition, would chip away at the "white supremacist ideology." Although many felt Henderson overstated his case, he firmly believed that Robinson, and those who would follow, gave white society a vested interest in the success of black athletes. If Robinson did well, Dodger fans gained, and therefore his accomplishments helped them. In addition, the public nature of sports, and the media which publicized events within it, allowed enthusiasts across the nation to see the feats of Robinson and the benefits to be gained from his inclusion and the inclusion of others like him. Because of their high visibility, black athletes contributed more toward spreading tolerance and integration than any other group of individuals and could develop the civil rights cause with greater speed. Athletics would transcend sport and unite people of all races, religions, and cultures around a common cause.[3]

Henderson did not argue his point alone. As time passed, and American viewers increasingly supported integrated teams, a wider range of analysts seconded his arguments. They wrote that the integration of sports made white America more accepting of racial mixing because it placed black achievement in its best interests.[4] Sports, particularly in the South, represented more than just entertainment; it represented, to a degree, the pride and heritage of the region.[5] As a result, victory on the field translated into superiority off the field as well, and spectators supported any measure which brought their team success. When integrated teams became increasingly unbeatable, even the most stalwart whites-only owners made the decision to recruit highly touted black athletes as a solution to declining records. They and their fans then had to choose between abandoning their teams, and the heritage associated with them, because of the decision to integrate, and embracing the black athletes which could improve the teams they supported.

Historians point out that, almost invariably, the fans would put aside their prejudices and cheer for the success of their team even if it did include blacks. That desire to win led much of the general public to accept integration, and, by the early 1970s, segregated teams disappeared because the fans wanted, above all else, to remain above the competition.[6] The white community, through sports, slid slowly into racial tolerance because of its foremost desire to win on the field.[7]

Beyond those issues, sports assisted integration by linking economic benefits with desegregated teams. It demonstrated that interracial teams were of immense monetary value to white owners. As businessmen, team owners and university financiers were single-minded in their drive to increase revenues and understood that winning teams rapidly met that goal. Therefore, athletes capable of producing wins, regardless of color, became highly sought-after commodities. Scholars such as Jay Coakley point out that if "black athletes had not made the turnstiles click, the racist recruiting policies of owners and coaches would not have changed as rapidly or as completely."[8] The same theory applied to colleges and universities that needed patrons and donors to support large athletic budgets. These men knew that winning teams would not only draw more white ticket holders but also attract African American fans; the revenue generated from that new market was significant.[9] That reality made businessmen ardent supporters of integration within sport arenas and field houses and demonstrated to other industries the financial benefits of integration.[10]

Other historians identified areas where sports made inroads into sectors previously closed to the black population. They pointed out, for example, that athletics accelerated the integration of collegiate education. White colleges, with a desire to field winning teams, would desegregate their campuses to allow for bi-racial rosters and the talent they could bring. Even the staunchest white campuses with historically strong athletic programs would push the issue of integration so they could return to athletic supremacy. To them, dealing with a few blacks on campus was worth the wins teams could accumulate. Although integrated college campuses threatened to steal the brightest scholars and athletes from traditionally black colleges, even black educators believed the benefits reaped were worth the negatives.[11] They understood that sports presented the best opportunity for black youths to receive a superior education, and the majority agreed that the chance to break into the white academic world was too significant to ignore.[12]

Beyond the educational advantages integrated athletics provided, the black community saw a chance to create relationships between blacks and whites in a manner acceptable to the mainstream population. The young men and women entering the integrated colleges could show whites that the two races could co-exist peacefully on equal ground. The president of the CIAA confirmed, "Athletics can play an important part in breaking down the barriers of discrimination ... and serve as ambassadors of interracial goodwill."[13] John Washington, now an educator in the Dallas area, agreed, saying, "Athletics was a good way of breaking down some barriers. The little bit of God-given ability that I had, I took advantage of ... and all my Anglo team mates respected us. We were winners, and that brings everybody together."[14] Although the integration of college athletics did lead to the decline of the black programs, educators were willing to make the sacrifice to change the racial landscape. In the end, the African American institutions were completely correct in their assessment. Black athletes, as well as other black students, rapidly gained entrance into recently all-white universities and access to the corresponding education they provided.

Lastly, sports played an important role in integration as, like the mass demonstrations of the main civil rights movement, they forced America to directly confront its racial issues. The struggle for civil rights had been an ongoing process and although the modern movement increased its visibility, athletics made every fan personally decide where he stood on the issue. Whereas the marches and demonstrations were distant to most Americans outside of Alabama and Mississippi and other hotbeds of conflict, athletic teams were everywhere and made individuals decide if African Americans, both athletes and fans, were equal to and deserved the same opportunities as whites. Randy Roberts and James Olson argue that "more than any other dimension of American life sport had projected black people into the white consciousness ... [and] brought white people face to face with their most entrenched racial attitudes."[15] As evidenced by the proliferation of blacks within sports today, the majority set aside their prejudices and conceded that African Americans deserved equality.

While a significant portion of the literature acknowledges a link between sports and integration, an equally vocal segment sees no correlation between improved racial conditions and athletic competition. These historians insist that although blacks and whites wore the same uniform, team interaction did not inspire any fundamental changes. To them, the idea that "on the playing fields the myopia dissipates and for two or four hours fans and players unite in one common victory ... is a fallacy [Americans] ingest daily."[16] These scholars attack every contention raised by their counterparts on the other side of the issue.

First, they assert that the achievements of athletes such as Jesse Owens and Chuck Cooper, rather than prove black equality, did nothing more than give way to a new form of racism.[17] Following the rise of star black athletes, white scholars attempted to objectify the African American race in a way that would discount its equality with whites and keep it entirely subordinated. Martin Kane, a writer for *Sports Illustrated*, promoted the theory of genetic superiority, a concept which argued that blacks excelled in athletics because they were genetically inclined to do so and not because of intelligence or discipline. White athletes achieved because they worked hard to achieve on the field, but blacks, although unintelligent and lazy, achieved simply because they had the muscles and speed necessary for athletic competition.[18] This idea, accepted by the mainstream presses, suggested that blacks did not possess traits and characteristics equal to whites and therefore should not garner the same treatment off the field. The blacks athletes were little more than work horses. As explained by Harry Edwards, athletics allowed "whites who [were] inclined to be racist to affirm ... the undeniable superiority of the black athlete and on the other [hand] maintain their definitions of black people ... as lazy, shiftless, and irresponsible."[19] It was believed that they should retain their second class status despite their show of skill on the nation's fields and courts. For these reasons, historians feel sports had little overall effect on the status of blacks.

Critics also refute the claim that economic benefits convinced people of the need for complete integration. David Wiggins suggests that integrated athletics actually hindered efforts at equality. He says that "sport often serves to maintain the interests of the power elite and can be an alienating rather than integrative force."[20] The economic powers that were used the athletes as a draw, benefited from the increased revenue, yet did little to nothing to improve actual race relations. Their central concern was, and still is, the preservation of the bottom line and nothing more.[21]

The most significant dissension arises over whether sports forced audiences to confront their own racial attitudes and behaviors. Observers attest that sport does not force a confrontation but only provides an outlet for existing biases. Fans could hurl insults at opposing black players, and the behavior would be dismissed as team zealousness. It is argued that within the teams themselves, whites and blacks never overcame racial prejudices; they only learned minimal co-existence. Richard Lapchick agrees, writing, "Prejudices are unlikely to evaporate with the sweat as [different races] play together on a team."[22] Despite the substantial number of former players that insist that a genuine harmony developed, others, such as Lew Alcindor, resent the token role they assumed and the lack of racial understanding between themselves and their teammates.[23]

The same point is made in relationship to the fans. Spectators, both black and white, did not root for the team as a whole but for the member that best represented their race. Games provided an opportunity to celebrate only the players who were "a credit to their race," which only further polarized the two communities.[24] The media did little to assist complete integration. They perpetuated stereotypes, emphasized the supposed lack of black mental competency, and consistently discussed black and white athletes differently in an effort to downplay African American ascendancy.[25] Although subtle, the tactics reinforced racism and gave audiences a way to retain their prejudices.[26]

Finally, historians point to today's sports world as proof of failed integration. The fields and courts contain diverse athletes, but the coaching and managing sectors do not. Kenneth Shropshire argues that "racism is ingrained in the sports culture ... and discrimination has only moved to the front offices where 'whites only' ideologies remain."[27] These commentators maintain that nothing has changed in or through sports, and, even after the sixty-plus years since Jackie Robinson's landmark integration, athletic teams remain, in practice, segregated.[28]

With all the debate swirling around, it is difficult to determine the exact truth. Sports absolutely facilitated desegregation in certain instances and lessened the gap between the races. It clearly opened doors for African American athletes and allowed them to enter areas of society they could not have entered otherwise. Black and white fans mingled and had a shared objective. But the process was far from perfect, and, as pointed out in the literature, issues did, and still do, arise which led to further inequality. Some athletes were objectified and used for the gain of others without receiving equal benefits. We must conclude therefore that any comment on the connection between sport and racial equality must be adjusted on a case-by-case basis. Each team and program must be individually examined before judgment can be passed on whether it eased or hindered race relations. The following examination of the University of Houston athletic program's integration will do just that.

1

UH Integration: A Fait Accompli

The University of Houston began as a community college in 1927 with a mission to provide an education to the middle class population previously unaddressed by the larger state colleges.[1] It made courses as affordable and convenient as possible, but, as was common in white institutions of the time, that desire to educate did not extend to the minority populations of Houston. The founder and primary benefactor Hugh Roy Cullen, a highly successfully oil man considered the "Father of the University of Houston" because of his large monetary donations, had a strong vision of who would and would not attend the institution he helped found and emphatically expressed that view, saying, "No nigger will ever set foot on this campus."[2] The Office of Admissions, following Cullen's directive, kindly rejected black applicants which resulted in little fanfare or challenge.[3] Non-whites understood the educational doors did not open for them and rarely even applied for admission.[4] That stance would serve as the official policy of the University for the next thirty-five years despite the *Brown v. Board of Education* (1954) ruling and the strong push for integration which grew increasingly vocal during the late 1950s and early 1960s. Not until the summer of 1962, after the death of Cullen in 1957, did the Board of Regents acquiesce and grant African American students admission to the campus. Even then, only a few unquestionably qualified graduate students enrolled.

So, what actually went into integrating classes at the University of Houston and what were the administration's opinions on the process? Did the president and Board of Regents truly support the move or did a need for state funding override any ideological objections to racial mixing? What other attempts at integration were made, and what prevented those efforts from transforming into policy? Although the University-wide integration may appear unrelated to the integration of the athletic program, the administrative debate grants insight into the racial environment of the campus and the administration that oversaw it.

In the years prior to *Brown v. Board*, colleges and universities across the South had few problems with African American students trying to penetrate the black/white barrier. Certain challenges to the "separate but equal" had surfaced, but overall segregationist practices were viewed as acceptable solutions to the question of racial interaction.[5] When the Supreme Court removed that safeguard, universities scrambled to understand what immediate changes had to occur on their campuses. The *Brown v. Board* guideline, a long time bulwark of racial segregation, now provided no assurances of protection, and the racial issue would be faced head on whether anyone wanted to or not. Several southern universities including the University of Texas, Louisiana State University, University of Oklahoma, University of Kentucky, and North Texas State University (University of North Texas) chose to comply with the ruling sooner rather than later and changed their admission policies with remarkable speed. Although limited in nature and still a far cry from wholesale equality in education, the changes did allow black students access to education and therefore complied with government regulations.

Institutions more entrenched in their racial boundaries, however, opted to stall any policy revisions and wait for direct legal orders to comply with the Supreme Court ruling. The University of Houston, like the majority of its southern counterparts, decided to avoid immediate integration in favor of a more tempered response. The presence of the all-black college Texas Southern University (TSU), located within walking distance of campus, buffered against any immediate challenges and granted Houston time to consider the correct policy. African American students had their academic needs met by the historically-black institution and therefore did not legally challenge the continued policy of segregation at the University of Houston. Despite the decision to remain segregated and the lack of widespread protest as a result of the policy, much debate did arise in the years following the landmark case and demonstrated a level of division among the administration and staff.

1. UH Integration

The integration debate on Houston's official policy began on 31 August 1955. With the press showing increased interest in the matter and black organizations more aggressively questioning admission policies, the school's president, Andrew Davis (A.D.) Bruce, formed a confidential exploratory committee to study the integration dilemma.[6] This group, comprised of ranking members of the University community had the task of studying the racial issue and determining what, if any, existing policies needed immediate attention to circumvent legal ramifications.[7] The committee examined the problem with great detail over the next six months and presented its findings to President Bruce by the end of February 1956. That two-page report, surprisingly small considering the severity of the matter and the time devoted to the study, recommended the use of stall tactics to prevent immediate integration even though it could lead to legal trouble. It further suggested that although legal council advised otherwise and the local African American newspaper *The Informer* threatened to bring forward a test case, all black applications already in house should receive the standard non-committal response which read, "No Negro has been admitted to the University of Houston."[8] In summation, the panel advised a continuation of the discriminatory policy in existence since the foundation of the University regardless of the legal responsibility it possessed.

Within a day of this report reaching the President's office, a new, more expansive committee formed to examine the issue further. Perhaps because of the brevity of the first report, or perhaps because he did not trust the advice of a small three member panel, Bruce quickly commissioned a new group to examine the issue. Also confidential in nature, the second panel included a larger number of faculty and staff to help provide a more diversified opinion. From the beginning, the committee ardently defended its strong southern ideals and ties to the established way of living. They wanted the UH community to know that they were not radicals looking to overturn the existing racial hierarchy on principle. All members possessed a southern and Texan heritage and let the public know upfront to prevent any controversy over its recommendation; warding off critics before they reared their heads was of greatest importance. If committee members ultimately recommended integration, they wanted it clearly stated that northern sympathies did not influence the decision.

The group approached the assignment more methodically than its predecessor and began by detailing the current status of integration throughout the nation. Members outlined which schools had already transitioned, what problems developed, what moral/ethical responsibilities existed, and what potential threats integration posed to the daily activities of the University. Although more thorough, the committee spent only a little over a month, a significantly smaller amount of time than the first group, considering the situation before presenting the complete report on 16 March 1956.

The findings and recommendations of the committee were quite specific. The University of Houston should integrate immediately and quietly with as little media attention as possible. Qualified African American graduate students could join the existing student population with considerable ease, and UH would have a "relatively quiet, dignified transition to integration."[9] The report contained numerous supporting facts. First, integration served as a prerequisite for the increased state funding the financially strapped University was actively trying to secure. Although already a four-year institution, Houston had yet to benefit from full state support and acquiring the designation of a state school ranked high on everyone's list of goals.[10] If Houston hoped to rise to the same academic level as institutions such as the University of Texas, integration would need to occur. Secondly, the committee feared the removal or withholding of academic accreditation because of continued segregation. Committee members pointed to the integration requirements of academic societies such as the American Association of Law Schools and unless it could demonstrate integrated facilities, the University would not qualify for membership in these and other similar organizations. The University of Houston had worked too hard establishing its academic credentials to lose its reputation over an issue such as integration.

Additionally, the committee expressed concern for the University's public image. On the one side, it desperately wanted to avoid any negative publicity from a segregation lawsuit and, on the other, hoped to gain a level of goodwill from the black community and progressive whites by integrating voluntarily. If integration occurred without legal intervention, the school could benefit tremendously from an otherwise difficult situation. If the University stalled, an ugly legal battle and public outcry could sink the school. Members of the committee saw an ideal opportunity to garner additional support from previously alienated segments of the population and hoped to take advantage of it.

In addition to the educational repercussions, the exploratory committee looked into the potential reaction of the student body and discovered a surprising response. On the whole, it determined that student opinion supported the issue of integration. While students clearly preferred maintaining the status quo, the majority would support desegregation when instituted. An additional report from the Dean of Men, J.E. Williamson, noted that racial mixing already occurred both on and off campus. For instance, the campus library allowed blacks to check out materials, athletic as well as academic teams played integrated squads, and campus organizations mingled with African American students from sister schools. He also pointed to an instance where UH and TSU students traveled together to a conference outside the city limits without personal incident His report did note that the interracial group encountered an "embarrassing situation arising at a drive-in en route when they stopped for refreshments. A waitress refused to serve the mixed group in the car" but that the group simply left the establishment without further issue.[11] The substantial level of black/white interaction which already occurred gave the administration reason to believe that full integration would cause no disruption.

Even with the majority of students demonstrating a relatively progressive view of race relations, the committee did identify small pockets of potential unrest. A few white students threatened to withdraw from the University, but even then, they did so because TSU provided a less expensive alternative to UH course work. If both schools offered an integrated environment, the cheaper of the two made the most sense financially for certain white students.

Despite the possibility of minor objections, the faculty members argued that the "overwhelming majority would support gradual integration" and that informing student leaders of the changes in advance would alleviate any major objections. Furthermore, the faculty would raise no objections over the presence of black students in their classrooms and would educate black and white students without distinction.[12] According to the findings, the University of Houston community appeared ready to surrender its "whites only" status should the administration move in that direction. Integration would proceed smoothly and without the unsettling level of disturbance seen elsewhere.

While his committee suggested otherwise, A.D. Bruce informed the Board of Regents on 12 June 1956 that the University would not immediately comply with the integration order.[13] His justification for the decision was relatively simple; integration was not as pertinent of an issue as asserted by either the committee or the public at large. He believed that the political season had severely inflamed the issue, and it served only as a point of political contention during the 1956 presidential election rather than a true issue affecting American life. Throughout the nation, Democrats and Republicans were jockeying for votes, and Bruce believed they used integration to accomplish that objective. Additionally, he argued that desegregation had not progressed to the level claimed by the nation's progressive population. The UH President asserted that certain highly publicized locales had made the transition, but those few examples did not qualify as the majority of society. He made this clear, commenting, "I do not feel that integration has progressed to the extent we first thought, and ... [the] political year [has made] it difficult to get a clear picture of the real problem."[14]

Secondly, Bruce felt that any national trend toward integration had stalled out and a step by the University in that direction would place it unnecessarily in the foreground of the fray. He insisted that "with the nation as a whole holding this matter in abeyance ... the young University of Houston should [not] take the lead in integrating."[15] This was not, in his estimation, the time for the University, already struggling with budgetary limitations and accreditation hurdles, to take a stand on an issue which had the potential to incite unrest and negative publicity. He would ensure his institution would not falter because of the volatile subject of integration. Although in direct contrast to the committee's recommendation, Bruce's policy was accepted by the Board of Regents. The President's decision, labeled as "wise in light of current events," gained unanimous approval and went into effect.[16]

Interestingly, the president made a point of discounting the role of personal racism in the decision. He included a note within the Board minutes which insisted the move away from integration was made "purely from a public relations viewpoint and what [was] best for the University, and not because of any prejudices or racial feelings in the matter."[17] Like Pontius Pilate, A.D. Bruce washed his hands of the matter and declared himself clean. He wanted to ensure that history would not remember him as a racist administrator unwilling to provide an education to all qualified but as a president solely concerned with the right path for the University. The administration agreed to remain segregated yet tried to convince itself and others that no personal racism influenced the retention of segregation.

Although he felt his decision served the best interest of the University of Houston, Bruce must have considered the ramifications of ignoring the Supreme Court ruling. The University could have found itself in the middle of a legal and public opinion battle over segregation which would have brought UH to its knees. Nevertheless, Bruce and the Board went ahead with their plans. They must have been certain that such an event would not occur and comforted by the unlikelihood of any serious challenges arising.

Fortunately for the administration, the black applicants seeking admission in the summer/fall of 1956 did not appear willing to take the matter to a higher legal authority and accepted rejection with surprising docility. One rebuffed student responded to the registrar's office that she "desire[d] no fanfare with respect to the application" and did not pursue her enrollment further.[18] Houston also minimalized the threat by misleading applicants in an effort to stem any outright challenges. The school simply implied that change would occur in the near future as to dissuade those interested in changing the system. Instead of the previously used response, rejection letters subsequently read, "If there are several highly qualified candidates for advanced degrees who would be willing to approach this delicate problem in a joint spirit of cooperation and finesse, it might be appropriate for them to meet with me personally to discuss the matter in some detail."[19] Of course, no discussions materialized, and these applicants disappeared from the picture. Other African American hopefuls, deemed academically unqualified, received letters of rejection which omitted any reference to race. In doing so, the Registrar's office effectively curbed any legal trouble.

Perhaps more importantly, Texas Southern University showed itself extremely willing to help its sister campus dispose of any potential problems. When two black students sought admission to UH because the courses they needed were unavailable at TSU, the TSU administration scrambled to establish the needed class so UH could avoid integration.[20] When the courses re-appeared on TSU's schedule, the black students willingly abandoned efforts to integrate Houston. This relationship helped Houston bypass integration on numerous occasions. Ultimately though, the President and Board of Regents recognized that by not moving forward with desegregation the possibility of legal action would always exist.[21] They felt, however, that protecting the University's image outweighed the threat of a lawsuit. If a suit arose, the school's legal council would handle it as positively as possible.

The decision to ignore integration communicates much about the underlying racial attitude of the administration. Neither the president nor the influential members of the University believed the moral weight of desegregation heavy enough to affect change and refused to lead the way in the pursuit of racial equality. They had a legal responsibility to integrate, a recommendation from the faculty committee to go forward with the process, and a campus community seemingly accepting of the transition. Furthermore, the limitations in place, including high tuition rates and stiff academic requirements, would ensure that even with integration black enrollees would not deluge the campus or constitute the majority. No spoken reason existed to avoid compliance yet, in spite of all the factors encouraging the change, the campus would remain segregated. The Board of Regents and President had no legitimate reason to delay integration, and therefore we must conclude that racial perceptions and prejudices did influence the decision. Ultimately, segregation remained because the majority of the administration desired that type of institution. This stance is a remarkable when contrasted against the integration which took place almost a decade later. Whereas the "young University" would not take the lead in 1956, it would set the pace for athletic integration by accepting black athletes well ahead of its contemporaries. The racial tone of the school would change dramatically within the next decade but not until the University experienced a change in leadership.

Although history cannot justify the decision to remain a segregated campus, perhaps it should at least acknowledge the circumstances surrounding President Bruce. To begin with, the University of Houston was indisputably a young school in a market dominated by the larger state institutions, and any unwelcome publicity could potentially destroy the small strides made in the thirty years since its formation. Bruce, as the president, had a responsibility to ensure the viability of the school, and it is possible that he sincerely believed such a step would cause irreparable damage.

Additionally, the school's primary benefactor Hugh Cullen held much influence over the University of Houston and remained heavily involved in its day to day operations. As the "Father of UH," Cullen contributed considerable amounts of money to the University and was vital to its fiscal solvency.[22] The loss of his support could severely handicap the budget, and Bruce might have been concerned that integration would upset the man who was the lifeblood of the University. Cullen made his racial prejudices perfectly clear and going against those wishes could have untold consequences. State funding would cover the budget needs, but it was not a certainty yet and, even if gained, could be years before state dollars entered the school's bankrolls. Therefore, we must at least consider that Bruce acted out of monetary necessity.

Moreover, Bruce did not show himself completely adverse to integration as he never hindered the interaction of whites and blacks in the University setting. Under his watch, the University of Houston did interact with African Americans in several different settings. It had a friendly working relationship with TSU, allowed its teams to participate in interracial athletic competitions and compete against segregated academic teams, and its students frequently kept company with African American organizations.[23] It appeared, at least on a surface level, that Bruce had little problem with those of other races. As influential as the detracting forces might have been, however, Bruce still had a significant number of faculty and administration who would have backed him, and he had a responsibility to make the correct choice on integration.

Because no direct challenges arose, the campus continued on as it had since its formation without incident. UH showed no propensity to take that important step toward racial equality until 1962 when a more forward thinking individual took control of the University and its integration policy. Dr. Philip G. Hoffman, who served as vice president under Bruce for almost ten years, assumed the office in 1961 and inherited the uncertain racial situation from his predecessor.[24] Although the segregated campus did not cause any turmoil prior to his appointment, the landscape had changed significantly in the preceding months. The Board, eager to end the financial woes plaguing the budget, had voted to seek the status of a state school, and the legislature had passed legislation to make it so in the fall of 1963. To make the step official and finally attain the state finances so desperately needed, the University would have to comply with state regulated integration policies. Hoffman knew that if UH was going to successfully jump from a small community school to a state-supported institution, the issue of integration would have to be broached once again. In addition, he knew that the University had tested the limits of Brown's "all deliberate speed" for far too long, and the probability of negative legal action increased exponentially with each passing semester. The 1956 committee recommended integration, and Hoffman and his staff knew change was inevitable. From the records, it is unclear whether the President raised

Dr. Philip G. Hoffman, University of Houston president (1961–1977).

the issue again of his own volition or because of pressure from elsewhere, but regardless it appeared on the agenda soon after his inauguration.

The first mention of limited desegregation appeared on 13 December 1961 when a newspaper clipping, an editorial piece from Dallas-based African American newspaper *The Dallas Express*, drew attention to the University's admission policy and passed through the President's office.[25] In it, the school was lambasted for its "absence of freedom" and for main-

20

taining a "barrier of color against American Negro citizens."[26] The author concluded by calling on the school, as well as other segregationists, to become "patriotic enough to join in making [the U.S.] truly a land of the free.'" Although this may not have influenced Hoffman's interest in integration, within the next month he requested and received a registrar's report on the status of applications from black students.[27] He was informed that one hundred eighty seven African American students had approached the school about admission, and, with the arrival of state-supported status, that number would increase significantly.[28] The report clearly affected Hoffman's stance because within a week of that memo he met with the Executive Board of Regents to discuss a program for immediate integration.

Emphasizing that the University was not under any immediate pressure, he informed the Board of his desire to "affect voluntary, quiet token integration" before its mandatory implementation in 1963. He asked that the step occur with "as little discussion as possible and with no publicity" beginning with certain governmental programs held on campus each summer.[29] Since the courses were technically an extension of the government rather than the University, objections to UH integration would be limited, yet the campus could acclimate to a black-white environment. The summer integration would then give way to the integration of the graduate program in the fall. Hoffman did not, however, intend to keep the process limited to the graduate level, and he made clear his desire to include undergraduate students in the process. Wanting to advance the position of the University, he aimed for complete integration believing the process should commence and conclude as quickly as possible so the school could turn its attention to more pertinent academic issues.

Had the Board of Regents not expressed concern over the proposed changes, complete desegregation would most likely have occurred in the summer of 1962. The Regents, although willing to acquiesce on graduate education, did not approve of full integration at such an early time. They felt a University-wide desegregation would overburden the students and faculty and requested a gradual process instead. To ease their concerns, Hoffman scaled back his plan and promised to shelve the integration of the undergraduate program at that time. Furthermore, he assured them that the number of blacks enrolling would be kept in check by a tuition six hundred times more expensive that of neighboring TSU and the excessively high academic requirements.[30] He also agreed that the admissions office would not actively solicit African American students to insure a smaller number of interested individuals would apply. Only those directly requesting admittance would receive information or consideration. At the start, integration would remain extremely limited because, after all, some integration was still better than complete segregation. Considering the president's adjustments appropriate, the Board approved the integration plan. Palmer Hutcheson, one of the prominent Regents, remarked of Hoffman's plans, "I can't tell you how much this means to me, that you have come to this decision on your own, openly, fairly, and squarely, and although we all knew this was inevitable your facing it the way you have without pressure is most rewarding to me."[31] It appeared as though Hoffman had caved in and embraced the philosophy of the Regents. But, perhaps he knew using the back door to accomplish integration would be just as effective as kicking down the front one. The Board of Regents and President Hoffman subsequently agreed that an integrated campus, even if only partly so, served the University's best interest and moved forward.

With these guidelines defined, the University set upon the path to integration. Although all approved of the move, they made a conscious decision not to formulate a formal policy to avoid any publicity which might stir up resentment. Even though his Board offered to pen one, Hoffman turned down the offer because he had "the benefit of their views, and with their permission, he would operate along the lines discussed and not put it on the basis of a formal motion or a new policy."[32] The process would begin in the summer of that year without any public record of its happening.

Despite the unanimous approval, Hoffman knew that racial adjustments would not occur easily and could evoke negative responses from the community. Entrenched racial attitudes would not be nonchalantly dismissed, and the chance of student protest and outrage had to be treated as a real possibility. Whites, used to the Southern way of life, often viewed any steps toward integration as a threat to their supremacy and aggressively disrupted the process. In light of that, Hoffman and his staff prepared for the protests of the surrounding community. Hoffman had the benefit of viewing the mistakes of other southern institutions, such as Ole

Miss, and had some idea of which actions to avoid, but, nevertheless, the University of Houston had a potentially treacherous road ahead.

To abate the possibility of violence, Hoffman took the initiative and called a meeting with black and white local leaders to discuss the best way to handle the situation. He told this group of fifteen which included newspaper editors and television and radio managers that the University would, without question, be integrated. The only issue unresolved was whether it would proceed "quietly or ... [similar] to something that resembled Mississippi or Alabama."[33] They, as the leaders of the community and the press, would decide which route the school would follow. After a discussion, "everyone there agreed that it was best to integrate the University peacefully.... The University [would] integrate quietly, and that is all there was to it."[34] When the integration actually occurred, it went forward without incident.[35] No students protested, overall enrollment numbers did not decrease, and campus life continued without interruption. Additionally, financial contributions, extremely necessary for a school not yet privy to heavy state funding, did not decrease and annual giving remained the same.[36]

The admittance of graduate students went so smoothly that those same plans extended to the undergraduate level in the fall of 1963. With the larger integration, President Hoffman wrote a formal policy to receive approval from the Board of Regents. It read, "The University of Houston, as a final stage in its continuing study of integration, will now accept qualified colored students at all levels. This follows the successful completion of earlier stages in which colored students were first accepted at the graduate level."[37] As in the previous integration attempt, this statement did not make it into the public hands in an effort to continue a quiet integration. The desegregation of the undergraduate program was, as was the graduate level integration, a non-event for the school. The community, accepting the necessity of these decisions, followed Hoffman's lead, refusing to agitate the situation. Students made no demonstrative protests, enrollment increased 131 percent from 1961 to 1971, and by the end of the 1963 fall semester the process was deemed complete.[38]

The school took great pride in the course of events. It commented, "Integration has been achieved here in a manner fair and equitable to all concerned."[39] UH also recognized the role the community played in the smooth transition as Houston's citizens refused to make an issue out of integration. Hoffman applauded community leaders for their "help and understanding in resolving what could have been a very complex problem." The integration truly came to completion in 1969 when the policy was publicized to the press and general public. The statement explained the tardy announcement as an attempt to shield the first black students from "any fanfare" which would draw undesired attention to an already tense situation.[40] It further described the process undertaken, the results seen on campus, and the growth of the black student population since 1962.[41] Through the cooperation of the university faculty, staff, students, and the city community, the University of Houston became an integrated campus offering an education to all regardless of color.

Although declared resolved, certain exclusions remained. As was common in southern environments, black students could not participate in extracurricular activities, including athletics, could not freely interact with white students in all campus facilities, including restrictions placed on integrated residence halls, and not a single African American student received an academic scholarship or financial aide.[42] But even those restrictions which limited actual racial interaction primarily to the classrooms would disappear soon. By the fall of 1964, the athletic department and residence halls became accessible to black students. These changes led to an increased number of African American students, and, by November 1966, the University of Houston would have more than four hundred black students enrolled, equally mixed between graduate and undergraduate students. Few other non-black colleges in the state had more.[43] Houston quickly made up for its late start.

Whereas the first integration debate yielded no change, the second mention of it demonstrated an administration willing to take the measures necessary to bring racial equality to the forefront. Although small in scale and by no means pioneering, the policy change signaled a new stage in the school's history. The University of Houston was finally integrated because it was the correct moral choice. Hoffman commented in later years that he pushed for the changes because "it made good sense politically and, more importantly, it was the right thing to do."[44] Unlike those motivated to integrate by economic or legal factors, Hoffman acted on his conscious and because of that deserves history's praise. Granted, the position of the

University had changed much in five years as Cullen had died, removing him from involvement in the school's business, and the status of state-school had been gained, which relieved much of the financial pressure. Still, Hoffman had no guarantee that a backlash would not occur and nevertheless pushed the issue forward. He placed the University of Houston on the path to complete racial integration. Hoffman, in breaking ranks with his predecessors placed a prime importance on educational access and worked to bring it to his institution.

The question remains then, what conclusions can one draw about the racial environment of the University, both from an administrative and student population standpoint? At worst, we can say the school was a typical southern institution beset by the attitudes and prejudices that dictated southern life. In the years immediately following *Brown v. Board*, A.D. Bruce and his contemporaries did delay the process, but they did not conduct themselves any differently than most others of their time. The administration and the school embraced the prevalent southern attitudes and behaved as one would expect. Houston was not any more or less threatening to African Americans than any other university.

At best, however, it was a relatively progressive place which pursued racial equality even when not forced to do so. There did exist, even at that early time, a segment which responded in a racially progressive way suggesting desegregation although not required by law or by threat of suit. The members of the larger exploratory committee weighed all the pros and cons and still believed integration a necessary event and even when overruled certain faculty members continued to push for the process. Thus, although still adherent to a policy of discrimination, the school did possess a few within its ranks which demonstrated a desire for racial equality. The marginal support for desegregation, rather than decline with defeat, grew substantially within the next few years. Those supportive of integration created the foundation for integration and would provide substantial support when it finally came.

Hoffman, in replacing Bruce, strove to implement desegregation almost immediately.[45] He not only pushed integration through but he managed to do so in a manner which made all involved, both black and white, comfortable. Although the school's racial experiment began slowly with a recalcitrant leadership, it quickly gained ground surpassing those institutions which began the process decades earlier. It would be this administration and city which would deal with the integrated teams fielded in the fall of the next year, and they proved themselves willing, perhaps more so than other cities, to accept such racial change.

The University of Houston community demonstrated an ability not only to accept black students but embrace them as well, and this attitude would carry over into the athletic fields. When three African American athletes, Don Chaney, Elvin Hayes, and Warren McVea, agreed to attend and play for the University, they had the backing of an administration willing to stand by racial progress. Even if the students and fans disliked the black athletes, those players would at least have the support of those running the University. But the integration of the athletic teams was still not a fait accompli. No one knew if integrated teams could work in the South, as thus far no major institution attempted it. Houston would not let that uncertainty keep it from pursuing the integration of its programs and made the decision to go forward just a little over a year after the undergraduate desegregation.

2

Rogue Athletics

Hugh Cullen made a commitment to the university's athletic program from the beginning. He believed that "an excellent athletic program [went] hand in hand with academic excellence," and he bestowed millions of dollars to start the program and see it grow.[1] In 1946, just eleven years after the school changed from a community college into a full four year university, the move toward fulfilling Cullen's desire for athletics began in earnest. A group of students, including the late Jack Valenti, future president of Motion Picture Association of America, successfully petitioned the administration to put together a small program.[2] The school's financial supporters, the administration, the alumni, and the students were all on board and with large contributions from Cullen and his son-in-law Corbin Robertson, the school started on its quest for prominence in sports.[3] The Houston Cougars were born.[4]

Diminutive and financially strapped by a first year budget of only $6.27, the department slowly began working within its resources to line up opponents and bring home victories. The program purchased used goods from Ellington Airforce Base, including football pads and worn footballs and baseballs, and rented second-rate facilities, but a vision had formed, and the school was on its way to developing a solid athletic program.[5] The first athletic director Harry Fouke felt that the "the athletic program should be of the same caliber as the total university" and worked tirelessly to find new sources of funding and support to bring the program up to the level of the other state schools.[6] Fouke knew what a good athletic program could do for a young school, saying, "The total recognition of the University is certainly not due to athletics.... It would be foolish to make that claim since no institution of higher learning should be measured on the basis of the success of its athletic program.... But, it would be equally short-sighted not to recognize the part that the athletic program plays in molding public opinion about the university."[7] He would take up the athletic cause and find a way to make it strong. Determined, he began climbing the athletic ladder.

The transition from a young program to a powerhouse did not prove as easy as many first thought it would be. With few financial resources and a conference membership in the less than spectacular Lone Star Conference (LSC), the Houston Cougars slowly trudged through second tier opponents, less than stellar facilities, and small scale victories. They matched up against institutions such as Sam Houston State University, East Texas University, and Stephen F. Austin University, none of which sparked the interest of sport enthusiasts or brought in the casual fan. During those first years, the school won with some regularity but its conference affiliation only allowed for so much success. Few cared much about victories over the likes of East Texas. The program was further damaged by a lack of facilities. It had to pay rental fees to use Rice Stadium and the Houston Independent School District's Del Mar gym and the cost of those venues offset any revenue pulled in.[8] If the Cougars ever hoped to achieve athletic greatness, they would have to find a way to get into a stronger conference and acquire their own facilities.

Fouke understood all those limitations and knew that Houston could not stay in the Lone Star Conference for long. He declared from the beginning that "as fast as [the Cougars] could get bigger and better, [they would] be moving out."[9] Hardly in position to bargain during those early years, Houston always made its bigger ambitions known. It would find a way to join the elite ranks through whatever means necessary, even if that meant rapidly jumping from one conference to another. AD Fouke had no qualms about that tactic and changed conference affiliations three times in the next six years. In 1951, Houston finally settled on the Missouri Valley Conference where it would remain until 1960. Even though it was not a long term solution to the need for a solid conference affiliation, the MVC at least allowed for a little better competition and slightly increased revenues. It was a good mid-major conference, and Houston would thrive in it at least for a few years.

While Houston would stay put in the MVC for almost a decade, the main goal remained admission into the state's most elite conference, the Southwest Conference (SWC). Organized in 1914, the SWC included University of Texas, Texas A&M University, Baylor University, the University of Arkansas, the University of Oklahoma, Oklahoma A&M (now Oklahoma State) University, Rice University, Southern Methodist University, Texas Christian University, and Texas Technological University (now Texas Tech). The conference had more funding, better competition, and press coverage unequaled anywhere in the South. UH set its sights on the SWC and made admission its central goal. Fouke made inquiries into gaining admission, but pleas for inclusion for were consistently ignored, especially by the school's sister institution Rice University which had boasted a football team since 1912. In the eyes of the SWC, Houston was too young and too upstart to be included in the state's most elite conference.

Despite the rejection of the SWC, Houston found a roundabout way to play opponents larger than those in the MVC. The Cougars lined up as many of the big name schools as possible trying to claw its way out of the cellar. While UH usually came out of those games on the losing end, the recognition it gained as a result proved invaluable. It found a way to play on a higher field of competition despite the limitations of the MVC affiliation. With all of the non-conference games UH played, many began to ask why Houston did not just strike out on its own and become an independent. They pointed out that the Cougars were functioning as a *de facto* independent anyway and should just leave altogether.

Fouke refused to consider operating outside of a conference alliance. He felt that the program "needed respectability ... and going independent ... might have given [Houston] the name of 'outlaw.'"[10] Taking that step would be a huge mistake because "the day of the 'independent' [was] dead." The athletic department was determined to stay the current course and wait patiently for an opportunity to work its way up through the conference ranks. If Houston wanted to maintain credibility, it would have to follow the established protocol rather than branching out on its own.

Unfortunately, the University would soon be forced to stray from its game plan. The Missouri Valley Conference, unhappy with the increasing popularity of Houston and its constant attempts to grow more and more powerful, tried to prevent the Cougars from scheduling non-conference games. Not previously required by conference regulations, the MVC ordered Houston to immediately take on a full conference schedule leaving no room for out of conference match-ups. The head office insisted that UH had a responsibility to play every MVC member annually and did not care that it would hamstring the Cougars' game plan for gaining national recognition. It knew that if the UH program agreed to the change and surrendered its current strategy, mediocrity would quickly trap Houston and likely end all chances of moving into the SWC. If Houston stood its ground, it would be forced to become an independent.

The AD tried desperately to work out a solution acceptable to all involved, but when a compromise could not be reached UH reluctantly withdrew from the MVC conference. On June 10, 1960, Houston took the leap of faith and declared itself an independent. Fouke and the University never wanted the program to strike out on its own, but, when left with no other option, made the best choice for the future of UH athletics. The University began as an educational independent and managed to succeed without help from the state, and the athletic program could do the same. It would make a name for itself without the support of any larger conference and would either find a way to survive on its own or fold.

As was feared in years past, the school was rapidly branded as a rogue program. It made the choice to become an independent working on the outskirts of the Southwest Conference, and its reputation suffered for it. But Fouke and his department felt the risk had to be taken. The program had to function on its own, with its own agenda, looking out for its own best interest. No one else was going to do so. Given the choice, Fouke and the UH administration would rather have an official conference affiliation, but they believed the school could still find its way to credibility without one through remarkable creativity and sheer determination.

And so, Houston continued its quest to join the country's elitist programs through scheduling. The strategy proved easy at first as the larger powerhouse schools, much like today, looked for easy wins against weaker competition. Even though the Cougars usually lost, playing those established teams at least brought attention to the program. Houston might gain a reputation as a losing program, but at least it would have a reputation.

Within a short period of time, the athletic department learned that exposure would only take the program so far. As the seasons flew by, the strategy was not making any substantial headway. Neither the SWC nor its counterparts seemed any closer to including UH. In the spring of 1964, Houston had its strongest case for admission but was denied due to the underhandedness of Rice. During Houston's most solid campaign for admission, Rice agreed to serve as Houston's sponsor, which was required for admission. The only thing Rice asked was that Houston not contact any other school for sponsorship. At the last minute, the Owls backed out of their commitment suggesting that Houston belonged in a smaller conference with less competent schools. Texas A&I (Texas A&M–Kingsville), Lamar Tech, and Sam Houston State, they claimed, would be much more suitable for the Cougars.[11] Houston was left without any hope of gaining membership and with no other choice but to remain on the outskirts of the SWC for a few more years.[12] In a move called "regrettable" and the result of a "bush-league attitude," Rice intentionally foiled Houston's bid because it did not believe an upstart program belonged in the well-established SWC.[13] The Cougars were no further along than when they first began.

Facing another dead end and still operating as an independent, Houston needed to once again rethink its game plan and find another, quicker way to capture respectability. Just scheduling the bigger schools would not work any longer. It would have to begin securing wins rather than simply showing gratitude for sharing a field with the University of Texas and its cohorts. UH had to find a way to dominate the surrounding sports world and force the larger programs to accept the Cougars as a legitimate equal. Houston had to find a way to win.

At first, recruiting efforts were increased to pull in more talented players. It struggled tremendously to win even the smallest recruiting victories because the "brand name" schools with their large boosters, elite conferences, and all the associated publicity easily tied up the best of what was offered. Cougar teams were simply not winning the recruiting battles and "when it came to getting good athletes, it could be kind of embarrassing."[14] The state's talent flooded to other institutions, the press all but ignored the small school, and the losses piled up while the big wins proved evasive. All of these factors combined to put a strain on the school's already tight finances, and the Board of Regents began questioning whether the benefits received exceeded or even offset the budgetary stress caused. Unable to extract themselves from the shadow of the state's bigger programs, the Cougars were willing to take chances and risks in order to create a niche in the athletic market.

The department, growing increasingly desperate to keep the programs alive tried a series of changes to revitalize the situation, including an influx of new coaches, but a spot among the state's elite programs seemed as though it would never present itself. Fortunately, the men's basketball coach, Guy V. Lewis, and his football counterpart, William (Bill) Yeoman, had a solid vision for their programs and knew what would pull their respective teams out of the doldrums: integration. The two Cougar coaches understood what other Southern coaches did not; recruiting highly talented African-American players would take even the most mediocre of programs to the pinnacle of any conference. Although a radical step for a school located in a town very much steeped in the racial attitudes prevalent throughout the South, neither coach was ideologically opposed to integration and had no problem treating black individuals as equals. If Houston could recruit from the wealth of athletes unwelcome in the South, the teams could realistically match up against their competition.

The majority of collegiate programs below the Mason Dixon line, including the proudly segregated Southwest Conference, did not welcome the black athlete and that reality grew increasingly apparent as forced integration spread during the 1960s. As the level of resentment grew, those universities staunchly regulated where the African American students could and could not go on campus and ardently denied them entrance into any area of campus not mandated by law. Dormitories, social organizations, recreation centers, etc. kept restrictions on integration and let black students know that their welcome did not extend beyond the classrooms. Beyond that, Southerners viewed the playing fields as the last bastion of white supremacy and vowed that without forced compliance, athletic integration would never occur.[15] Certain exceptions to that sentiment did exist including Texas Western University (University of Texas–El Paso) and North Texas State University (University of North Texas) but those locations hardly qualified as major programs.[16] They were small institutions with small athletic programs and neither ventured into the main athletic venues nor competed for national recognition. Therefore, the only options for a southern black athlete to excel at the university level were to either settle for a small tier institution, an all-black program, or travel north to the programs which had integrated in the early part of the twentieth century. Southern African American athletes could not play close to their homes and families and, for the most part, left for the north in droves. So, in the minds of the coaches, welcoming the black athlete into the fold was a logical choice. The decision to integrate would open a crucial door for Houston.

To be perfectly clear, the turn toward integration had nothing to do with the theories of genetic superiority being volleyed around the sports world at that time. No one on staff believed that the black athletes were genetically crafted to excel athletically any more or less than white athletes. They did believe that an increased recruiting pool would have to draw in better talent. Yeoman and Lewis sensed that the large number of talented men residing throughout the South represented an untapped talent pool which Houston could monopolize. Recruiting those athletes would be significantly easier than trying to draw in the white talent which could choose from the full spectrum of programs. It was also time to end the domination of the northern schools. Lewis and Yeoman recognized that those programs consistently relieved the South of its best unwanted athletes. *Sports Illustrated* described the standard procedure writing, "Northern recruiters, their carpetbags loaded with grants-in-aid, [expected] to hop on a big ole Delta jet and come right on back, you hear, with [tremendous talent]."[17] The spectacular athletes which helped the northern powerhouses, including the University of Michigan and Ohio State University, establish themselves were not welcome in the South, and, if Houston could draw some of those players in, it could begin winning the big games and gaining the respect and financial benefits of a successful program. The athletic teams could finally accomplish their nearly twenty-year old goal of significance. It was time for the Cougars to start winning, and the athletic department knew it was time for drastic measures.

Fortunately for Houston, the school's undergraduate integration in 1963 at least allowed the discussion of athletic integration to occur. Since the student population, faculty, and university supporters had already grown accustomed to black students on campus and in the classrooms, an extension of the policy would be more likely to occur without incident. But the path was not completely open. The athletic department would still have to gain approval from the administration and convince the university community that such a move would quickly bring accolades to a program in duress. University President Philip Hoffman had shown himself open to progressive changes, and that made the coaches hopeful that the idea would garner his approval. The integration of the campus had proceeded seamlessly as the threat of violence and exaggerated demonstrations had not materialized giving the athletic department further reason to expect the best. So, the athletic department quietly began discussing the possibility of expanding the University's integration policy to include its two major sports teams: basketball and football. Once the change occurred, the possibilities would be limitless.

To the surprise of many, integration gained approval from the administration in 1964 without much fanfare. The coaching staffs had the go ahead and immediately began seeking their first African American athletes. Although approved out of desperation, the decision to integrate the Cougars' football and basketball programs revolutionized southern collegiate athletics. It brought into question the whites only policies which dominated most universities throughout the south and challenged the most basic racial attitudes. The change forced other universities to examine their segregation policies and decide how, or if, they would amend them. Ultimately, Houston's decision would force the powerhouses to decide whether they would integrate and prosper or stand firm on segregation and grow increasingly obsolete. It would be a landmark case which turned the world of the traditional, exclusively white, sports upside down in the southern region.

As influential as the UH move toward integration was to collegiate athletics, the decision also changed the city of Houston as well. It demonstrated to citizens that black and white teammates could not only share a field and a locker room but could work in tandem, as true equals, to produce tremendous results. The men of these teams and their coaches proved to themselves and others that racial perceptions and attitudes, regardless of how entrenched they may be, could change and true interracial relationships could take root. Local fans saw week in and week out that integration could work, and the Cougars' integrated sports facilities allowed them to experience that as they sat among co-mingled black and white spectators.

The process was not perfect as opponents of the decision, including some media outlets, tried to sabotage the integration through provocative reports and negative opinions. Despite those obstacles, however, Houston's desegregation radically changed race relations within the city and more importantly within the world of collegiate sports.

3

Hunting Cougars

Bill Yeoman entered the UH football program in 1961 with a mission to turn a struggling program around. A graduate of the West Point Military Academy and a former assistant at Michigan State University under established coach Duffy Daughtery, Coach Yeoman struggled for two seasons to field winning Cougar teams. He encountered some success but consistent victories proved elusive with the types of recruits signing with Houston. The team could train and practice ad nauseam, but the coach believed that without an influx of talent to his rosters, no amount of heart or discipline could overcome the physical discrepancy displayed in the on the field match-ups. "I looked around," Yeoman recalled, "and saw we just didn't have the quality of kids, they were great kids, but to beat Ole Miss, Alabama, Auburn, etc., we weren't going to get it done, and there's no sense in playing if you're not going to beat the best or [try] to be the best."[1] He knew from past coaching experience that only improved talent would provide a permanent solution to the problem and aggressively began looking for athletically endowed men willing to pass up other programs with more to offer and sign on with the University of Houston.

Unfortunately, the larger more established institutions had sufficiently locked up the white talent and tied up the recruiting inroads, so Yeoman had to find other resources for talent. His attention logically turned to the black population of the South. For some time, Yeoman had been scouting out talented African American athletes and directing them toward northern programs, especially to his former employer Michigan State. Because of the exclusion of black athletes from southern teams, "too many [black] athletes [were] going to waste," and Yeoman tried his best to help these men capitalize on their talent.[2] He convinced them that if the South would not embrace them, the North certainly would. The northern schools offered the best opportunity for achievement and an escape from the traps of the South, and the incredible success those programs experienced with the African American talent only made the step toward integration more obvious. Yeoman was certain he could win with the quality players he was funneling to the north and now it was time for Houston to capitalize on those athletes. The young coach could see the solution to Houston's ailing programs just over the horizon. Integration would solve Houston's problems.

In his push to integrate, Yeoman never claimed to be on a civil rights mission. He made clear his sole motivation was a winning Cougar squad, adamantly insisting that it was not a "great crusade" but simply an intense desire to beat the nation's best schools. Yeoman remarked, "I wanted to win football games. I would like to tell you that I thought about [the moral responsibility] and [that] there was all this pressure, but I did it to win."[3] He knew from experience that if he ever desired to achieve victories with regularity, he would have to find extremely talented men willing to pass on the larger programs and take a chance on Houston, and the African-American athletes were more likely to do so precisely because of their limited options. He had considered integration previously but the time had not been right; he could not wait any longer.

Bill Yeoman came to Houston after a stint with Michigan State. He is still the winningest coach in Cougar history (1965).

Guy V. Lewis, while not directly connected with northern programs or southern black athletes at that point in his career, also understood that drastic changes were needed within the program. He had been a part of the school's basketball program since its inception in 1946, first as a member of the University's first basketball program and subsequently as a coach, and understood with tremendous clarity the unique difficulties the University faced.[4] Though his teams achieved a greater level of success than their football counterparts and brought home a handful of conference titles over the years, they too failed to make it on the bigger scene, losing recruits and tournaments to the more established schools.[5] He wanted to make more significant strides, to make it deep into the NCAA tournament, to capture national titles, and knew that doing so would prove nearly impossible without better talent. Like Yeoman, Lewis previously passed on tremendous African American talent interested in the Cougars because of the existing policy of segregation. As his wife recounted, Lewis "wanted to integrate before with David Latin ... but [he] couldn't take him because UH (athletics) was not integrated at that time."[6] The more recruits that passed up on the Cougars, the more Lewis begged the University for the freedom to sign all qualified players. He expressed a sense of powerlessness in the process as he requested permission repeatedly yet was denied at each attempt.

When the approval finally came, Lewis took no credit for it. He said, "I can't say I was instrumental in the decision to recruit [black] athletes 'cause if I'd really been instrumental, we'd have had them long before we did."[7] But, the department placed more stock in his requests than Lewis realized, for the Information Director Ted Nance credited his efforts with nudging the integration debate to the forefront. He, along with the rest of the athletic department, understood that "a lot of things were changing in sports history," and Lewis and Yeoman emphasized to them that the University of Houston would have to move along with them to remain valid in the public eye.[8] The decision remained a year away, but the process was already in motion behind the scenes.

To be clear, both of these coaches pushed for integration because of a desire to win rather than out of any larger commitment to the civil rights crusade. They wanted to be successful badly enough to turn to alternative sources, even if that meant dealing with an upset community or unhappy opponents. That should not, however, overshadow the progressiveness they displayed during those early years. They had the ability to look past skin color in a day when few other white contemporaries could or would. Part of that stemmed from their upbringings. Yeoman, for example, was raised in Arizona and was exposed to a diverse community which included a multitude of ethnicities, and that early exposure, combined with his years at the U.S. Military Academy and time coaching in the north, gave him a unique perspective on desegregation. "I never had a problem with what people were. When I was growing up in Greendale (AZ) we had a Russian community, we had a Mexican community, a Basque community, we had a bunch of Polish.... I never ever realized that [race] was something I should pay attention to when I was growing up."[9] That early acclimation to multi-ethnic interaction prepared Yeoman for his later role in the integration. Lewis was not much different. While one might expect an east Texas upbringing to cultivate discriminatory attitudes, the young couch did not harbor those traditional sentiments. When the time came for it, no adjustment time would be necessary; both men were ready to field athletes of all colors without distinction. They would do make whatever adjustments would allow them to win.

Yeoman and Lewis gave the athletes an equal opportunity to prove themselves and to gain access to the Southern world of sport which had always been closed off to them. And, although the primary motivation was the teams' success, their sacrifice should not be overlooked. They still risked their livelihoods on an integration that may or may not produce victories. These men lived in a South not yet liberated by the successes of the Civil Rights Movement and not yet changed by the landmark national legislations. They had no guarantee that their efforts would prove successful or of the reaction of the white community, but they backed it nonetheless and were willing to invest in the players' lives even if the wins did not come. For that reason they deserve credit for their role in breaking through the athletic color barrier regardless of their stated reasons for doing so.[10]

After years of requesting racial integration without any visible headway, Yeoman decided to take control of the situation. Certain his plan of integration would work, the young coach decided not to postpone his plans any longer simply because he lacked formal University approval. He took the lead and began recruiting an African-American athlete without even informing the department of his intentions. Yeoman's logic was clear; he was not "going to get the answer [he] wanted so why ask?" No one within the administration understood the situation at Houston as intricately as he did and furthermore did not know what moves would save the struggling program. He just "wasn't really interested in listening to anybody else because [he] didn't think they understood what had to be done."[11] That is not to say that he did not comprehend the gravity of the decision. He fully understood that he was risking his career on integration, but, in his estimation, it had to be done if the expected success was to be attained. He walked into the office of Athletic Director Harry Fouke and informed him that Warren McVea was being actively recruited and would be signed if possible. He would not be deterred, and the department let the issue slide uncontested.

Lewis took a more traditional route in his quest to integrate. He discussed his plan with Fouke, who in turn took the matter up with President Phillip Hoffman.[12] The administration, in a surprisingly progressive move, agreed to the changes for both programs with no recorded resistance. Despite the almost sacred nature of southern sports and its traditional all-white status, Hoffman and others believed "the time was right and were very supportive."[13] Fouke said later, "The Board of Regents had decided to integrate the school, and [they] wanted an athletic program representative of the university."[14] The administration also shared the desire to win and ultimately decided that "winning athletic teams were more hip than *lily-white* teams," which cleared the way for Yeoman and Lewis to fully undertake the process.[15] With approval from all sides recorded, the plan went forward without hindrance, and both coaches were free to recruit the best athletes available regardless of color. At that point, the programs quickly moved to find their chosen athletes.

The University of Houston community agreed to the change, but all knew the transition would not be an easy one. Schools throughout the South did not welcome the black athlete, or for that matter blacks in general, into white society and expected segregation to continue indefinitely. It was acceptable for African American athletes to excel in the all-black colleges, specifically designed for them, or in the northern schools which had no problem with black and whites playing side by side, but Southern fields and courts were exclusively for white men. That racial viewpoint was prevalent throughout Texas as well. Yeoman recalled numerous conversations with Southwest Conference coaches where racial prejudices were openly communicated. He remembered that those "stupid oafs from some of these other schools would tell some very critical black jokes, and we'd have three black waiters standing [nearby]. I'd have to stay after and apologize for [the coaches]."[16] Yeoman and Lewis, in acting as pioneers, knew that these prevalent racial attitudes would be amplified in competition and completely understood that they would have to field the majority of dissatisfaction which would surely arise.

Wanting to ensure as smooth a process as possible, Yeoman decided against a wait and see approach and instead took a proactive stance. He called together the prominent members of the African American community, including the director of the Houston Y.M.C.A. Quentin Mease, to discuss the changes taking place on the UH campus.[17] Like Hoffman had done with the graduate school integration in 1961, Yeoman wanted the major community leaders in agreement so misunderstandings from either side would not hamper the attempt. "When we sat down and got comfortable I said, 'I want to tell you guys something right off the bat. I'm prejudiced. I'm prejudiced against bad football players.' And you know, there was a little sucking of wind through their teeth [at first], and then we all got along great."[18] Although broached with levity, Yeoman communicated to these men that the University of Houston was breaking rank with the other major programs in the South and granting their young athletes "an opportunity to compete with everybody" color or race excluded.[19] Even though it impeded on the territory held by neighboring all-black college Texas Southern University and threatened to strip it of its best athletes in the major sports, the leaders decided that in the end an opportunity to play on a larger stage was more important than maintaining the competitiveness of the all-black college just blocks from the Houston campus. It was time, they felt, for their young men to garner the same benefits and opportunities that white athletes had received for decades without leaving their homes completely behind. Houston offered African American athletes that chance, and the black leaders would support the process in whatever ways necessary.

Lewis and Yeoman now had the green light to proceed with recruiting from the black and white talent pools, but they would have to select their first athletes with caution. Not just any player would be able to walk into an all white environment and navigate through the tough situations that were sure to present themselves. These athletes would have to deal with teammates upset about losing playing time, with Deep South teams and fans staunchly protective of their white traditions, and opponents less than enthusiastic about sharing a field with blacks. The Cougars, in particular the newly recruited black athletes, would have to face that adversity without reaction and perform perfectly in the face of it. Additionally, their athletic talent would have to be unparalleled because the performances of those few would either bolster or destroy the attempt at integration and the coaches' careers in the process. Fans and opponents alike would judge the viability of integration based on those first recruits, and they would have a heavy part in determining whether athletic integration would flourish or flounder in the south. The pressure would surely be immense, and therefore the selection of athletes needed careful deliberation and much precision.

Yeoman nixed an earlier attempt because the right young man for the situation had yet to surface. He remembered that "there was another youngster the year before but [we] had to have a certain young man to get this done positively.... [We] had to have a guy that was sensitive about what the people around him were like, and get it done.... I would hate to bet my family on his being able to handle whatever came his way."[20] Lewis echoed those sentiments as he knew his job depended on "finding an athlete able to handle the situation with temperance."[21] With these qualifications established, the search was on for those special young men with the talent and intelligence to handle the situation properly.

Coach Lewis selected and signed his men first. Through a tip from the basketball coach of Texas Southern University, Isaac Morehead, Lewis and his coaching staff heard of two outstanding black athletes playing high school ball in Louisiana. Don Chaney and Elvin Hayes each had amazing athletic talent, led their high school teams to acclaim, and would be tremendous additions to any team.[22] Either one of these two would be incredible additions. TSU provided so much help to the Houston staff not out of friendship but out of simple self preservation. Recognizing he lacked the ability to recruit the talented duo for his own program, Morehead decided instead to keep them as far away from his competitors in the

Southwestern Athletic Conference as possible.[23] He would push the athletes away from the all-black programs to avoid defeat during conference play. Morehead reasoned at the time, "We know we can't get him so anything we can do to help [Houston] recruit him can only help our basketball program. Lord knows we didn't want to spend four years watching him come after us."[24]

With a letter of introduction from the African American coach in hand, Lewis and his assistant coach Harvey Pate went down to Louisiana to look at Hayes in Rayville and Chaney in Baton Rouge. As expected, he found two young men with incredible levels of athletic talent who consistently lifted their respective teams above the competition. With a state title and all manner of scoring records to his name, Hayes had an amazing combination of basketball skills rarely seen in a single athlete. Chaney, who Pate gushed was "a good one," also had a tremendous ability to play basketball against the best.[25]

But perhaps more importantly than any on-court feats, Lewis and Pate discovered men able to deal with difficult racial situations off the hardwood. Hayes, the more athletically celebrated of the two, came from an intensely segregated rural society where white/black interaction never occurred without negative consequences. He learned how to endure the taunts and jeers of racist whites without reaction, and that skill would be much needed to fulfill the role of pioneering athlete. Chaney came from the more metropolitan city of Baton Rouge and knew better about interaction with the white community. While race relations were by no means progressive in the state capital, Chaney did learn how to handle himself in mixed society and how to walk in between the black and white worlds. If both athletes would agree to join Lewis's Cougars, the strength of one would complement the other's weakness, and together they could meet the challenges facing them in the UH basketball program. Now Lewis and Pate had to acquire their signatures.

Despite the fact that both had verbal commitments to other universities at the time, the coaches immediately began trying to convince them that they belonged in Houston instead. The basketball program began recruiting both athletes immediately and tried desperately to convince them that Houston was the place for them.[26] The athletic department, desiring as little turbulence as possible, did not want two African American

Head Basketball Coach Guy V. Lewis and Assistant Coach Harvey Pate, 1965.

basketball players that first year, but Lewis refused to pass up on either one. The staff exhorted both Hayes and Chaney to accept the offer to play at a Division I university in the South, close to their homes and families. At Houston, they were presented with an opportunity to blaze trails in the sports world and make names for themselves in the process. Lewis knew that acquiring talent of that caliber appeared impossible to most observers but "didn't think too much then about how hard it was" and just focused on making the opportunity appear as lucrative as possible.[27] The sales pitch worked, and by mid–April Lewis had secured their signatures on scholarship offers.

As with the school's integration, the press, both black and white, did not cover the event. The two slipped quietly onto the team almost without notice, and neither the coaches nor the administration minded the unexpected silence. The campus newspaper, *The Daily Cougar*, did run a brief article on the coming of the players, but it did little more than extol their playing abilities and hype their potential contributions to the team.[28] While the football integration would bring unprecedented press coverage a few months later, the first two black basketball players came without significant comment.

At the same time, Yeoman began the search for his star athlete. Unlike Lewis, Yeoman had an idea of exactly who he wanted to sign and did not need any suggestions. He had seen and heard of an amazing running back from the San Antonio area that had been breaking school and state records in replay-worthy fashion since he began playing high school ball. Warren McVea, as a member of the Brackenridge High School team, possessed a natural talent heralded by all who watched him on the field. In his senior year alone, McVea scored 315 points, rushed for 1332 yards on 127 carries, and was selected as a member of the all-state team.[29] Contrary to his basketball counterpart, Yeoman did not discover an unknown; he sought after a phenomenon noticed by the majority of the nation's large programs. The rest of the football following country was fully aware of this young man's talent evidenced by the seventy-five plus scholarship offers he received from universities nationwide.[30] Schools from the North understood the value McVea could add to any team and the number of wins he could help tally over three years of varsity play. With the conditions in the South such as they were, all recruiters and press outlets certainly expected him to sign with an established northern school. He had too many outstanding qualities to sign with any lesser program.

Because of those factors, Yeoman, as the coach of an arguably insignificant program, had a tough fight ahead of him if he wanted to secure McVea. And want him he did, but not only for his quick feet and sharp eyes. He desired McVea on his roster because he believed the speedster had the ability to step into a potentially hostile situation and still perform as well as, or better than, expected. According to Yeoman, McVea "really had all of the things you had to have.... He was comfortable in crowds.... He could go into a room of people, and, in ten minutes, he could

tell you exactly what he could and couldn't do with every one of them....
He was a difference maker, and that's what you had to have." He knew
after speaking to the recruit for a few minutes that "he was the one to get
[integration] done."[31] Furthermore, McVea already had experience with
integrated teams as his high school squad was desegregated. He knew how
to interact with white and black team mates, how to play against segregated teams, and how to continually produce points in light of all those
issues. Yeoman knew he had found his man; he just had to find a way to
lure him away from the larger conferences which assured an abundance of
television coverage, guaranteed winning seasons, and promised teammates
already comfortable with integrated squads.

Without any of the leverage points held by the northern schools, Yeoman eagerly set about on the uphill battle to recruit McVea. He was not
deterred by the stiff challenge because he had one positive selling point
the others did not: proximity. Yeoman decided that exploiting Houston's
geographical relationship to San Antonio would be his best chance to lure
the young athlete onto his roster. When he first visited the runner in his
home, the UH coach recognized almost immediately that McVea was
incredibly close to his mother, Mattie, and eight siblings and leaving them
for a place like Michigan or California would place a significant mental
strain on him. Yeoman began working the angle, continually pointing out
that Houston was relatively close to his hometown and frequent visits to
his family would pose no problem. If, or when, he became lonely, home
was just a few short hours away. Yeoman's calculation was correct in that
McVea, despite the urging of his mother, could not bring himself to move
several states away because his homesickness always pushed him back to
the Lone Star State.[32] If he wanted to play outside of the black college system and simultaneously be close to his family, the Cougars were his best
choice. Yeoman did fear, however, that St. Mary's University, a private college in San Antonio, would revive its football program and sign the athlete he had already decided on. Luckily for him and his program, the
revival never occurred and only then did McVea seriously consider signing with Houston. Before long, he had done so and was on his way to
Texas's largest city.

In all the discussion, however, the issue of integration was only briefly
brought up. The sole mention came as Yeoman reportedly told McVea,

"We can be a first. You'll be the first Negro football star to stay home, and I'll be your coach. We'll go down the road together."[33] All understood the underlying racial issues and what would be involved in McVea's signing, but Yeoman did not dwell on the subject figuring it would not be an issue. He knew he could control his own players, removing the threat of intra-squad tensions, and, while trips through the South promised racial disruptions, he decided not to allow the possibility of such events to influence his recruiting decision. In addition, he knew that the Houston boosters completely supported the decision to bring in the star running back, a fact which would help remove or at least minimalize the presence of detractors from the situation. He said at the time, "I've never had so much pressure put on me by my McVea boosters. Hundreds ... of Houstonians have called and written me asking that I make a strong bid to sign him. I don't think he'll ever regret coming to the University of Houston. He will be welcomed by all."[34]

On 11 July 1964, McVea and Yeoman committed to each other regardless of what those surrounding them thought and were determined to make the situation work. McVea would go to Houston, face the racial challenges, and continue his stellar career with Yeoman's Cougars. The University of Houston now had the last member of its integration squad in place, but his arrival would not be treated with the same silence that greeted the basketball stars.

Unlike the signing of Hayes and Chaney, a firestorm erupted when McVea made public his decision to attend Houston. Speculation had been floating around for months as newspapers and sports writers constantly guessed and second-guessed which avenue McVea would go down. They ran exclusive after exclusive and tirelessly questioned when he would announce his decision. Newspapers followed his every move, including off court activities and injuries, and quizzed his family for hints about McVea's preference or about any impending proclamation.[35] In all the speculation though, no one realistically expected Houston to come out on top in the recruiting wars. It was too small, gained too little attention, and, perhaps most importantly, had no conference affiliation to guarantee worthy competition and recognition. Yeoman and his rogue program could not possibly gain McVea's signature. All those speculating were dead wrong.

In spite of all those seemingly significant drawbacks, McVea did select the underdog school to display his talents and announced his story through one of the local newspapers. In an exclusive, the *San Antonio Express News* first informed the watching sports world that "the long battle of bids for the football services of Warren McVea, ... the most furious scramble to sign a high school athlete Texas has ever known ... came to an end."[36] The *Houston Chronicle*, which had earlier described McVea as "a half-back with more moves than a belly dancer," followed suit the following day and reported that, "Now that [he] has signed his intention of remaining in his home state, there will be weeping and gnashing of teeth in other parts of the country, where football coaches felt they had this hipper-dipper touchdown maker signed and sealed."[37] The black presses also covered the signing with excited bylines that read, "He will help strike terror in the hearts of Cougar opponents."[38] They went further by acknowledging the financial benefits Houston would reap saying, "The Cougars will suddenly find more money in the box office every time the Cougar freshmen play a game at home."[39] Thus far, all commentators appeared surprised yet gleeful that Houston had won the recruiting battle.

Interestingly, none of the reports focused on the integration of Houston, highlighting instead only the sensational abilities of the athlete headed the Cougars' way. Neither the black nor white press questioned the racial change at hand or emphasized that Houston was the first major institution in the southern region of the nation to integrate. The decision was neither heralded or criticized; it was simply ignored as the school had hoped it would be all along. It was not looking to make any type of racial statement.

For one day, the news remained positive and upbeat about McVea's selection of a smaller, less established school to display his talents at, and it looked as though the process would proceed more smoothly in the public eye than anyone anticipated. But, less than twenty-four hours later, the situation escalated into a media nightmare for UH and McVea. The signing became a highly controversial event as certain newspapers, upset about either the integration of Houston or the refusal of McVea to choose what they considered the right school, challenged every aspect of the event and of the speedster himself. On 13 July 1963, the *San Antonio Light* ran a feature story which claimed that McVea, rather than being a prized recruit, was in reality an undesirable athlete who "had little choice when he signed to enroll at the University of Houston."[40] It claimed that McVea, because of his lack of intelligence and appalling displays of discourteousness, had to sign with Houston out of desperation because all of the Big Eight coaches had agreed to a hands off policy and withdrew their respective offers well before signing day.[41] The members of that conference, which included mostly mid-western schools including the University of Oklahoma, Oklahoma State University, and the University of Colorado, blackballed the athlete since he moved "past the realm of discourteous and was [darned] rude."[42] He made appointments and broke them without advance notice, refused to commit to any one school and kept all recruiters in the dark as to his ultimate decision. Perhaps most telling, the source said that "conference's coaches felt the loss of dignity, both for the school and the coach, would be greater than any good [they] could get from the boy's playing."[43] The alleged rudeness from a black athlete was simply too humiliating for any white coach to endure.

Finally, the article insinuated that Houston used illegal practices in their recruiting process and promised an NCAA investigation was soon to follow. At the urging of some unnamed Southwest Conference school, the paper claimed, the collegiate governing association would launch a full-scale investigation in response to the signing. Yeoman and his staff had allegedly gone beyond the realm of accepted NCAA practices by giving the running back an undisclosed amount money, a new car, a lucrative employment deal, and other illegal perks as payment for his signature on recruiting papers. After all, how else could an independent school like Houston steal a five star athlete out from under the more elite institutions? The Cougars, it predicted, would be slapped with sanctions for its illegal recruiting methods, and any visions of greatness they hoped to achieve through McVea would be short-lived. The NCAA had the authority and the ability to destroy a program overnight through sanctions and suspensions, and detractors hoped that would be the case for the newly integrated Cougars. This single story quickly snowballed into the media's biggest controversy and soon newspapers throughout the state covered the underhanded signing of Houston's first black football player.

The reason for the negative publicity is curious. When McVea was thought to be heading north, no objections surfaced. He was a polite young man with amazing talent worthy of the most elite athletic programs, and a long and prosperous career stretched out before him. When he remained in the South, however, the whole story changed.[44] Johnny Janes highlighted this change in attitude commenting that the paper considered him "the greatest bar none" when the University of Southern California was believed to be his destination. The simplest explanation, although a bit too clean, reduces the controversy to a question of professional jealously. The story-breaking *The San Antonio Express and News* scooped all other newspapers in its coverage of the decision which everyone anxiously awaited. It has been argued that the *San Antonio Light*, upset about losing the lead story to its rival, tarnished the name of the player in the center of the publicity to minimalize the importance of the news story. The negativity, therefore, was little more than sour grapes.

That explanation is not completely satisfactory. The evidence suggests that the Associated Press knew the signing was eminent and instructed news services to remain close to the story only days before it broke.[45] The *San Antonio Light* had to know the announcement was coming and could have easily matched the coverage provided by its competitor.

A far more plausible answer is rooted in the question of race. The timing of the negative remarks and the accusations levied suggests the publication of the story was racially motivated. If the newspaper had all this information, and clearly it would have to have had it well before 12 July, it could have had its own lead story well before the signing occurred. So why did editors wait until Houston won the recruiting race to publish the alleged information? Would McVea's supposed rudeness or the blackball or the payouts offered not be of interest before he had chosen a school to represent? The answer must almost certainly be attributed to race. Integrated sports programs were acceptable as long as they existed only in the North where they belonged. As soon as McVea crossed over that racial line, he ceased to be San Antonio's favorite athlete, and "their boy" became little more than a low level performer unworthy of the recognition he received. They had no use for a player who did not understand his place and challenged the whites-only system that had been in existence well before the Civil War. So, the press used the full force of its pens to denigrate McVea.

This became even more evident when it was reported that McVea's discourteousness led to the blackball. Even if true, surely these coaches had encountered white Prima Donna athletes before, but their discourteous actions never provoked a blackball. Why would rudeness from a black athlete be any different than the same behavior from a white athlete? As one columnist argued, "Maybe [McVea's alleged actions] would get bad marks from Emily Post, but breaking an appointment with a visiting coach is hardly new for avidly-sought high school athletes ... nor is it against NCAA regulations."[46] Clearly, the supposed bad behavior was only unacceptable because of McVea's color and his selection of a Southern program.

Other newspapers pushed the race issue further by pointing to the school's playing agreements with deep South universities and question whether these teams, such as Mississippi State, Auburn, and Mississippi, "which have shown a decided reluctance in the past to schedule games against integrated teams ... will react to any suggestion [that] the schools prolong their series [past 1964]."[47] The writers knew they were provoking a racial reaction from their readership and ran the pieces regardless of the negativity they would cultivate.[48] They wanted nothing more than to cause Houston trouble for its radical change.

Furthermore, why would a SWC team, none of which were even considering the player because of staunch segregation policies, spearhead the NCAA investigation? If those institutions could not recruit the player, and therefore Houston did not rob them of an athlete they wanted, why would they care where he signed or what methods were used? The only logical conclusion remains that they did not want to face integrated teams and more importantly did not want Texas football to become the new home of black athletes. Football in the South belonged to the white community alone, and that was how it should remain. *Sports Illustrated* hinted at this element of racism within the state commenting that "most of the rumors were started by rednecks, of which Texas still has many despite its plea that it is a southwestern state, as opposed to a southern one."[49] Clearly, Texas, or at least many parts of it, was not ready to accept athletic integration carte blanche.

Whether the naysayers within the newspaper staff, disgruntled about the turn of events, concocted the story of the blackball or whether a detractor, upset about losing the prized recruit to a lesser school, made up the story to punish the one that got away is uncertain. The fact remains, however, that all involved in the cloud of negativity tried to harm the heralded

African American running back for his decision to play in the South. They turned McVea's signing into a racial ruckus to prevent a smooth integration at Houston and to diminish the likelihood of other schools following suit.

As provocative as those reports were, not all members of the press reacted in such an incredulous manner. Many contemporary columnists acknowledged the attacks and questioned why McVea had suddenly received such ire from those who had praised him most not a day before. They saw in the strange turn of events a more sinister motive than simple professional jealousy. A columnist for *The San Antonio Express* wrote about the negative campaign saying of the *San Antonio Light*, "This newspaper, a part of the nation-wide Hearst chain, is throwing all its power against a 17-year-old boy, in an obvious effort to prevent this Negro boy from obtaining the education it is his right to have."[50] John Hollis of the *Houston Post* remarked scathingly, "Through all this, [he] must be a thoroughly confused and unhappy [17]-year-old boy. All he did was make an honest choice of the college he preferred to attend, stipulating his reasons at the time. And then he awoke the next morning as a middleman in a newspaper battle, a feud begun before he was born."[51] Dan Cook, the sports editor of the newspaper which ran the exclusive story of McVea's signing, was clearly upset about the scuttlebutt and grew apologetic. He said, "I wanted the story but I had no idea it would hurt the boy like this. I wouldn't have had this kind of thing happen to him for anything."[52]

Even the black newspapers, usually minimalist in their sports coverage, came to the defense of the athlete. One wrote, "The many rumors of McVea's discourtesy to coaches who were seeking his signature are utterly ridiculous."[53] Furthermore, the article commented on the racially motivated nature of the allegations writing, "Because of the color of his skin, some coaches could not understand why McVea could say no to them or could be busy when they, the "big-shot" wanted to see him." It went on to say that he was the Jackie Robinson of college football in the South, because he would have to fight the same level of racism playing the sport he loved for the team of his choosing.

With many writers coming to his defense, McVea was obviously not alone in this fight. Those members of the press he had impressed during the preceding months quickly sprung to his defense since he could not defend himself. Some of them went a step beyond defending the young man and took an offensive stance. They tried to invalidate the claim that a gentlemen's agreement, provoked by McVea's unacceptable behavior, had kept him out of the larger schools. In fact checking, writers questioned the coach of Big Eight member University of Oklahoma, Gomer Jones, about what events actually took place in the preceding days and discovered that no such "hands-off" agreement existed among the member schools. They wrote, "Jones, one of the [most] active of the would be recruiters ... refuted the broadside attack fired at the 17-year-old Negro boy ... [saying] 'we here at Oklahoma would have been happy to have signed the boy right up until the moment he signed with Houston.'"[54] The Sooner coach also refuted the alleged excessive rudeness. Jones insisted, "The boy certainly was never discourteous to our staff in any way ... We found him to be a very high type of young man."[55] Through the tenacity of other reporters, it soon became clear to most observers that the story had no substantiating evidence supporting it.

For the University's part, it had little comment choosing instead to remain above the groundless reporting. Yeoman kept comments to a minimum and simply informed the press that McVea "behaved in an exemplary fashion while he was in Houston" and tried to discount the story: "I'm sure there'll be 900 million stories started about him."[56] In regard to the recruiting violations, he adamantly asserted, as did Athletic Director Harry Fouke, "In all our recruiting we do everything we can to stay within the framework of the NCAA regulations."[57] That was the end of the story as far as they were concerned, but the contrary protestations did little to protect the university. Ultimately, the detractors were successful in harming both McVea and the University of Houston and by the end of McVea's first varsity season, the NCAA had thrown the book at Houston.

On 28 September 1964, the NCAA informed Houston that it was under investigation for recruiting and financial assistance violations. The NCAA committee, which formed only three days after McVea signed with Houston, began its investigation because of, among other things, an undisclosed athletic director's allegations and the questions raised by the press following McVea's commitment to the Cougars.[58] Among the supposed violations listed were free transportation for recruits and their families, excessive entertainment expenses on recruits, and illegal out-of-season practices. The University responded to the charges in a nearly thirty page response and disputed all of them except three. It admitted that the department provided five student athletes and one athlete's family transportation on one occasion and that the supervision of recruiting policies had been lax on occasion.[59] Despite its claims that the NCAA report was full of "many errors of fact and misconceptions," Houston's football program received a three year probation in January of 1966.[60] The NCAA penalty forbade the Cougar football team from competing in post season play and from appearing on television until the 1969 season, a year after McVea graduated. The restrictions ensured that Houston would only been seen locally and that national audiences would not be privy to the Cougars' style of football. Houston may have landed a stellar athlete, but the NCAA saw to it that few would notice.

Interestingly, none of the charges were directly related to McVea's recruitment. Despite that, a member of the violations committee announced to the press that Houston had in fact transferred funds to the highly sought after athlete and that illegal activity served as the impetus for the sanctions. Walter Byers, the executive director of the NCAA, informed the *Houston Post* that the infractions undeniably included "illicit cash payments to ... McVea."[61] Although later forced to publicly retract his statement because of blatant inaccuracy, Byers's comment ensured that the sports world would link Houston's trouble with an underhanded, illegal recruitment of Warren McVea. The program had recruited the athlete by the books, or at the very least by the same standards followed by the other collegiate institutions, but because of negative press stirred up by McVea's and Houston's detractors, the entire program was penalized.

The timing of the probation, the severity of which only three other schools in NCAA history had received, clearly shows a connection between the punishment, the integration of the program, and the charges raised by those upset with Houston disturbing the racial situation.[62] It was a probation unjustified and, as printed in *The Daily Cougar*, "The Cougars received the NCAA lashing largely because they belong to no major conference and have no large pressure group which protects the UH general welfare."[63] Those opposed to integration had seemingly succeeded in their effort to thwart the process, but Houston would prove resurgent in the coming years despite the setback. They would experience their most fruitful seasons while on probation and make a statement as to the viability of integration nonetheless. Yeoman and his restricted, integrated, Cougars would force the nation to take notice regardless.

It is interesting that the basketball program received neither the negative attention nor the probation that the football program received. It made the same racial changes as the football team and pushed the racial boundary further by bringing in two African American athletes simultaneously, yet the coming of Chaney and Hayes did not even appear on the radar. The most logical explanation lies in the relative importance of the two sports to Texas. In the South, football was the premier sport and received the majority of attention from the media and fans. Spectators lived and died by the wins and losses on the football fields and derived a strong sense of personal identity from the performance of their team. Wins equaled a sense of superiority.

Basketball, on the other hand, was not associated with Southern culture or heritage and did not evoke such a passionate response from Southerners. It clearly took a backseat to anything that happened on the gridiron, and therefore one can only assume that the discussion around basketball's integration was minimal because it was not linked to a sense of self. The arrival of Chaney and Hayes did not challenge tradition like the arrival of McVea did and subsequently did not incite a level of ire. They slipped onto the team without too much notice.

In 1964, the University of Houston athletic department allowed Yeoman and Lewis to move ahead with the integration of its two major programs without formal comment. It was a risky move but the hope of increasing public interest, expanding financial funding, and securing an invitation to a better conference made the calculated chance worthwhile. Even if the integration attempt failed and the program collapsed as a result, the fledgling program's demise would not be so earth shattering. As already noted, it had secured minor victories here and there but none significant enough to firmly root the program, and realistically, its disappearance would not accomplish anything which the Board of Regents had not already contemplated. It is not surprising then that the coaching staffs made their move to desegregate, and the University in an act of desperation allowed it. Two coaches now had the task of melting two colors into one.

4

Coach, Meet My Mother

For UH, the process of integration held the promise of the tremendous success with few drawbacks. The first African American athletes on the contrary had practically everything to lose. Products of the Jim Crow South, the black athletes were raised to respect the long entrenched racial boundaries and completely understood that free interaction with whites was not a permitted behavior. When in public, they should avoid the gaze of whites and certainly never speak to those not of the African American community unless directly confronted. Not even their stellar athletic talent could immunize them against the racism present within the lower half of the country or the rules of engagement, and thus all three minority recruits shared a common underlying goal-escaping from the South. With any luck, they would excel through sports, receive collegiate scholarships, and head north away from the epicenter of prejudice and oppression which had dominated their lives for so long, unless persuaded otherwise.

Coming to Houston in lieu of any northern locale, Hayes, Chaney, and McVea were risking their futures and their abilities to escape the lives which had trapped them for so long. If Houston did not work out, all would be lost. So, what pushed these men to accept the challenge of integrating the small program? Why would they agree to put themselves at the forefront of such a large racial controversy when they could gain an equal amount of acclaim, if not more, at a prestigious northern university without having to deal with the added pressure of being the pioneering athletes? Furthermore, why would they risk their athletic careers on an uncertain racial situation at a school with unproven results?

On one hand, they had a clear desire to challenge the racial system which had handicapped them and their families for decades. They were tired of the dead ends repeatedly handed them and desperately wanted to break away from the stranglehold not only for themselves but for those who would follow. But they also saw in Houston an open opportunity for greatness. The UH record books were simply waiting for an athlete to write his name in its pages and leave a mark on the program. For these three athletes, the Cougars offered an invitation to prominence.

The journeys from their hometowns to Houston were not easy ones. These athletes had their own sets of racial perceptions which impacted their views of UH and influenced their reactions to their coaches and teammates. They had real fears and concerns about embarking for Houston and putting themselves in the middle of tense situations. Only through much deliberation and soul searching did they finally sign on the dotted line and don the scarlet and white uniforms.

Elvin Hayes, a native of Louisiana, grew up in Rayville, a typical Jim Crow town about two hours east of Shreveport, Louisiana.[1] Similar to almost all other southern rural towns, black residents, as well as other minorities, occupied the very small second-class space assigned them and limited all interaction with the white community as nothing positive ever came of interracial fraternization. The Civil Rights Movement had to yet to affect any of its landmark legislative victories and the apartheid system, replete with its intense discrimination, segregation, and constant threats of violence, was still very much entrenched in the south.[2] Life in Rayville matched, and in many ways exceeded, the brutality seen elsewhere. African American residents encountered aggressive discrimination, common violence, and intense police terrorism daily and had to find ways to exist under the white radar. Blacks constantly aimed to remain out of sight thereby bypassing any chance for harassment altogether. Unquestionably, the two races had a fractured relationship, with strict codes leaving blacks with few rights of citizenship and a great level of trepidation. Hayes recalled, "Violence was always with us. People were always getting killed on Saturday nights in Niggertown. They'd slave all week on one of the big cotton farms, breaking their backs from dawn to dusk. Then they'd come into town on Saturday night with their week's pay, knowing they could get drunk.... They'd wind up getting shot to death or stabbed to death."[3] The presence of an overbearing police force only made the situation worse as officers would harass black citizens and often corral them into forced labor under the threat of jail time.

During his childhood and youth, Hayes was not immune to those adverse elements. A child of a single parent, the result of his father's premature death, he had to rely almost solely upon his mother's experiences and advice to navigate safely through a bigoted southern society.[4] She refused to let her son, or any of her other children, fall into the traps of poor scholarship, bad company, and run-ins with the white-controlled police. Under her stern direction, he kept up with his schooling, even at the cost of practice time on the court, kept away from the wrong crowds, and remained focused on staying out of the Rayville trap. She would not allow her son to falter as she knew first-hand of the life awaiting uneducated African Americans in the small Louisiana city. From experience, she was cognizant of the cotton fields needing harvesters and of the railroads needing manual laborers. Because only the low wage jobs were available to black workers, she struggled constantly to financially care for their household, and she always told her children that she "wanted them to have a better chance than [she] did."[5] Ultimately, Savanna Hayes succeeded in her mission as the majority of her children, including Elvin, obtained a college degree.

But even the strong oversight of a caring mother could not shield the youngest member of the Hayes family from the harsh reality which surrounded him. Racism undeniably existed in Rayville, and to his hometown, he was nothing more than a black youth, regardless of his athletic or intellectual abilities. He remembered his life there vividly and how he would have to stay out of sight of the white community and act overly submissive when interaction occurred. The memories of the threatening tone of white men and the dictatorial nature of the police ingrained themselves into Hayes's memory, and they would not easily be erased.[6] Even when he returned to his hometown during the height of his college years, Hayes feared going against the standard racial expectations. On one particular trip home with his white teammates, he jumped into the backseat of the car and hid from sight afraid that a bystander would see him cavorting with white men and raise an issue with it.[7] Although a figure on the national scene, Hayes feared upsetting the black/white status quo and the consequences it would bring. In Rayville, "whites had been taught to hate blacks, and blacks had been taught to hate whites" and that lesson bred "so much hostility in [him]."[8] Hayes would not easily overcome those racial perceptions.

Poverty, which plagued the majority of blacks in the South, only exacerbated the Hayes family situation. Like the rest of the African American population in his hometown, Hayes went without luxuries as his mother, the sole supporter of the family, could only secure menial, low-paying, employment. She managed to keep the family together and fed; however, life in Rayville was not easy and stressed the black population which resided there. The combined effects of all these elements battered Hayes, and he would take those attitudes with him to Houston.

The combination of racism and poverty served only one positive purpose, to motivate Hayes to get himself out of Rayville and out of the south through whatever means possible. In addition to prejudices and racial attitudes, rural Louisiana cultivated a desperate desire to escape from the quicksand environment. Despite the situation which he found himself in, or perhaps in spite of it, Hayes determined to leave behind the life which had trapped his mother and threatened the same for him. Hayes, in his youth, would "walk from Niggertown to U.S. Route 80 and watch the cars with out-of-state tags go by, right past Rayville ... or [he'd] read about far-away places in magazines, and swear to [himself] that someday, somehow, [he] was going to go to a better life."[9] The need to leave Louisiana turned his attention toward his strongest ability: athletics. His natural talent and size quickly pointed him toward basketball and away from baseball, his first athletic love. He threw himself into the game practicing every free moment he had and slowly but steadily learned the basics and perfected those skills. At that early age, Hayes did not realize that his athleticism would be the way out. He simply knew "there was a better life out there beyond Rayville and North Louisiana.... [He] had no way of knowing that basketball was going to be the vehicle ... all [he] knew was [he] was going to find some kind of vehicle."[10]

By the time he finished high school, Hayes recognized that "basketball was to be [his] savior as well as [his] ticket out of Rayville."[11] His domination on the court, which included a 67-point game, a 54-0 senior season record, and a state title in the black high school division, brought him to the attention of a plethora of college recruiters despite the local newspaper's refusal to cover black athletes.[12] Hayes had made a name for himself and was certain that his days in Rayville were numbered. With offers pouring in from those universities willing to accept African American

athletes, which consisted primarily of black institutions and those outside
the South who had heard of the athlete from deep Louisiana, Hayes had
to make a decision as to which environment would provide the most
benefits. He could accept an offer from the black colleges, of which Grambling State University was at the top of the list, or head north to well-
established integrated programs. In his eyes, it was a win-win situation
for any university would allow him to trade in Rayville and Jim Crow for
a lucrative career outside of the Deep South.

While the University of Wisconsin ranked highest on his dream list,
Hayes more realistically considered places such as Grambling State University and Southern University, where one of his sisters attended.[13] Because
of its non-integrated status, Houston, and places similar to it, never entered
into the equation. "Growing up where I did in northeastern Louisiana,"
Hayes noted, "playing at a place like Houston wasn't something that ever
crossed my mind."[14] Southern white institutions were not welcoming
places, and Hayes had no reason to assume they would come calling for
him. The black universities offered the most realistic shot, and Hayes nat-
urally assumed he would attend one of them.

When the delegation from Houston arrived the situation changed
entirely, and soon a different course of action had been decided upon.
Hayes, or more realistically his mother, determined almost instantaneously
that Houston's offer would be accepted over all others on the table.[15]
Savanna Hayes, unconcerned with her son's athletic preferences, selected
the institution which would provide the best educational opportunity and
essentially dictated to him which offer he would accept. He remembered,
"My mother said 'you're going out there with Coach Pate' and that was
it.... When your mother tells you something that's what you're going to
do.... It really wasn't up to me."[16] As much thought as Hayes put into the
decision, it ultimately was not his to make. His mother had decided on
the Houston Cougars.

Mrs. Hayes's choice to send her son to Houston stemmed from two
factors. First, the coaching staff completely won over her trust. They
entered her home and although white men treated her, a black woman,
with an unheard of level of respect. As Hayes recalled, the coach was one
of the first friendly white people who ever came into his presence. Pate
"respected people ... it was like he was from across the street."[17] The

ability to so quickly entrust her son to the race which had ruled so harshly over her and her family speaks to the genuineness of the Houston coaching staff. They convinced her that Elvin would be safe, as well as athletically prosperous, and that they would provide him with an honest chance to escape the oppression of rural Louisiana and have a career in professional basketball. The situation would not be perfect, no integration process could be, but Houston would make it as comfortable as possible for Hayes and could protect her son from the racial negativity when and where it arose.

It is also possible that Hayes's mother believed his life in Rayville already exposed him to the worst racial environment. He grew up and learned to survive in the heart of repression, and Houston could not present much more of a challenge. The thick skin and an ability to avoid dangerous situations cultivated during his youth would allow him to survive in any city in the nation. His mother must have thought her son could fend for himself and stay out of trouble.

More importantly, Mrs. Hayes believed Houston provided the best opportunity for Elvin to receive an excellent education. Even more so than a chance to play ball, she wanted her son to have a legitimate shot at a solid education as that was, in her estimation, the only guarantor of an improved life. "My mother didn't care about me playing basketball. She said, 'I want you to get your degree. You need an education more than you need basketball.'"[18] Hayes knew exactly where his mother stood on the issue. Education had always been of utmost importance to Hayes's parents; his father, even on his deathbed, instructed Mrs. Hayes to "keep them children in school" and to not worry about the details because "the Lord's gonna make a way for you to do it."[19] The University of Houston, although a new member to the funding and benefits of the state educational system, offered a better education than any of the other schools recruiting Hayes. Elvin's mother would see to it that her son's athletic ability would grant him full access to the best education possible.

Even though willing to accept the opportunity presented by them, Hayes did not fully embrace the white coaches who sat in his living room that day. He had grown up as a second-class citizen, had been taught his place well, and these men offering the world seemed suspicious to a young man entrenched in the southern way of life. How could he trust the very race that had always treated him like less than a person, forced him to lower his eyes on the sidewalk, and deprived him of even the simplest rights? How could he know with absolute certainty that the Houston coaches would give him a fair chance? Ultimately, he had to take a step of faith. As dominating as the race issues were, they could not deter him from accepting the challenge of joining a previously all-white athletic department, and he resolved to conquer whatever challenges existed in Houston. This was his opportunity to break away, and he would accept it even if it made him uncomfortable. His high school coach Melvin Rogers believed Hayes accepted the offer to the University of Houston precisely because of the racial challenge. He said, "The fact that he would be in the first group of Negro athletes to play for the University of Houston was another [positive] factor [for] it was a challenge to him and he thought he could do it. Elvin always had an unbelievable amount of self-confidence."[20] Determined to overcome the racial issues, Hayes acquiesced to his mother's decision and agreed that Houston would provide the best opportunity for him to escape the intense racial suppression which had loomed over him for eighteen years.

But Hayes had another motivation in attending Houston. Although his student questionnaire listed a good education as the primary reason for attending the school, Hayes admitted that the lack of great men in its history ultimately convinced him. In the absence of stellar athletes, his accomplishments, or lack thereof, would stand or fall on their own merit.[21] The Cougars provided him with a wide-open canvass to showcase his athletic talent, and ironically their largest weakness became their greatest selling point. He wanted above all else an institution where his accomplishments could stand alone. Neither supporters nor opponents could dismiss his talents by comparison, and commentators could not negate Hayes's abilities by pointing to the prowess of white athletes like Bill Bradley.[22] If he attended Houston and fell short of greatness, no one would have paid much attention or cared. If, on the other hand, he found tremendous success, detractors could not use former athletes to diminish his accomplishments. Either way, Hayes could determine his own fate and either establish the small program through his skills or fade quietly into the background of an old team photo. The coaching staff came back to Houston with his signature partly because of the Cougars' less than stellar records. Its largest detriment became its largest selling point.

Finally, the most racially significant issue which affected Hayes's decision was the encouragement Houston coaches gave him to make his own decision irrespective of the outside pressures. For the first time in his life, white men validated Hayes's opinions and pushed him to express them. While the black coaches tried desperately to steer him toward their universities, the UH coaches warned the young star not to allow others to pressure him into a decision he was not comfortable with. It is interesting that the African American coaches did just that and tried to dictate his course of action while the white coaches, although having the social authority to do so, encouraged the athlete to attend whichever school made him most comfortable. For so long, the white community lorded over the black citizens and informed them exactly what they would do and when they would do it. When Houston came calling, they told Hayes that the decision was entirely his own He should choose whichever program would make him most happy. That encouragement by white men enticed and intrigued Hayes. For the first time in his life he was allowed to make his own decision like a white man. Lewis treated the potential recruit as a thinking adult capable of making a decision on his own regardless of the color of his skin; he treated Hayes as an equal. Houston seemed to offer everything he desired and, even with the issue of integration looming overhead, presented the best opportunity for a stellar career.

Hayes did have one contingency which Lewis needed to address before he could secure a commitment. He wanted assurance that Howie Lorch, the team's student manager, would room alongside him. Although most assumed the two black athletes would room together, Lewis had definite plans to the contrary. He had already determined that Hayes and Chaney would not stay together to avoid any perpetuation of segregation, and Hayes knew of the requirement before signing. Because of that, Hayes wanted to select which member of the opposite race he would room with, and Lorch was it. The two met during a recruiting trip where the team trainer served as his campus guide and introduced him to Houston, both the school and the city. Lewis, afraid that certain players might try to intimidate Hayes in an attempt to keep their spots on the roster, asked his manager to take him around, and he willingly took on the responsibility. Lorch, who grew up in New York and had a real understanding of the evils of prejudice from his parents' escape from Nazi Germany, had no problem with the race of the latest recruit, and the two became quick friends.[23] Even though he had never associated freely, much less lived, with whites, Hayes felt comfortable and at ease with Lorch and wanted to make certain he would spend his college years with him. He wanted to ensure his roommate would be someone he already knew and could count on in a new world which would frighten away most young men.

Although Lewis already decided that his integration would be complete, he had not yet fleshed out the details of the plan, and the request caught him by surprise. He had not asked any of his players to take on the additional responsibility beforehand and did not know whether or not his manager would agree to the living arrangement. The entire signing hung on Lorch's willingness to take on a black roommate, and, on the eve of the decision, he received an unexpected call from the coach. During that phone call, Lewis said plainly to his student, "'Howie we [have] a big problem with Elvin.... The only way he's coming to the University of Houston is if you're his roommate.... I can sure understand if you don't want to do it because you know it's asking a lot.'"[24] Lorch, already acclimated to integrated environments and without racial reservations, accepted the task without a second thought. He told Lewis that he would take on the responsibility and said to Elvin over the phone, "I look forward to having you as my roommate next year ... [and] that was the beginning."[25] This relationship between an African American and a Jewish German did not end with graduation as the two remain friends to this day.

The desire to make his own decision along with the dictum issued by his mother and the level of comfort he felt with the staff and students pushed Hayes to sign with Houston. He did not know exactly what awaited him there, or how he would be able to handle himself away from the only life he had known in segregated Louisiana. Nevertheless, the allure of the unknown drew him in, and, with the encouragement of his family, he set off to make a new life for himself and to overcome the racial barriers that kept him and others like him away from the major playing fields of the South for so long. He agreed to be a pioneer in the integration movement and to do so with the Cougars.

Donald Chaney, most commonly known as Don, is a much larger mystery in the picture. His youth in Baton Rouge, although still spent in a segregated society, was unquestionably less hostile and less restrictive than Hayes's. His hometown remained a southern city, but its urban environment lessened the repressiveness of discrimination and segregation. Those elements were still there resting just under the surface of society, but they did not dominate everyday life. Chaney, unlike Hayes, learned how to co-exist with whites even if only minimally. As he noted, "Baton Rouge is a small town, but it [is] the state capital, so I was exposed to a lot of different things [Elvin] didn't see in the small Louisiana town where he grew up."[26] He knew how to live in segregated society without being noticed by whites and could take that with him into any situation. That is not to say, however, that Baton Rouge, or any other southern town for that matter, was a comfortable place to live for any African American family. It was after all still the South. His college roommate, John Tracy, recalled that Chaney's experiences did affect him as a young man. He remembered how Chaney would recount "stories about growing up with the KKK marching through [his] neighborhood ... [about] never [having] a relationship or speaking to white people.... [How] he didn't speak to white people unless he was spoken to or told what to do."[27] Chaney knew how to survive in mixed society, but he still struggled with integrated environments. The situation in Houston would certainly be an adjustment which required much effort, but he was not as burdened by racial attitudes as his counterpart and was better prepared to handle the situation.

As far as his home life, Chaney, like Hayes, was raised by a single mother who wanted only the best for her son and worked several jobs to ensure all her children had a decent living. The family resided in an all-black neighborhood and in the absence of his father, Chaney's uncles served as father figures providing him advice on which decisions would prove most beneficial to his life and how to avoid the most harmful mistakes. Also similar to Hayes, Chaney had a stellar high school career at an all-black high school which quickly brought him to the attention of numerous institutions able to recruit him. Although Chicago's Loyola University appeared his most likely choice, he had offers from all across the north as a result of his strong athletic career. Chaney was aware of the athletic doors within the state closed to him due to his skin color. He recalled, "I grew up in Baton Rouge, a block and a half from the Louisiana State University campus. I could sit on my back porch and listen to the crowds at the football games, but I couldn't go to school there because it wasn't integrated."[28] Although leaning toward certain institutions, the scholarship he would ultimately accept depended on the recruiting process and on the different benefits and drawbacks of the offers that rolled in. He, like Hayes, ended up choosing the school which appeared least likely on the surface.

The Houston recruiting team came to Baton Rouge ready to acquire its second black athlete.[29] Coaches Lewis and Pate, again with help from the TSU basketball coach, approached the situation slightly differently than they did with Hayes. Whereas Mrs. Hayes's remained concerned foremost for her son's education, the Chaney family wanted its star athlete to become a pioneer for black athletes. According to Chaney, his mom Gladys had "always been a pioneer, and she wanted [him] to be one too."[30] He should select the school which best allowed him to challenge the racial barriers evident within southern athletics. Education should not be minimalized, but his role on the court would provide the way out of the poverty and repression of Louisiana and the South. The coaches tailored their pitch accordingly. They explained to the Chaneys that Houston provided a chance for him to make a way for himself through a career in basketball and chip away at the system of segregation at the same time. He could be the Jackie Robinson of southern college basketball if he would commit to Houston and take his place alongside Hayes. They assured the Chaney family that the coaching staff and school administration would be there to assist him on the journey and stave off as much negativity as possible. Mrs. Chaney "believed in someone stepping up to take the initiative of being the pioneer" and told her son he "[had] an opportunity to help [his] people."[31] Like Hayes's, Chaney's decision was made primarily by his mother. "[Lewis and Pate] impressed my mom and my [high school] coach by telling them I had an opportunity to be one of the first black players ... I came home and [she said] 'Coach Lewis from Houston was just here ... that's where you're going.' I never had a choice."[32] Lewis presented Chaney with a chance to shake-up the Texas sports world, if not the athletic world of the South, by accepting a scholarship to the University of Houston, and his mother made sure he would accept the offer. Even if he did not see the significance in the move, his forward thinking mother did. She knew the opportunity would open doors to a solid future for her son and others in the process. Don Chaney could, with success, create tangible improvements for blacks in the South, for athletes and non-athletes alike, and the potential for change was too great to pass up. Her son committed to Lewis's squad of Cougars. This was his chance to step to the forefront, and Chaney would not argue the point.

Aside from the larger significance, Chaney reached the moment where he could finally improve his own personal situation as well. Signing with the Cougars provided an excellent opportunity to fully enter into white society and not only learn how to navigate through it but take full advantage what it had to offer as well. He grew up in a metropolitan sector of segregated Louisiana, but he and his family always wanted more for him outside of the confines of prejudice and labor-intensive jobs. His family,

> talked it over and agreed it would be a great opportunity. The University was growing and trying to build its program [and it was the only way] he was going to get out of the neighborhood he was in. His other choice [was] to grow up with black people, work in the black industry, just live his life out the way he grew up. So, if you're going to get out in the world and mix in with white people, when is that going to start? So maybe this was a good opportunity to make things happen. [33]

It was decided. He would go and make his way in Houston, because it was an open field of opportunity ready for him to take advantage of. This was the fastest way out of Baton Rouge, and, like others who had the chance to leave the state, he would accept it.[34]

As tremendously exciting as the chance to play for Houston appeared, Chaney did not have any delusions about the transition ahead. Houston, much like Baton Rouge, had its own racial problems with racism seeded just below the surface. Direct affronts were rare and open hostility simply did not present itself on a daily basis, but racism's ugly head could rear at any point without notice. He could not completely let his guard down just because he crossed over the Texas border. Furthermore, as a pioneering athlete additional stresses would weigh down on him. He would not only have to take care of his academic and athletic careers, but he would also have to deal with observers who opposed his presence and would rejoice in his failures.

On the positive side, he would not have to bear the brunt alone as Hayes, who he had already met during high school all-star games, had also joined the team, and they could face the potentially volatile situations together. He did not know at that point though that he and his fellow African American athlete would occupy different rooms. Coach Lewis would not reveal the race of Chaney's roommate until his arrival in Houston. It is not certain why Hayes knew of the arrangements while Chaney did not. Upon learning of the room assignments, Chaney reconsidered his decision to attend Houston worrying the integration could be some form of a trap. Ultimately though, Chaney decided that making a racial statement held more weight than his personal comfort. Though he had yet to find out exactly how hard the transition would be, he became the newest member of the Houston program. His roommate recognized the courage it took to make that decision and said of Chaney, "I think Don was really brave. He had never left home, he had never traveled. I remember telling him that this would make him a better man ... and be the best experience he ever had."[35]

Chaney and Hayes, with the complete support of their mothers and families, prepared to take on the challenge together. They would not share a room, but they were certainly joined by common experiences. The two of them would become the first two African American Cougar basketball players side by side for better or worse.

Warren McVea, the last African American athlete to sign with Houston, was the most surprising recruit of the three brought in that year. While the two basketball stars were incredible additions to the team, a nationally recognized athlete of McVea's caliber choosing a program like Houston was unheard of. With offers proliferating, no one seriously expected Houston to win the recruiting competition, and from a logical standpoint McVea's decision made little sense. The young star risked his athletic promise on a questionable program with an uncertain racial situation; his reasoning had much to do with his strong attachment to his family.

McVea was a unique athlete, different from each of the other two African American recruits. He came from a different home environment, grew up in a different type of city, and had different goals and aspirations for his future. His family lived a relatively stable life, with both parents present and the family finances solid, in a town more moderate than most, where McVea and the black community lived peacefully with the whites around them. Unlike the other two athletes, the football star's hometown did not conform to the racial norms of the South. San Antonio, about 200 miles northeast of Houston, did not portray the characteristics of a Deep South city and mirrored more of the moderate western attitudes. With a black population under 10 percent and a Mexican-American population which served as the middle ground between the black and white communities, the city never had serious racial tensions.[36] *De jure* segregation disappeared by 1960 and did so with little fanfare as public schools, lunch counters, busses, etc. easily fell to integration. *De facto* segregation did not last too much longer either and soon the three races exchanged niceties in public and made life tolerable.

As a result of the relatively progressive environment, McVea attended an integrated high school, played on an integrated football squad, and had no problems moving through white society. The successes he achieved on the gridiron only made his entry into the white community that much smoother. He became a favorite among all the races, and citizens of all colors loved him because he brought acclaim to their city. McVea was the hometown favorite, and that celebrity provided him an added level of immunity to whatever racism existed within the small Texas town. The city's citizens embraced him because of his ability to run and score, and the level of support within the town was incredible. When McVea played in the Texas High School Coaches' Association all-star game, a record crowd followed him to Ft. Worth for the game.[37] These elements combined to make McVea much more comfortable with his surroundings, and he felt no intense urge to leave his environment. The South he lived in did not threaten him, and he had no problem remaining in it. Content with his surroundings, his choice of college was based purely on which place best met his needs.

McVea's difference was apparent in that his athletic prowess was not hidden within a rural area, neglected by the press because of his skin color. McVea had the advantage of a media machine which made his athletic feats known throughout the state and the nation. The local and state press highly publicized his abilities, and all in the sports world knew he was, without question, a top athlete capable of carrying any program to a higher level. A plethora of scholarships awaited his signature, and he knew he could practically write his own ticket anywhere.

At the beginning of the recruiting process, McVea explored all of his options, visiting major schools along the east and west coasts including the University of Kansas, the University of Southern California, the University of Nebraska, and the University of Oklahoma. Enticed by the well-established programs and the media attention and success they could all but guarantee him, McVea figured his transition to college fame would come easily. He would sign on with the most prestigious university, have a tremendous career, and move on to a professional team without discussion. The university he chose was not all important because with his natural athletic talent, all roads led to greatness in the professional leagues. College was just a stepping stone on his way to the top.

So, how did Bill Yeoman convince McVea to join his program? What did he offer that none of the other coaches could? Not surprisingly, when Bill Yeoman appeared among the list of suitors, McVea gave little to no thought to the coach from such an undistinguished school. McVea had "no idea who the University of Houston was ... [and] had never heard of them."[38] In his own mind, he was destined for incredible feats, and such a small institution "[wasn't] even in [his] plans."[39] When first contacted, he practically scoffed at the contact. Upon Coach Yeoman's arrival, McVea thought inwardly, "You've got to be kidding me, I'm the top player in the country ... U of H? Nah."[40] The Houston coaching staff graciously accepted his rebuffs and determined to wait patiently for a chance to convince him further. They understood that the slim to none odds made signing McVea a near impossibility but decided to try nonetheless knowing they had found the right player for integration.

Little by little, they spoke to him and his mother of the school and the benefits it had to offer. True, it was a small school, but as they explained it was just waiting for its first great athlete and for that pivotal player to lift the entire program to new heights. Plus, as the only major institution in Texas accepting black athletes, Houston provided the perfect environment for someone wanting to stay close to home. Remaining low key and refusing to enter into the negative campaign tactics used by other institutions, Houston slowly began gaining the trust of the McVea family. Warren recalled of Yeoman, "The more I got to meet him, the more I got to like him, and the more I trusted him.... He never badmouthed any other school ... [and only] talked about U of H."[41] The Houston staff remained on the periphery of the recruiting process and kept promoting Houston as the best choice within a few hours of San Antonio. Eventually, they hoped, McVea would choose his family over the larger schools and join the Cougar team.

For McVea, the Houston pitch gradually began to make sense. He was after all extremely attached to his family and home environment and did not feel any pressing need to leave his home state. San Antonio provided him with a fair, unrestricted, lifestyle and thus he had no need to escape the South. Further, his tight-knit family, which included six siblings, was of immense importance to the young star. Never having been away from home, the reality of living alone hundreds of miles away from them proved a huge dilemma, and the more he visited the distant schools the more he missed his family. On recruiting trips to the more athletically prestigious institutions, McVea's homesickness would quickly set in. "I found myself every week wanting to leave the next day I was so homesick.... I said, '[what] if I go [to school] away from home?'"[42] Slowly it became clear to him that if he wished to remain close to his comfort zone, Houston presented the only reasonable possibility.

The larger schools, such as the University of Texas and Texas A&M University, did not have integrated programs and showed no propensity to change that tradition any time soon. The black colleges, despite their best attempts to compete with the more elite programs, simply could not adequately support his athletic dreams. The opponents, facilities, and press were less than suitable for a rising star and could not support an athlete of McVea's quality. Thus, like the two basketball players, his best choice rested with the Cougars. Houston had drawbacks, and McVea knew he was sacrificing certain things to play there. Despite those detractions, it at least offered the possibility of a stellar career and a location very near his family. After weighing all the options before him, he agreed to sign with Yeoman's Cougars. He would play close to home and make a name for himself, both on and off the field, at the same time. Plus, he believed the institution itself would not determine his future, because it was, in his mind, already set. McVea knew he was bound for greatness regardless of where he attended, so the decision was not all that monumental. Houston would suit his needs as well as any other school.

Interestingly, McVea's mother had a negative reaction to her son's decision. Chaney and Hayes both had the support of their mothers in selecting Houston, as they seriously pushed their sons to accept the offers from Lewis and the University of Houston. Each of those women believed scholarships provided a way of escape and encouraged, or more accurately dictated, Houston as the destination for their athletes. McVea's mother, however, had the opposite reaction when Coach Yeoman came calling. She understood the racial situation at the University of Houston would be tumultuous and feared her son's athletic career would be caught in the middle of the black / white struggle. He had enough talent to attend any previously integrated school he desired, and she saw no need for him to bear the brunt of the pioneer stigma, especially in a town which could racially erupt with little notice. Houston did not present any direct racial threats but all knew that racial unrest sat just below the city's consciousness, and there was, in her opinion, no reason to unnecessarily risk his career to challenge that status quo. Mrs. Mattie McVea wanted her son away from the South and the evils it could perpetrate. "She wanted me to go to some place like Missouri ... because Houston was bad, Houston was tough.... [It had] blacks living in one section of town and whites in another section of town."[43] Tom Beer, a northern athlete who played alongside McVea, also noted the tense racial situation that existed in Houston during those times. He remarked, "I was very surprised to find the city of Houston [so] extremely polarized [with a] black college, black living areas, black clubs, etc. I was even shocked to find a white beach and a black beach in Galveston. Houston was indeed a bigoted city."[44] But for McVea, none of those realities could negate his devotion to his mother. He decided the University of Houston, with its location so near to San Antonio and his mother, best fit his needs and nothing could keep him from going.

In all the discussion McVea never seriously considered the racial aspect of his commitment. While the media emphasized, and on occasion criticized, Houston's integration, the black athlete at the center of it all did not pay much attention to the racial changes his signature brought forward. "The racial aspects didn't really bother me too much," he commented. "I thought everyone was making too big a deal out of it."[45] Even when Roy Hoffheinz, the individual primarily responsible for the building of the Astrodome, encouraged McVea to come play in his state-of-the-art, integrated, stadium, McVea's cognizance of racial progress did not surface. He understood that the black fans could watch him play without being relegated to a colored section, but it just did not influence him one way or another.[46] Whereas the other two black recruits saw Houston as an opportunity to challenge the color barrier, McVea did not pay attention to the issue. "I really didn't feel much like a pioneer by staying in Texas," the running back said, "[because] the big thing was being close to home."[47] McVea's life in an integrated environment made race a non-issue for him. He interacted with whites all through high school and had no reason to pay attention to a subject like integration. He would go to Houston because it made the most sense to him rather than because of the improvements it would provide for his race. He was not there to change the South's race relations or improve the condition of black athletes; he was there to make a name for himself and get out. Yeoman and McVea both had the same goal for integration-consistent victories.

But, another factor under girded McVea's choice to attend the University of Houston. Coach Yeoman, much like Lewis and Pate, walked into McVea's living room and earned his confidence almost immediately. The coach did not try to buy McVea's signature, as other programs did, but he promised McVea that if he committed to Houston, he would stick with him from that point forward. McVea said, "The main reason I came to the University of Houston was Bill Yeoman. After I got to know him, I trusted him, I honestly trusted him.... He offered something nobody else did.... He told my parents, 'If he comes here, I will be his friend for life.'"[48] The offer of friendship was not simply a recruiting tool as Yeoman remained true to his promise even forty plus years later. "Coaches say anything to get players," McVea reflected, "but this man said it and actually stuck to it.... He's still my friend.... I'm most proud of that than anything."[49] Houston's coach gained the trust of a young man being offered the world by other programs and, as a result, gained his commitment signature. It would mark the beginning of a lifelong relationship.

McVea, contrary to what would be expected from a high school student, was resolute in his decision even after the negative hype exploded throughout the state's press outlets. Despite the press reaction and his mother's strong objections, McVea refused to reconsider his commitment to Houston. That was partially because of the comfort Yeoman provided. He knew the coach would stand with him at all cost and would see him through whatever may come. Yeoman remained true to his promise and even when the NCAA placed Houston on probation two years later, no blame was ever assigned to McVea. To this day, McVea still does not believe responsibility for the school's problems was ever placed on his shoulders. He had made his choice, and he would not turn back.

These three athletes, coming from varied backgrounds and with different racial views, agreed to come to the University of Houston and change the nature of collegiate sports in the South. They all understood the risks involved in committing to the Cougars but still agreed to take on the challenge wholeheartedly. The toughest part remained, however, as Chaney, Hayes, and McVea still had to go into a potentially hostile environment and perform brilliantly. Everyone would watch to see if integrated teams could overcome their own racial prejudices and learn how to succeed against the all-white programs prevalent throughout the South. Critics, which were plentiful, anxiously awaited their miserable failure to prove blacks could not effectively compete with whites. They hoped that the Cougars' implosion would end all further discussion of athletic integration and quench any future attempts. At the same time, though, there were a substantial number of Cougar faithful hoping the day of Cougar athletics had finally arrived. They would be present to cheer their athletes on.

Before facing full out competition the coaches and their newest players would have to integrate the program itself. They would have to live and play together despite their different skin colors and learn how to see each other as equals and as friends. No one knew exactly how things would pan out, but Houston would give its best shot. Lewis and Yeoman, after striving toward integration for years, had finally blurred the color barrier and brought African American athletes into their programs. The move came with a significant amount of debate from the public and sanctions handed down by the iron fist of the NCAA, but the change came regardless. That was only half of the battle. Now, the coaches had to prove that integrated teams could win games and defeat the opponents which had handed them losses for years. They had to convince both the fans and the community through substantial victories that the radical move had paid off. It would be a long road.

5

"Two Different Races ... Two Different Sides of the World"

The integration plan carefully crafted by the two coaches and their supporting staffs appeared, at least on paper, ready to go. In principle, it would proceed smoothly as three of the most talented and capable African American athletes signed on in the spring and summer of 1964, and two progressive-minded coaches had fully committed to see the process through. The athletes' previous experience dealing with racial hostility only increased the odds of success. All of those positive factors could not guarantee that Houston's integration would proceed seamlessly or at all for that matter. The athletes had agreed to come, the University of Houston had agreed to let them play, but either party could instantaneously retract their decisions and immediately collapse the process of integration. Further, teammates, roommates, classmates, and the entire city of Houston still had to adjust to the racial changes and the athletes pushing it forward. They would ultimately control the pace and ease of the process and dictate whether it would succeed at all.

Regardless of the potential problems, the time for planning had passed, and it was time for the racial experiment to move forward without delay. Mercifully, the first year of play for these men would not be on varsity teams as the NCAA regulated that all freshmen had to serve a year on the junior varsity teams, away from the major spotlight. They had one short season to work out any personal or athletic kinks before hitting the big scene, but, even on the small scale, that first year of integration would set the tone for the next three years. The only question still on the table was not whether the integration would go forward but how it would progress.

It would either be a marvelous year with many victories and few problems, or the University of Houston would reject the integrated teams and stymie the process before it ever got off the ground. The first season would set the tone and serve as the trial run for the impending full scale integration. That year could transport the Cougars into victorious heaven or a riotous hell.

Kittens Basketball

Immediately following their high school graduations in May 1964, Hayes and Chaney set out for their new home of Houston. Although acquainted from their high school playing days and comforted by the fact that they could rely upon each other for support in Houston, their adjustment to the city would not prove all that easy. For Hayes, the acclimation would take more effort. His life in Rayville had severely impacted his ability to interact with the white community and left him severely fearful of new environments. His initial reactions to the city did not bode well as his small town upbringing left him feeling vulnerable in such an expansive city. "It," Hayes said of Houston, "was a very scary place because I had never seen anything this big or been around this many people in one place at one time. So for a kid coming from a double A school, it was just a massive, very scary experience for me."[1] His trepidation was strong enough to drive the young Hayes back home to his family on more than one occasion. "The first time they brought me over," he recalled, "the next day I was back over in Louisiana, and they would come back and get me and I was gone again."[2] After a few such retreats across the Texas border, Hayes's mother sent her oldest son Arthur to Houston alongside his younger brother with the instructions that Elvin would remain in Texas for good. She would not allow him to pass up the best opportunity he had to make a better life for himself because of his fear of whites. Hayes's brother would make certain that there would be no more unscheduled trips to Rayville.

Eventually, Mrs. Hayes's tactic paid off as Elvin slowly acclimated to his new surroundings and felt at ease remaining at UH. He came to realize that "the Houston people offered [him] an education and a watchful

eye" and that they were in place to help him if needed.[3] With the start of
the fall semester and the arrival of the rest of the squad including fellow
black recruit Don Chaney, Hayes finally felt comfortable enough to release
his brother from his companionship duties and sent him home.[4] Basketball would be his new companion and his teammates his new brothers.
Even still, the desire to be around the family which had provided him protection from the world and unconditional support his entire life never
completely left him during that first year. Lorch recalled one practice in
particular where the pressure proved too much, and Hayes almost surrendered his career at the University of Houston. Although determined to
head home, Lorch wisely exhorted Hayes to stick out the year: "If you
pack up and leave now you're going to be a quitter the rest of your life."[5]
He had found a way to escape Louisiana, and if he abandoned that opportunity now, he would most likely never have another opening. The threat
of losing that chance for good was enough to convince Hayes, for the last
time, that he needed to remain in Houston and finish the role of integra-
tor he had agreed to fill. He had dreamt of this fortuity since he was a
child, and thanks to the encouragement of his new found friend, he would
not forfeit it.

Hayes did not completely leave his mother behind as he always kept
her sage words of wisdom with him. Ted Nance, the Information Director, recalled that the young athlete always acted as though his mother
stood right beside him. When offered a cigarette on one occasion, Hayes
responded, "My mother'd whip me if she saw me with [one]."[6] Mrs. Hayes
had trained him well.

Chaney, on the other hand, did not have as difficult of a transition
as his fellow black teammate. Coming of age in Baton Rouge did not
severely traumatize his childhood or his perceptions of race. He had a
healthy respect for racial divides and knew his place but was better able
to deal with his new situation without an excessive amount of inner turmoil. He understood that contrary to Hayes his transition would not prove
overwhelming, commenting, "It was harder on Elvin.... I was exposed to
a lot of different things he didn't see in the small Louisiana town where
he grew up.... He came in with a chip on his shoulder."[7] Although not
completely comfortable with the new situation and still rather ill-at-ease
with his new surroundings, he was capable of coping and at least keeping

the angst he felt pent up and managed. Chaney could survive in Houston, could adequately take care of his grades and, most importantly, grow and nurture his athletic career even if he did not feel entirely at ease living so closely with the white community. He came into the program ready to play basketball and firmly secure his future. Outside of that, nothing else mattered.

From the beginning of the integration process, Guy V. Lewis took complete control of the situation. He understood that players, black and white alike, had to learn to treat each other as equals and refused to allow any form of segregation among his students black or white. These men would live, play, and study together ignoring the color of skin. Lewis had made up his mind from the word go that "if [they] were going to integrate, [they] were going to integrate."[8] Blacks would stay with whites and whites would stay with blacks both on and off the court. It is also possible that Lewis was also concerned about outside perception. He hoped to avoid outsider claims that his black athletes lived segregated from the rest of the team, and that the integration did not extend beyond the bouncing of the basketball. Players, coaches, and spectators would all know that blacks and whites were on the same footing across the board. To begin the process, he assigned his two black players white roommates.

Initially, Hayes felt disappointed with the living arrangements. Although he knew beforehand of the rooming situation and had pre-selected which white student he would reside with, Hayes still longed to share a space with his black counterpart. He believed he and Chaney shared a common past which no white player could possibly understand and rooming together would be the best arrangement for all involved. He felt Chaney would understand on all levels where he was coming from and the mental anguish that came as a result of that baggage. Instead, he was staying with one of the whites he had long feared and would have to learn to deal with him on an intimate level, one on one. Despite his overwhelming reservations, he wanted to play at Houston so he reluctantly moved his things into the dorm room he would share with his white roommate Howie Lorch. Although not completely disastrous, the two of them, like many other roommates, did encounter some problems along the way. On a few occasions, Hayes threw Lorch, along with his belongings, into the halls of Baldwin House, the athletic dormitory.[9] Almost like two brothers sharing a small room, the two had to go through an adjustment period just like any other newly matched roommates.

Those disagreements did not extend beyond the rows of any two dorm mates, and ultimately they learned to live together not as adversaries but as friends. Both men, in retrospect, only remembered one truly racially-related argument. During this incident, Hayes was heading out of the dormitory when Lorch, seeing his black hand on the door, called out to him. When Hayes realized his friend identified him only by the color of hand, his temper flared. Despite the innocent nature of Lorch's comment, after all there were only two African American basketball players residing in the dorms, Hayes did not appreciate being identified, yet again, by the color of his skin. Even though the dispute did not cause any lasting damage between the two, and was over almost as soon as it began, clearly both young men struggled with the issue of race and exactly how they fit together into the new environment.

Even with the necessary adjustments Hayes had to go through, Lorch never faulted his friend because he knew of his past and understood the effect it could have on anyone much less a young man. "I certainly understood [Elvin's behavior]," he said later, "I think he had a lot of pent up anger.... Over the years he had been really mistreated.... He had a lot of frustration built up." Lorch simply gave his roommate as much space and understanding as he needed and waited for him to acclimate to his surroundings. He understood where Hayes's anger stemmed from; life in Louisiana was extremely difficult, and he knew those experiences would not fade away overnight. He said of his friend, "It was harder on Elvin. He came in with a chip on his shoulder."[10] Hayes's fellow black teammate tried to stand in the gap for his friend. Coach Lewis begged Chaney to calm down Hayes and get him to focus on the team effort. Chaney did his best to help his fellow black athlete, and with time Hayes did adjust to the situation.

While Hayes acclimated to his white teammates with few serious altercations, his relationship with Lewis did not transition as smoothly. Early on, Lewis called Hayes on the carpet for his negative attitude toward himself and the entire coaching staff and summoned him into his office one day demanding an explanation. "Why do you hate me?" Lewis forcefully asked, "I put my job on the line.... I try to do everything I can for you. What is it with you?"[11] Lewis could not understand why Hayes projected such negativity toward him despite all the help he had granted him. He comprehended the racial burdens Hayes had been raised under, but he was not the enemy. Lewis had given the young Hayes a chance no one else would, and while he was not expecting overwhelming gratitude, he did not expect animosity either. In that moment, Hayes was forced to confront his own prejudices toward the white community. As he contemplated the question there in Lewis's office, he realized his life in Louisiana had seriously affected his perception of and reaction toward white authority, and he had been working under those auspices. Hayes recognized that "because [he had grown up] in a totally black environment, and [he had] never been around white people that much. [He] always kind of shied away from [whites].... [He] brought a lot of baggage with [him].... A lot of the things and experiences which [he] had in Louisiana [he] brought ... with [him] over here."[12] With a reasoning ability more advanced than his years, Hayes understood that he had no concrete reason for disliking his coach, or any other member of the white race. His epiphany that the daily prejudices he experienced all through his younger years created anti-white prejudices in him as well. That meeting forced Hayes to re-examine his attitudes and "totally changed [his] life [as] all the anger [he'd] held in left."[13] Hayes had a defining moment and determined racism would no longer control him or dictate his behavior.

From that point forward, Hayes and Lewis had a mutual respect for each other and developed a sort of father/son relationship. Lewis and his family would make sure Hayes was taken care of and even drove him home to Louisiana for summer vacation. Hayes later credited Lewis's handling of the situation for the seamless integration of the University of Houston, calling him a "visionary ... [who deserves] a lot of the credit for integrating the sports program."[14] Lewis returned the compliment saying of his two first black athletes, "I can't express how much I admire [them] they handled it so well that it was probably an easier integration here than anywhere else."[15] The Cougar athletes and coaches were learning to interact as men without color.

Whereas Hayes knew before setting off from Rayville that his roommate would not be another African American, Chaney did not have the slightest clue he would be staying with a white athlete instead. His roommate John Tracy, a freshman raised in New York, had been hand selected by Coach Lewis to stay with Chaney prior to his commitment. Lewis knew the white player would have to be special with experience in integrated situations and an ability to handle the unique pressures associated with the integration. Ultimately, he chose a northern athlete because of the level of racial interaction which transpired there. Lewis knew that "New York was a multi-racial city [and] thought [Tracy] had a little bit more understanding in the area ... [of] knowing a [black] athlete [and] being a teammate."[16] The coach figured that Tracy, like Lorch, could not only make the transition easier for Chaney because of his progressive racial attitude but because he could serve as an intermediary between Chaney and the rest of the white team.

The reason Lewis kept Chaney uninformed of the living arrangement prior to his arrival is undetermined; however, the athlete's ignorance of the matter was in retrospect an excellent decision. The room assignments almost drove Chaney away from Houston.[17] When he arrived in Houston and realized the living arrangements set up, he quickly reconsidered his choice of schools. He feared that the integration, which Lewis and Pate had pitched as a great opportunity for him and others like him, was in reality a trap. Although the concern was unfounded, Chaney's life experiences gave him reason to suspect otherwise. He immediately called his family to discuss the situation, and they warned him to approach his new roommate with extreme caution. His uncles, who served father-figure roles, instructed him to "be careful, kind of sleep with one eye open" and to be wary of his new roommate because "[he] must be getting paid.... Why [else] would a [white] guy ... take this on if he wasn't getting something out of it?"[18] Taking his family's concern and wariness under advisement, Chaney agreed to stay, even with his white roommate, but the tension between the two of them did not dissipate easily.

Their relationship would remain strained for a while as Chaney kept conversation to a minimum and limited interaction to the court and the hours devoted to sleeping. Tracy, although exposed to integrated situations previously, was not quite prepared for the effects the years of oppression had on Chaney and was taken aback by the nervous nature of the relationship.[19] He had agreed to take on the assignment earlier in the year, but he never imagined the arrangement would prove that difficult. Tracy did not quite understand the reason for Chaney's standoffishness or that his roommate "associated the white person as the enemy and all of a sudden, [he] was rooming with the enemy."[20] Chaney, like Hayes, was struggling to overcome his own racial demons and making it hard for others to grow close to him.

That uneasy relationship, with each intentionally avoiding the other whenever possible, continued until Tracy took the first step toward true friendship. At the urging of his father, the white youth opened the conversation one night after both had retreated to their beds. He suggested that the situation would never work, that they were simply not compatible and needed to end the awkward arrangement. They should immediately speak with Lewis about a change. Tracy had forewarned Lewis that the rooming situation was not necessarily a permanent assignment; he left himself an escape clause if things did not proceed as planned. He told Lewis from the beginning, "If this doesn't work out it's not going to be because he's black but because we're not compatible.... I didn't want [to] add any distraction to my education [just to prevent observers from saying] 'they let the blacks in but they put them in the corner by themselves.'"[21] Tracy told Chaney that the ten months remaining in the school year could prove torturous without a drastic change. Since that adjustment did not seem immanent, he would talk to Lewis in the morning.

Lying in the dark that night, Chaney thought about the awkward position both he and his roommate had found themselves in. While not entirely comfortable with the situation, Chaney had to decide whether living with Tracy was a lost cause. To surrender would lead to a continuation of his life in Louisiana, apart from the white world around him and without much freedom. To stay would provide the opportunity to finally break that old pattern of the past. As Hayes had done in Lewis's office, Chaney determined right there to embrace the chance and open up the conversation rather than run from it. Chaney began explaining to his suite mate that his southern upbringing had taught him that blacks did not interact with whites, and they certainly did not speak without first being spoken to. In his world, blacks and whites never mixed on friendly terms and were cordial at most. That conversation opened the path of communication between the two, and they slowly began discussing their lives, finding the commonalities and differences, and forming a genuine friendship.[22]

From that point forward, the two had no racial problems and coexisted without incident. They learned through their close living quarters that, despite the different colors of their skin, they were two young men who enjoyed playing basketball and wanted a future for themselves and their families. Even when Chaney surpassed Tracy on the basketball court, their friendship flourished. By taking a chance, they each found a true companion that they would remain in touch from that day forward.

For both Chaney and Hayes, sport tore down part of the racial barrier their upbringing had instilled in them. To say that it completely erased their negative perceptions of race and race relations would be an overstatement, but it did unquestionably eliminate at least some of the animosity which existed. These men became true friends who stuck together through it all. Lorch would coach Hayes in public speaking so that his Louisiana accent would not hinder him in interviews with the press, and Hayes would take Lorch home with him for holidays. Lorch remembered meeting Hayes's family and friends and enjoying a Thanksgiving dinner of opossum. Tracy and Chaney became so close during their years together that they considered each other "blood brothers" and keep in touch to this day.[23] We cannot doubt therefore that true change was transpiring under the auspices of athletics.

Despite all initial reservations and the work required of those involved, Lewis resolutely stuck by his plan to keep the two black athletes apart. He knew that self-segregation would hinder integration just as much as a forced separation and refused to rethink his strategy. As a result, the young men soon bonded with their white room partners, despite their racial differences, and all learned to respect each other as friends and teammates. Ultimately, Lewis's strategy paid off and just may have been the key to the successful integration. He forced these four athletes to look past skin color and upbringing and see each other as men, as friends, and as teammates. While the living conditions did not immediately appeal to either athlete, they, in retrospect, applauded Lewis's decision. If given the choice, Hayes would have stayed with Chaney, but he soon realized it would have been the wrong decision. He would have been living just as he was in Louisiana with the same adverse ideas about race relations. Chaney expressed the same sentiments saying that although he and his roommate were "two different people, [from] two different backgrounds, two different races ...

[and from] two different sides of the world," Tracy became closer to him than any of his other friends, black or white.[24] They learned to see themselves as equal members of the team and of society rather than mere pawns in the integration process.

Despite the white athletes seeming acceptance of the situation, Hayes realized that they most likely felt the same uneasiness he did as they had never actually lived so closely with blacks before that point. He knew many white players came out of the north, but they had not really roomed and lived with black athletes so closely. It was a new situation for a lot of them and a significant transition. Chaney recalled the initial situation with a bit more tension. He commented, "There was some turmoil for a while.... The basketball players wouldn't even talk to us or even look at us. There was some racism there, no question about it," but, he was quick to add that "things changed quickly."[25] So, the understanding swung both directions, for, while the white athletes recognized the difficult situation the black athletes found themselves in, the black athletes also acknowledged the unusual position of the white athletes. They were as much a part of southern society as anyone else and would have to make certain adjustments regardless of how accepting they were of the black population, and Chaney and Hayes decided to cut them some slack as a result. Arguably, that dual-sided understanding made the attempt at integration viable.

The other factor contributing to the smooth desegregation was Lewis's expectation that every player demonstrate equal commitment and dedication to the team. Everyone contributed the same level of physical output and discipline, and Hayes and Chaney, despite their heralded status and special role within the University, were not exempted from Lewis's standard.[26] No player, regardless of their star rating or race, attained special treatment from the coaching staff, and that placed everyone on the same plane. Although historians such as Richard Lapchick claim that "prejudices [are] unlikely to evaporate with the sweat as [the different races] play together on a team," the Houston basketball team proved that athletics could do just that.[27] The team lived together, played together, and became friends despite the different colors of their skin.

While Hayes and Chaney became acclimated to living on the university campus, dealing with the city of Houston still presented problems. Even though the University of Houston welcomed its newest African

American stars, Houston remained a segregated southern city. The possibility of continued discrimination did not deter Hayes as he had grown accustomed to a second-class status in his hometown and believed himself capable of handling potential difficulties. He recounted that "[Don Chaney and I] knew what we were getting into, but we had endured racial prejudice before and were confident we could do it again while breaking down some old barriers."[28] But even in their confidence, Hayes and Chaney were glad they did not have to face the situation entirely on their own. Hayes remarked toward the end of his days with the Houston Cougars, "I'm glad that Chaney came along with me. With two of us undergoing similar pressures, we were able to help each other when the going got tough."[29] Sadly, if there was one aspect they knew how to handle adequately it was oppression and discrimination. Anything they would see in Houston could not be worse than what they came from.

Fortunately, no insurmountable problems or overt discrimination occurred with any regularity. As minimal and passive as the racial prejudices remained however, both players and their teammates encountered problems while interacting with Houston citizens during that first year. Lorch recalled one evening at a restaurant near campus when several of the white patrons protested their presence to the owners and asked for their removal. Although the restaurateur refused to remove the athletes from his establishment and continued to serve them as though nothing had happened, that type of attitude, prevalent throughout much of the city, was always there. The Cougars knew just enough of the feelings and perceptions of those around to make the situation uncomfortable for the integrated team. On campus, some students expressed displeasure with the situation through more blatant means such as refusing to share a sidewalk with the black athletes or tossing around derogatory language just on the edge of earshot. In other instances, the white team members would be taunted because of their affiliation with the black athletes. Students would posit questions such as, "Are you some kind of nigger lover or something?"[30]

In other situations, the racial affronts were even more direct. Tracy recounted times when Chaney would be denied entrance to movie theaters and other establishments because of his color. Facility owners would remark to the group of athletes, "You guys can [come in] but not the Nigger."[31] Although well acclimated to the racial rebuffs, the rejection seemed to sting the black athletes more because of the mixed company they carried. When these things happened in Louisiana, they were not challenging the line of racial separation and remained within their acceptable spheres. In Houston, however, that was not the case. They were challenging the system by associating with white teammates in public places and opened themselves up to attack. This was a different situation entirely. One teammate recognized the increased level of discomfort felt by the two black stars saying, "[They] got a little embarrassed [about being] told that in front of [their] teammates or [their] peers in mixed company as opposed to being in front of a bunch of black guys who were used to it."[32] This was new territory for them.

To its credit, the athletic department did not let these situations continue unchecked. It challenged the establishments which did not welcome all its athletes and cracked through their policies of segregation.[33] The University of Houston had a responsibility to the players who had agreed to enter its system, and it would do everything within its power to make the process as comfortable as possible for all involved even if that meant dealing directly with segregated facilities. These racial problems would change within the year, but the first few months in Houston did betray a significant level of disapproval at the integration.

Despite those incidents, the overall attitude of Houston's white community pleasantly surprised Hayes. In Louisiana, racial problems were an everyday event that the black population could not escape, but in Houston, the events were at least isolated. There were moments of racism but "there wasn't anything sticking out so blatant as it was where I just had left ... [Houston and Rayville were] day and night and a lot of those things I never saw [in Houston]."[34] For whatever indignities these players experienced, Houston still provided a greater environment of equality than Louisiana.

In order to help Hayes and the other black athletes further adjust to their new surroundings, the University made a conscious effort to incorporate the black community, including prominent business leaders, into Hayes's and Chaney's lives. Both athletes knew, therefore, that they had a bridge that they could cross over and a place where they could go to escape the pressurized situation. Things were not bad at Houston but the constant adjustments necessary and stress of the integration would wear on the most resolute individuals. Texas Southern University provided a nearby location for Chaney and Hayes to leave the all-white environment if even just for a few hours. The University of Houston made every effort to bring comfort to its athletes because it sincerely cared about their well-being. It did not want to simply use its athletes for athletic glory but wanted them to develop into well-educated, prosperous men and did everything possible to bring those goals to fruition.

The time had come for the integration to extend beyond the four roommates as the white team members also had to adjust to sharing the court with black athletes. These white players had to confront whatever prejudices they might have inadvertently carried and learn to interact with members of the African American race on a regular basis. As the team primarily came from the northern areas of the nation, the integration process did not prove overwhelmingly difficult. Many of them had played with African American athletes in high school and did not view the situation in Houston as unusual. Gary Grider, an athlete out of Indiana, had a measure of surprise when he discovered the black players on the roster but was not in any way turned off by the situation. "I was told," he remembered, "that there were no blacks on the team [but] it didn't matter to me one way or another."[35] Leary Lentz, whose freshmen records were eventually broken by Hayes, reacted much the same way saying, "Since I grew up in the North and went to schools which were already integrated I never felt it was significant ... I was naive ... and didn't realize the impact [of the integration] until much later."[36] From their perspectives, integration was a non-issue.

Overall, the team's white players did not seem concerned with the situation, but they were cognizant that the ease of the integration was directly related to the level of athleticism the first black players possessed. "The first ones that were recruited," one member of the team assessed, "were outstanding athletes, they had to be to ease the process."[37] White athletes could accept Chaney and Hayes in part because they knew those two men would help them accomplish their goal of winning games and championships. With increased talent, especially of that magnitude, those concerned with winning could not help but be pleased. The team managed to practice and play together without incident and soon gelled into a functioning unit with a common cause: winning.

Soon, the preparation for the season and the start of the fall semester preoccupied the team, and the integration began in earnest. The duo had adjusted to their teammates well enough, but now they would face basketball audiences who would expect much more from them than the average athlete. They would have to play in front of primarily white audiences yet simultaneously demonstrate an incredible level of discipline and athletic ability. No one knew exactly how the community would respond to the integrated squad, especially if the team failed to perform up to expectations. McVea had navigated through his first season with little difficulty, giving hope that the basketball season would be equally easy, but much uncertainty lingered on. Although not a comfortable situation by any approximation, Chaney and Hayes had come to Houston to play basketball, and it was time to fulfill that responsibility. Lewis too could no longer just promise future success, he and Coach Harvey Pate had to produce victories. All involved now had to focus on the 1964-65 season and perform as promised.

In their freshman year, the two, like all other players who had come before, had to put in a year of playing time for the junior varsity team called the Kittens. The Kittens would travel throughout the state playing mostly junior colleges who did not care for and did not welcome the interracial squad. Hayes recalled, "You would get called the 'N word' by people and it was just a norm, it was just a phenomenon that's what happened... One night against Jacksonville Junior College ... I heard a little boy say, 'Mommy! Mommy! Look at the Niggers.'"[38] For Hayes and Chaney, the experiences of their past granted them an immunity from such comments and taunts, and they brushed off the insults without much thought. It was nothing new.

Despite their treatment of other teams' black athletes, the Cougar fans welcomed Chaney and Hayes as all-star athletes able to lift their team to the pinnacle of competition. The team manager explained how the Kittens consistently drew in larger numbers of fans than the varsity team. "People would line up at the entrances [and] ... there would be a packed house," he explained. "I tell you the University of Houston fans embraced them right away because gosh they were so good."[39] The freshman team brought so much excitement to the campus that the campus newspaper labeled them as "the fabulous five" and as the "brightest spot on the

Kitten Elvin Hayes demonstrates a backwards dunk in 1965. Teammate Don Chaney watches from below.

basketball horizon."[40] Even when Pate's freshmen came home with a loss, the media still praised their skills, in particular those of Hayes and Chaney. Winning helped, but according to Lewis, their demeanor and rapport with fans and students of both colors mattered just as much. According to his perception, the fans could not do anything other than accept the two African American athletes because "by golly, they were just gents.... You couldn't help it, being nice to Elvin and [Don]."[41]

Although both black players had a successful season, Hayes became the team's standout player in that first year. His exploits on the court broke seven freshman records, including point total, scoring average, and total rebounds, and garnered him the nickname which would remain with him for the rest of his career.[42] The "Big E" showed the Houston fans that indeed he could take the team to the top of the NCAA heap and would do so sometime in the following three years.[43] Houston, under his watch, began demanding the attention of the larger conferences, including the ever illusive Southwest Conference, and the nation at the same time by slashing through opponents in style. For those reasons, Hayes, despite his color, quickly became the hero of the Cougar basketball team and the bearer of everyone's hopes.

With the successful Kittens' season, the future of these black athletes seemed strong. Even Hayes felt his on-court skills facilitated true racial acceptance from the fans, commenting, "I think [the fans] came to see how the Negroes were doing, but later on I think they accepted us on our ability, not on our skin color."[44] The University of Houston appeared as though it would support the integration when Hayes and Chaney made their varsity debut. They would have to wait through the summer to find out.

Football Drills

The first year of football integration, despite all the misgivings created by the ruckus which surfaced following McVea's signing, proceeded with greater ease than anyone could have anticipated. Because of all the negative media attention which surfaced just a few months before the start of the season, everyone realistically expected the worst. Warren McVea, though, never second-guessed his ability to win over the staunchest opponents with his athletic abilities. Throughout his high school career, he ran, scored, and out-maneuvered his way into the hearts of many foes with little problem. Even when he stumbled every now and again, his on-field skills were strong enough to override those mistakes.[45] His college coaches knew that the collegiate level would not prove so easy to master, especially with the uncertain racial situation present in Houston, and tried to prepare him for the difference. They understood that the issue of race could trip McVea up because he was not responsible for breaking the color barrier in his high school. In San Antonio, someone else had already undertaken that task, and he, along with other African American athletes, simply stepped into the integrated situation. At Houston though, McVea would not have the benefit of someone else's work; he would have to win support both on and off the field, and he would have to do it alone. Whereas Chaney and Hayes at least had each other, McVea would tackle the situation solo. Despite the concerns of his coaches, McVea was not threatened by the reality before him.[46] He had enough confidence in himself to know that he could take on the team, the city, and football programs across the South all on his own.

As far as meeting with the team, Yeoman, like Lewis, chose not to discuss the matter with the other members of his squad either before or after the decision to integrate. He believed in the integration, acquired the right athlete for the task, and the players' opinion of the situation did not hold any significance to him. From interviews, however, none of the athletes had a problem with the changes anyway. Dick Woodall, the team's starting quarterback during the 1967 season, explained that when the team learned of the integration, it did not have too much concern over it. He said, "I don't ever remember hearing one [negative] comment about black athletes coming in.... We knew we were recruiting good athletes that were going to help the team ... [and] any reaction was excitement about them improving our team."[47] Even those members who had not previously played with African American athletes did not make an issue of the integration making comments such as "I welcomed [him] as a teammate and had no problem at all."[48] Ultimately, the team integration did not lead to any uncommon disruption. For all the planning and preparation, the desegregation of the football team yielded no negative consequences. Kenneth

Hebert said of the situation, "The University of Arkansas had handled the action of integration poorly, and I wondered what the situation [at UH] would be ... it turned out to be a non-factor."[49] Much like the basketball integration, it seemingly past without notice from the white athletes and coaches.

Some of that smooth transition is attributable to the stern direction of Yeoman. While the coach did not discuss the integration with his players, he did firmly instruct them that prejudicial behavior would not be accepted from any member of his team. According to McVea, Yeoman set the tone for the integration early on as he "laid down a foundation [saying] 'Do not mess with this boy ... I'm telling you right now.'"[50] All understood that Yeoman had the most to lose if the situation ballooned out of control and because "this was his decision, and his decision alone, he was determined to make it work."[51] His athletes would either fall in line or quit; either way integration was proceeding as planned.

According to all responding team members, racial tensions and outbursts simply did not occur following the issued directive. McVea, who would have been privy to any negative behavior, only remembered one minor incident during his junior varsity season. With Yeoman absent from practice, a white player decided to test the limits of the previously established policy. This athlete physically challenged McVea, who responded in turn. Although a black man physically challenging a white man was not acceptable by societal standards, McVea decided to establish his equality early on. According to McVea, the player "looked at [him] like 'he's not afraid' and it was almost like 'hey, I better lay off because I know the rules.'"[52] After that brief set-to, the two athletes became friends, working out together and sharing football tips. From then on, racially motivated disputes did not arise among team members.

As much impartiality as Yeoman required of his athletes, he fully exhibited the same level back to them. From the beginning, he demanded equal participation and discipline from every athlete regardless of color. Yeoman explained, "We just didn't pay attention to color.... If a kid could play, he'd play.... I didn't care what color he was."[53] Although certain reports claimed that McVea did not receive an equal level of discipline from the coaches, players such as Michael Barbour claimed otherwise. They insisted that Yeoman and his staff treated every squad member with equal rigor.[54]

The media's claims to the contrary were arguably only attempts to exacerbate an already tense situation. McVea himself admitted that his coach required him to perform according to the same expectations and demanded complete obedience to orders at all times. During one game, McVea decided to challenge Yeoman's command and was told right away, "You've got about fifteen seconds to put your [football] pads on or else I'm going to beat you up right here on the sideline."[55] Within fifteen seconds, McVea had himself back on the field. If he chose to break the rules or not follow orders, he too would receive the chastisement of his coach without exception.

The ease of the transition should not be overly simplified. These young men, although not overtly racist and more racially progressive than many other southern athletes, still had to deal with the temper of the times. The prevailing societal attitudes did not look favorably upon the black community or its constant striving for equal rights, and those attitudes had to at least minimally influence the white students. Racism was, after all, part of the culture and the majority of people were not so sheltered as to not assume some of those attitudes. One team member did admit that "a few of the white athletes had a historical southern view of the blacks [but] these feelings were not pronounced publicly."[56] McVea, although unquestionably comfortable with his fellow teammates because they never made him feel unwelcome or out of place, understood that some on the team subconsciously reflected the majority opinion about black athletes. He remembered one incident when a few guys used derogatory language in a conversation without even realizing the racial connotations associated with the words. McVea recalled, "They had got so used to me being in the room that I was one of them, I became one of the guys [and] ... [the N word] slipped from a guy's mouth one night."[57] Although they did not intend to offend McVea or his race, they did demonstrate their unconscious perpetuation of the traditional southern ideology. The incident did not overwhelmingly bother the black athlete because he understood these white players had to adjust to the integration as well, and further, they were products of their time and environment.

Even at that though, other members of the team were sensitive to McVea's situation and made sure to speak with him about it. Following the aforementioned event, Mike Pate, an athlete out of Odessa, Texas, took time to encourage his teammate and said, "You've got to forget about that ... [and] stop letting [those comments] upset you." He exhorted him further, commenting, "You made your decision to come here [and] you're doing something for your race, you're doing something for yourself, [and] your doing something for your family."[58] The words of his friend convinced McVea that he could and should let the thoughtless comments go unchecked. After all, he knew his team accepted him without regard to his skin color, and their actions were simply the repetition of learned behavior. Like Hayes and Chaney, McVea made a conscious effort to grant a measure of understanding to his fellow team members. Both sides of the racial divide were consciously making an effort.

The city of Houston as well as the school campus, although not as abrasively racist as most other cities in the deep South, did present problems for the heralded runner, more so than it presented for the basketball players. Perhaps because of his high profile or perhaps because football reigned supreme in Texas, he experienced increased levels of negative attention from all directions. In regard to the city itself, McVea found himself harassed with regularity. The police department stopped him frequently while driving, both alone and with his white teammates, and often questioned his presence on Houston streets.[59] On campus, the insults also surfaced during the first year, although they were never directly aimed at him. He would hear derogatory language from a distance but never to his face. In keeping with the passive discrimination of the city, McVea only experienced subtle racism which could not be directly challenged. So, the only African American football player turned a deaf ear and refused to let the little things deter him from the issue at hand. All that mattered was winning football games and earning an education.

With the outside situations under control, Warren McVea and his fellow freshmen teammates continued solidifying their friendships and readied themselves for junior varsity competition, which consisted of a four game schedule. Like the basketball team, the football team had to show Cougar fans that they could win even if only on the small stage. Unlike Harvey Pate's basketball freshmen, the football freshmen would have the nation's eyes trained on them and could not hide their performances, either good or bad. The excitement surrounding McVea's career would bring added interest to the team, and should it fail to live up to expectations, the next three years could prove difficult.

McVea's athletic career began relatively quickly following his move to Houston as the season kicked off in late September 1964. Beginning with the annual red/white game, the fans immediately came out to see their newest and greatest athletic wonder. Local press covered the event closely, although team scrimmages hardly qualified as newsworthy sporting events, and expected much from the athlete everyone had spoken so highly of. Twelve hundred fans turned out for that debut, yet the unusually large crowd left extremely disappointed as McVea did not play a single down. Citing injury and bad field conditions, Carroll Schultze, the junior varsity coach, and Yeoman opted to keep the program's greatest star out of the game. McVea had slightly injured himself during the off season and played a part in the decision to remain inactive. He felt his injury left him unable to perform up to his ability. Yeoman said of McVea's absence, "He knows how much people expect of him, and he doesn't want to get out there unless he can do his best."[60] Although necessary, his lack of play led to a rocky start.

White reports brushed off McVea's time on the bench understanding it was after all only a freshman scrimmage, and McVea had too much talent to risk on such a minimal event. They would simply wait for the next outing. The black media, on the other hand, did not take the letdown so well. It insisted that the fans present, which consisted primarily of those from the African American community, had been tricked by the UH athletic department into attending a game featuring only white athletes. Reports described how the fans, "which booed lustily" during the game, would not be wary of UH. McVea supporters felt "the magic of Warren McVea has not diminished but the confidence of football fans has been bruised."[61] The black community was not pleased with McVea's absence from the Houston line-up.

The reaction of the black community, which bordered on anger, is surprising. It would seem as though African American spectators would be appreciative of the coaches' desire to avoid an injury to McVea during a game without significance. If the athletic department had wanted to exploit the young man, it could have played him regardless of the injury he nursed and risked his future career just to satisfy UH fans. Nevertheless, it appeared as though the black spectators felt entitled to watch "their boy," and paternalism was working in reverse.

Warren McVea displays his running abilities against the Air Force freshman team in 1964. This 20–14 win was covered by *Sports Illustrated*.

For whatever disappointment the fans felt about McVea sitting out of the first scrimmage, they felt equal elation when he made his first appearance a little over a month later. In the game against the Air Force Academy, McVea played brilliantly in front of a crowd over eight thousand strong. His on field exploits, which included two lengthy touchdown runs, even led to a feature article in *Sports Illustrated*, an occurrence almost unheard of for freshman games. It praised his athletic abilities and emphasized the unusual interest he garnered: "Tickets to freshmen games are now in far greater demand than those of the varsity, and those fans who cannot get seats perch themselves atop the scoreboard or simply stand."[62] McVea finally began demonstrating to his fans and critics that he would perform brilliantly for the Cougars. His shows of athleticism during that game brought so much support that the Cougar program arranged to have the game film aired on pubic television so the entire Houston area could view McVea's spectacular displays.[63] In his freshman year, McVea was performing as all had hoped he would.

At the conclusion of the season, McVea had further convinced the fans that he would take the Houston program to the top of the collegiate sports world. He knew though that he could never let his guard down and would have to continue performing consistently and perfectly. He expressed this clearly saying, "You never forget that people are watching you and that some of them are waiting for you to mess up." But, he did not attribute that constant scrutiny to any issue of race. In his opinion, he was not being treated than any other athlete. He said, "They do that with all athletes."[64] Despite all the challenges ahead, McVea knew from the beginning that he would find success in Houston.

The overwhelmingly successful first years did not completely comfort Chaney, Hayes, or McVea. They had achieved much in their respective sports, won over the support of the majority of fans, and acclimated to their teammates and life in Houston. All the indicators signaled that the seamless integration of the freshman teams would carry over to the varsity teams as well. But none of the three players or their coaching staffs rested on the laurels gained knowing that varsity play was an entirely different entity. The media would train its sights on these players and quickly pass judgment should they fail. Competition would increase, opponents would more vehemently protest their racial composition, and the team's unity would be tested. The 1964-65 seasons were only a starting point.

The 1965-66 seasons would be the true test, and the athletes recognized that. Hayes acknowledged the pressure: "We were in the same kind of situation Jackie Robinson found himself in when he became the first man to play major league baseball ... on a smaller scale of course but a similar situation.... The pressure was on us."[65] Yet, such a challenge did not deter Hayes because he, like Chaney and McVea, knew that he could perform up to anyone's standards. With the start of his varsity career, Hayes gathered his resolve and "determined, with a burning fire inside [him], to prove myself against all those white players.... They were white and accepted and talented.... We were talented but not much else."[66] The next three years would give them all, coaches and players alike, the chance to demonstrate conclusively that integrated teams would acquire a tremendous level of success and would do so at the expense of white programs unwilling to embrace the black athletes.

6

Ready or Not,
Let the Redvolution Begin

The 1964-65 seasons, although a significant period for the racial issues within the team itself, was realistically only a warm-up for 1965-66 when fan and media attention would focus squarely on the integrated squad. The Houston Cougars, with three black athletes on the rosters, took to the courts and fields understanding that they fought not only their weekly opponents but racism and prejudice as well. The coaches knew the time for talk was coming to an end, and there would be no more grace period. They understood the existence of the UH program rode on their perform- ances both on and off the court and extensively planned and prepared to make certain they did not fail. By the end of the season, one way or the other, all those uncertainties would no longer exist.

Under the Domed Lights

The fall of 1965 was a huge time for the Houston Cougar football team. Bill Yeoman and his athletes would take the field inside the newly minted Astrodome, hyped as the "8th wonder of the world," and, with Warren McVea in tow, the team was expected to have "an offensive threat unequaled in its 20-year history."[1] It would obliterate all teams that came against it. McVea would serve as the headline athlete and carry the team to the top of the national rankings. Sports writers fueled the hype writ- ing furiously of the season's nationally televised opener against the Uni- versity of Tulsa. They insisted that McVea would perform super-human

Top: The 1965-66 Varsity Basketball Team photograph. Howard Lorch is on the front right and John Tracy is on the front row, fourth from right. The team had a 23-6 record. *Above:* Two young Coog fans cheer on the home team. With McVea on the roster and the strong team efforts, attendance soared to all-time highs (1965).

Athletes line up to speak with NBC Sports prior to the 1965 game versus Tulsa. McVea's lackluster debut in the NCAA game of the week was not the start anyone had expected.

feats of athleticism and said, "Here's hoping the TV people have their instant replay camera on our boy all the time."[2] The national media bought into the McVea phenomenon and had the opening game moved to an earlier start time so viewers on the East Coast could watch Houston's wonder athlete. With a near capacity crowd of 38,000, the city of Houston along with the rest of the nation sat down to watch Houston's first integrated team play its first game in the newest, most advanced, and most expensive stadium in the nation.[3]

Despite the heavy publicity, not all observers wished the team so well. Certain media outlets highlighted and emphasized the consequences to be met if the team faltered against Tulsa or any other of its upcoming opponents. They wrote, "The Cougars are embarking on the most important season of their football history and if they stumble and fall the first crack out of the box, a lot of folks are going to be sadly disappointed."[4] Reports also commented on the potential damage to the Cougars' reputation should the final scoreboard not show a Houston victory. One remarked, "They will be performing for the first time in *living color* before a nationwide television audience.... [They] have a lot at stake."[5] The *Houston Chronicle* took a more subtle approach in its coverage. It placed McVea on the cover of its "Texas Magazine" football insert to seemingly hype the impending game but instead insulted the African American athlete in the process. In what it claimed was only an editor's mistake, the article misspelled McVea's name in all mentions of him. A San Antonio reporter insinuated that the mistake was more than a simple error and that the direct affront would detract from McVea's varsity debut. The writer commented that now as McVea "nears his biggest moment in football ... he will be known in some places as McVey." He called the editor to task, saying, "May the editor who permitted this sin to be committed escape with his life if nothing else."[6] Much like the subtle racism prevalent in the city, ugly undertones obviously existed and those upset over the integrated Cougars tried to undermine the process whenever necessary. Should the team fail, detractors would exploit its failures to the fullest extent.

With all the attention swirling around him, McVea understood the precarious situation he was in. Responsibility for the team's performance, good or bad, would belong almost solely to him. He admitted this, saying before the first game, "I'm getting a little nervous.... I never really thought I'd be a marked man as a sophomore [with] all the publicity and things in the magazines and papers."[7] The team deflected the attention away from McVea as much as possible and consciously presented a united front to the media. Regardless of how the team performed, the members made it known that it would be a team effort. Dick Post exemplified this as he remarked before the season, "It's a heck of a threat having [McVea] back there.... I think [McVea and I] can help each other, but most of all, I think we both can help the team."[8] Yeoman echoed those sentiments in his responses to questions concerning the centrality of McVea. He reminded the press, "We've got to be careful about losing our heads.... He's still going to have to acclimate himself to the speed with which the defense moves."[9] The team let it be known that it took the field as a solitary unit and would win or lose as such.

The unity of the varsity team was clear from the onset of the season. Whatever minor racial problems existed among the freshman team the previous year had dissipated by 1965 and when the sophomores joined the varsity team no racial issues surfaced. The majority of team members had no objections to integration and played alongside McVea without any qualms. To propose that none of the white athletes needed a period of adjustment would be naïve and inaccurate. We can claim, however, that those objections were never openly articulated. As noted by one team member, "A few of the white athletes had a historical southern adversarial view, however, these feelings were not pronounced publicly."[10] The coaching staff, aware of the standard cultural attitudes of the South and the acclimatization certain white members would have to make, worked to keep serious tensions in check and to facilitate racial acceptance among the athletes. Athlete Pat Pryor said of the coach's effort, "[Yeoman] does not have a bigoted cell in his body, and he would not permit it to ever become an issue."[11] Ultimately though, the staff made it clear that racial discord would not be acceptable. Pryor continued, "Without ever saying a word about it, it was a given that racial squabbles would not be tolerated."[12]

Perhaps more effective than the coaches' directives, McVea's personality helped convince those athletes reticent about desegregation that he was just like them. Fellow athlete Tom Beer attributed McVea's catching persona as the most persuasive factor, saying, "[He] had a wonderful personality, [he] was smart and well spoken, had an infectious sense of humor and dressed impeccably well. You could *not* not like Warren."[13] Pat Pryor had a similar view: "While not a Jackie Robinson clone, he was close enough.... Although not overly chummy, he was never sullen or isolated, and once you saw him on the field it was, whew, whoa."[14] Dick Woodall confirmed that sentiment commenting, "We became friends before we even kicked off the first game of the season.... From my perspective, I [didn't] see any skin color. When you have a teammate and a friend, it just [didn't] matter."[15] Whereas other institutions had significant documented problems between black and white athletes, Houston's varsity adjustment progressed without incident.[16] Genuine friendships developed among the players, and, when the season began, those relationships would keep the team together despite the best attempts by outsiders to pull it apart.

The 1965 season, full of expectations and demands for perfection, began in disaster as every Cougar's worst fear came to fruition. Despite the hopes to the contrary, the team lost five out of its first six games and was outscored by an embarrassing point margin of 142 to 33. McVea and the coach who brought him to the team took the fall for the gridiron failure even though coaches and athletes emphasized team play. After the loss against Tulsa, in which McVea sat on the sideline for the entire second half, the critics pounded the sophomore star with comments such as, "It is doubtful if ever a sophomore heralded or unheralded ever had a worse day or disappointed people more than did Mac the Knife" and "He bombed out, to put it mildly. He fizzled so completely the first half it became embarrassing to everybody."[17] The criticism did not relent for most of the season as the press constantly belittled McVea by writing, "It remained for [him] to provide a new way to blow [a game]; he didn't remember to down a kickoff in the end zone."[18] The newspapers even defended their hounding of the sophomore athlete from those who questioned why the young star received more than his share of the blame. One reporter wrote, "It perhaps is unfair to judge a 19-year-old sophomore so quickly, but that is the price such a bally-hooed entertainer must pay."[19] The majority of the media was mercilessly hard on McVea throughout the losing stretch and felt no need to lay off. This was the opportunity they had anxiously awaited, and they would not let McVea out of their cross-hairs.

Members of the press with ties to the young speedster did step forward to defend McVea from the attacks. Dan Cook, who first broke the story of McVea's signing with Houston, pointed out the immense level of pressure resting on the athlete and suggested that it was seriously impacting his game. "Maybe the pressure of his first collegiate game," he wrote, "finally snapped something inside the boy's nerve system.... He looked as though the whole dome of this great stadium pressed squarely on his back."[20] Others tried to pass off his poor performance on the artificial grass which filled the Astrodome. The first of its kind, the synthetic turf appropriately named Astroturf was harder than anyone had anticipated, and all of the athletes, even those from opposing teams, complained that they could not get a proper footing. Astrodome officials scrambled to rectify the situation, and some objective reporters tried to forgive McVea's weak performances based on the rock-hard ground. They remarked, "Mac the Knife gave the only real dull performance of his career through no fault of his own.... Wonderous Warren tried to make the moves that made him famous and defenders look silly and there was [no grass] there to hold his cleats."[21] Still others pointed to the poor performance of the rest of the team and the effect of that ineptness on McVea making statements such as, "The blockers weren't providing [him] with any room for fancy maneuvers" and "the Cougars [despite McVea's flashes of greatness] unveiled all sorts of new problems and their ills appeared beyond cure."[22] McVea had a few allies in the press, but the detrimental reports were obviously in the majority.

The Houston fans did not take the failure well either, and they, like portions of the press, directed their disappointment and disgust at McVea. They were loud and vocal about their unhappiness with his performance and let Yeoman and his star know of their sentiments.[23] Reporters referred to Houston as "a team with more coaches in the stands than the law allows," and with fans like "wolves [who] let Yeoman know who should be in the game by their cheers and boos."[24] During the Tusla debacle, McVea was jeered each time he entered the field, even when only seconds remained in the game. The whole team played poorly but McVea had to take the brunt of the fans' dissatisfaction. They made it entirely clear what they would and would not accept from the Cougars, and a non-contributing, error prone McVea was not acceptable.

Amidst all the criticism, the team attempted to defend its beleaguered teammate and his athletic abilities. Yeoman pointed out to critics that "Warren played a good game, you can't just expect a sophomore to come on right away. He'll come along.... He's just got to adjust to varsity ball."[25] Bum Phillips, the defensive coach who went on to coach the Houston Oilers, also emphasized the team nature of the game. "This is a whole team game," he stated, "not an offensive team and a defensive team." Yeoman seconded his thoughts, saying, "[All] our boys are capable of better football.... We just didn't play well at all."[26]

McVea, not used to the large number of detractors or more so his own poor athletic performances, reacted to the situation with remorse. The media noted his sense of embarrassment and commented how apologetic McVea was. They quoted him as saying, "I know I have let my teammates down. I guess it's my fault for not coming back in better shape," and noted that he "[offered] a final apology to anybody listening."[27] The star athlete did not even complain about the significant level of criticism he received and informed reporters that his disgraceful outing merited all the criticism the fans could muster. He had let them down and would take their berating comments like a man. After the fifth loss of the season, however, it became apparent that the intensifying pressure was affecting the athlete. A reporter noted this: "He still walks with the same old strut but his nose has been lowered out of the clouds."[28] Those wishing to put McVea in his place were slowly succeeding.

Although he tried not to let anyone know that the criticism grated on him, McVea felt the full sting of its commentary. "That was the worst press," he remembered, "I didn't know that people could be so brutal. I had never had bad press and I saw this article where it said, 'The Astrodome might be the 8th wonder of the world, but I guarantee you Warren McVea isn't the 9th.'"[29] For an athlete who could do no wrong before, his unexpected failure and intense criticism wore on him and his resolve to keep going. Fortunately, he refused to give up.[30] His coach, understanding the unenviable situation his first black athlete found himself in, encouraged McVea to keep his head up and not adopt a downtrodden demeanor. "Don't look for a place to hide," Yeoman told him, "Don't let this get you down. All athletes make mistakes. It's the way you react that makes you and I want you to know I'm going to keep right on putting you right out there in the spotlight because I know what you can do."[31] McVea, trusting his coach almost as much as a father, took Yeoman's advice and kept pushing forward week after week despite the ultimate score. If only by sheer determination, he would work through his struggles and remain resolute even with all the mounting pressure.

McVea was not the only Cougar under attack as Yeoman too received a fair amount of negativity from fans and boosters. Integration had been Yeoman's brainchild. He had pushed for it, promised it would lead to tremendous results, and understood from the beginning that he would take the fall if it failed. The plan which he had so much faith in was seriously faltering early on as his team lost to squads throughout the southern states. Cougar fans and the city of Houston found the football program unacceptable and aggressively questioned Yeoman's decision to bring McVea on board. Calls for his job began surfacing after the first two losses. Fans demanded a change in the coaching staff, and rumors quickly circulated that the University, following a secret meeting by upper-level officials in the underbelly of the Astrodome, was firing Yeoman via a contract buyout because of the poor team he fielded.[32] President Hoffman ardently defended the battered coach telling the press that "there is nothing to [the rumors] at all.... [He] is our coach, and we have full confidence in him. I am going to be out there rooting strongly for him Friday night."[33] Corbin Robertson, a former member of the UH Board of Directors and a strong supporter of the athletic program, also defended Yeoman from the rising detractors saying, "My gosh, two games don't make a season. I can't understand what these people are getting excited about." He further made a direct statement on the integration, applauding Yeoman's racial strides by commenting, "[He] is doing a lot for this school in a lot of ways."[34] Although the school's representatives determinedly denied the rumor, it continued to swirl through the city.

Cougar alumni and supporters were not alone in their dogging of Yeoman as UH students, and even some members of his team, questioned whether Yeoman could live up to his promises of success. After the loss to Mississippi State, two unidentified players remarked that the team could not win with Yeoman. Their comments began innocently enough as they despaired over their record: "We're through, we'll be lucky if we finish 1-9 now." But they went beyond a sense of disappointment as they said of the coaching staff, "None of the players have the respect of the coaches." The students came to the same conclusion and pointed out that "the talent is obviously there [but watching] all of it going to waste, seems unfair to the boys who take the lumps in vain."[35] On campus, an anonymous student group hanged Yeoman in effigy from the school's flag pole. Hearing the rumor that "Yeoman might be sacrificed to irate, win-hungry alumni," the group put together the display to demonstrate its, and the rest of the students', dissatisfaction with the direction the team had taken.[36]

Yeoman, showing an understandable level of irritation, defended his position and the racial diversification of his team. "I'm not quitting," he said, "my daddy didn't raise a quitter. I'm particularly not quitting in view of the things we've accomplished here. We've put in a lot of work and we've got a lot of things done."[37] He also refused to get upset about the press reports because he understood that "they [weren't] interested in [simple] reporting but in creating controversy."[38] Neither the press, nor the fans, nor even his own athletes, would not distract him from his team or the fulfillment of his vision.

Even with such resoluteness, Yeoman was undeniably in a precarious situation. If he wanted his job and the integration he established to remain intact for at least another year, Yeoman needed to find a way to fulfill all of his off-season promises. That task would not be easy as the Cougars' remain-

McVea, the hero of the UH. Ole Miss match-up, is carried off the field by a crowd of his white peers. Houston scored 17 points to grab their first ever win over Mississippi (1965).

108

ing four games included perennial powerhouses such as Ole Miss and Florida State. With his back against the wall and precious few supporters remaining, Yeoman rallied his troops and made them focus on the upcoming games, one at a time. The past blunders did not matter nor did the bad press that had been hounding their play. They just had to chip away one yard at a time. The majority of the team trusted their coach and focused on the task. To the surprise of most, the team did what only a few remaining supporters still thought it could and what all had been expecting since the start of the season. It went toe to toe with the teams and produced three straight victories and one tie outscoring its opponents by a point margin of 94 to 31.[39] Finally, the Cougars were winning in dramatic fashion against many of the top athletes and programs, and the fans' negativity quickly transformed into celebration. Victories automatically pacified the majority of the watching public.

From the fans' perspective, the dramatic turnaround fixed all ills. Once the team won with regularity, they had no problem with the coach, the players, or the integration. With the success of the team, the "Coogs' fans were thoroughly aroused [as they] howled gleefully as the scoreboard exploded."[40] After the defeat of Ole Miss, crowds, primarily white in composition, rushed the field to carry off their one-time scapegoat in heroic fashion. Yeoman had been under attack by the fans before but now found "[his] office crowded with well-wishers and happy students and alumni [and realized] nothing [brought] back fans like a couple of big wins."[41] The campus newspaper, *The Daily Cougar*, "called for unconditional support for the Cougar team and an end to [all the] rumors and discontent."[42] Members of the Cougar Club, the organization dedicated to the support of the athletic program, showed up in significant numbers to watch game film and hear Yeoman speak about his athletes. During an event which "premiered the movie of [the Ole Miss] miracle," the packed room was filled with "a hand-clapping, knee-slapping, red-coated crowd."[43] The surging attendance numbers provided the most concrete evidence of bolstered fan support. By the end of the 1965 season, even with the rough start, the team broke the existing season attendance record.[44] The Houston fans wanted to see their Cougars beat up on the opposition and as the team demonstrated it could do so with regularity, the fans turned out in increasingly large numbers.

At the completion of the 1965 schedule, the fans were sold on the

Cougars, but had unequivocally demonstrated that they would only lend their support if the team won consistently and convincingly. It is perhaps unfair to say that integration made the fans so fickle. As quarterback Dick Woodall observed, fans reacted to losses in the same matter regardless of the racial status of the team. He recalled, "When you start losing ... people get testy because they want to win, whether they're black or white. I saw more fights between white people [before McVea came] than I ever want to remember."[45] At the very least then, we can say that integration gave fans a target for their ire. When the team failed, McVea would almost exclusively reap their disappointment.

As they did in defeat, the Cougars made sure the media recognized that winning came as a result of a team effort. The end-of-season run was not about the miraculous play of McVea or about the amazing coaching schemes of Yeoman but about a group of diverse individuals learning to come together and overcome the obstacles placed in front of them. When the team seriously faltered, the Cougar camp always focused on the problems of the team, and when the team learned how to win, the team's focus did not change. Yeoman reiterated that point saying in response to an inquiry about which players made the most impact, "The group on offense and the group on defense."[46] And, no athlete was above playing a supporting role. For example, the first Cougar touchdown of the season came as McVea, who was expected to be the leading scorer and little else, provided a block so Ken Hebert could take the ball into the end zone and demonstrated that he was not above fulfilling backup roles.[47] After another game, players traded compliments as McVea stated, "I owe everything to [quarterback] Bo (Burris) tonight," and Burris responded, "[McVea] got open.... You can't over throw a guy like that."[48] Even those players who lost starting positions to McVea hoped for his success. Mike Spratt, a halfback who found himself on the bench due to injury, was seen "throwing tape, yelling, and singing" and said after the win, "My boy came through. He's an old veteran now. No more nervousness for Warren."[49] The athletes knew that only in a complete effort could they attain their ultimate goals. As one member explained there were no stars or scrubs, "there [was] no black or white in a huddle, only players."[50]

The press, minimally acknowledging the contributions of the other Houston athletes, severely overlooked the larger team effort. Creative

The Cougars in action in the Astrodome. Ken Hebert scores a touchdown in the 38–21 win over University of Kentucky (1965).

descriptions proliferated and placed the spotlight solely on McVea. The reviews read, "Warren skittered inside ... with arms grabbing and missing from all sides" and "the little speedster dodged, weaved, faked, and bobbed, leaving [Kentucky] Wildcat players sprawling on the turf with nothing but handfuls of dirt."[51] Other reports more directly tied the success of the team to McVea: "[The] University of Houston popped the cork on its 'secret weapon' Saturday night."[52] Write-ups credited McVea with full responsibility for the wins saying bluntly, "Where all the [Cougar] heroes were valiant, McVea carved a special niche" and "UH found that happiness is Warren McVea."[53]

During the course of that first season, the issue of desegregation did not go unnoticed by fans in the South.[54] McVea chipped away at the color barrier, took the field against institutions which embraced the traditional southern attitudes, and faced a significant level of opposition from many sides in the process. In his sophomore season, McVea was the only black athlete in eight out of ten games, and southern fans did not take the integrated team lightly. When it came to defending their segregated fields, many went to extremes promising that "that Nigger [will be shot if he] sets foot on our turf."[55] The Klu Klux Klan called McVea's room and informed him he would be killed if he went ahead with his plans to play Mississippi, and "nobody would ever look for the shooter."[56] For McVea, the anti-integration reaction did not come as a surprise; he had expected such derogatory statements and volatile responses.

The same level of preparedness did not apply to the white members of the team. The Southern reactions they encountered made them, many for the first time, truly aware of the cultural boundaries Houston challenged.[57] Tom Beer said, "We [heard] racial slurs and epithets from the stands, especially behind our bench ... calling us 'nigger lovers' ... [and saying] 'ya'll get the nigger-kill em.'"[58] For these white young men, the experiences demonstrated precisely how their fellow Southerners viewed black athletes and those who fraternized with them.

Yeoman and his Cougars tried to limit public interaction while away from home, even going so far as to re-route travel plans. Yeoman recalled that the team would fly out of its way to avoid set downs in southern towns including "fly[ing] to Shreveport, [to] land and re-gas so we could get all the way to Florida State [without stopping]."[59] During unavoidable interaction, security guards and chaperones remained near at all times to protect the young men.[60] There was no reason to take unnecessary risks while in hostile territory. McVea took the situations in stride and Information Director Ted Nance applauded his self-control: "The thing that impressed me about Warren is how he handled himself [on the road].... He was treated very poorly by some crowds."[61]

The racial hostility was not limited to away games. Houston faced prejudiced fans at home in the Astrodome as well. They attacked Warren with slights inferring that he would never perform better than the white athletes and mocking him when he struggled.[62] Those more direct about their dislike of the integrated Cougars, such as the Florida State fans, "went after [them] with a lot of heart ... [and] showed it even before the kickoff waiving signs like "kill" and similar endearments."[63] In defeating Deep South schools, Houston directly challenged the racism those institutions espoused. Jerry Wizig picked up on that parallel writing after a victory, "[Houston] lynched Ole Miss to the Domed Stadium's yardarm."[64] Undeniably, the Cougars were under attack because of McVea, but they would all fight the racial battle together.

Although the majority of spectators chose not to recognize or applaud the racial struggle playing itself out on the field, some supporters did highlight the significance of McVea's racial accomplishments.[65] *The Daily Cougar* ran two articles which explained the difficult situation McVea faced that year and the hypocrisy of the Houston fans and media. It first pointed out that he made it through a rough year where "one week he is everyone's scapegoat and a big heel of a fellow with too much publicity, the next week he is 'our boy.'"[66] The writers noted the unfair media treatment he received, the attacks hurled at him when the team performed poorly, and the burden he carried as "an ambassador" of his race. Further, they credited the team for remaining unified during the season and Yeoman for encouraging McVea to keep his head up during the downward spiral. Finally, the article sent a message to Cougar fans who "do not like [McVea] because of his race," saying "that particular type of fair-weather and prejudiced fan is the kind not wanted or needed." Frank Schultz, Jr., a young *Daily Cougar* columnist, heralded Yeoman as "a head football coach [who] refused to panic when his squad looked dismal" and praised McVea because he "[failed] to fold and kept working [despite] hearing many a catcall."[67] McVea had stumbled out of the gate, but along the way he gained the respect of some of his fellow students and sports fans through his perseverance during those hardships.

The 1965 season ended with a 4-5-1 record and no post season berth. Late season speculation had placed Houston in the Bluebonnet Bowl, but when that fell through and the bowl chose two other schools, the Cougars' season ended. It would be McVea's and his fellow teammates' only chance to attend a bowl game as the NCAA suspension, which banned the team from postseason play as well as any further television appearances, went into effect the following season. That suspension would not slow down the team's progress, and the 1966 season saw increased on-field production. The '66 team won eight out of ten games and outscored their opponents by a point margin of 335 to 125. While that second season would undoubtedly produce positive results, it did not have the same effect as McVea's senior season with the team. That final year would split the sports community apart and expose the reality of race relations among fans and foes. It would also cement the integration at Houston and throughout the South.

Stepping onto the Hardwood

With the end of the football season, the basketball team began its warm-ups. The Cougar Cagers began the 1965 season under tremendous pressure as the success of the 1964 Kittens squad elevated expectations to an all-time high. Conversations of the team's strengths and abilities rose dramatically in the days leading up to the start of the season, and the newspapers only added fuel to the frenzy already in full swing. They gushed about the new and improved line-up: "The Little People are gone from the University of Houston basketball.... [It has] lost its gnome court advantage" and has been replaced with "large people who wear triple-X shoes, sleep in outsized beds and have to be careful with their noggins when they walk into a room."[68] The school newspaper concurred; it said, "Gone are the Lilliputians of the past. No longer will the Cougars have to look up to any team."[69] Outside of the adjective laced descriptions, the media filled its pages and reports with statistical analysis and insisted that the '65 Cougars were the best team ever assembled under Lewis.[70] Season tickets flew out of the ticket office as more fans wanted to see the Cougars play than the Del Mar Gym could hold. It was the city's hottest ticket, and Cougars clamored to get their hands on them. To help with the seating limitations, a local radio station, KPRC, agreed to broadcast each of the twenty-six Cougar games that season so all who wanted to hear them could. Houston was clearly ready for the start of the basketball season and ready to see their Cougars dominate the competition.

With all the attention surrounding the season's commencement, Lewis feared the high expectations placed on his team and desperately tried from the onset to temper thoughts of perfection. He openly acknowledged that the team's talent exceeded that of any of his previous squads; no one would believe otherwise anyway. With sophomore standout Elvin Hayes and his supporting cast, including Don Chaney, Lewis could not deny that "as far as material is concerned, this is the best, overall, we've ever had. It's also the tallest."[71] He stressed that even with the strong athletes immediate success may not be realistic. Part of his concern stemmed from the schedule the team faced. Of the twenty-six teams lined up, only seven of those finished with losing records the prior season and many others, including season openers University of San Francisco and Brigham Young University, perennially contended for the NCAA title. He explained in advance, "I wouldn't want to think our whole season will be judged on two games. Even if we lose our first two games, I still feel we'll have a good ball club."[72] Lewis also wanted fans to understand that the difficult strength of schedule would challenge his players and that they "could still be a better team and wind up with a worse record."[73]

His second concern stemmed from the newness of the team. With five new members on a twelve man squad, Lewis wondered if the team chemistry would develop quickly enough to produce immediate wins. Even with amazing talent and athletic abilities, if the varsity team could not learn to play together, he knew victories would be few and far between. Lewis forewarned, "We're not a basketball team [right now]; we're a bunch of individuals.... I'm hoping we 'jell' pretty soon ... [especially since] they're going to require a period of adjustment to the competition we'll face."[74] Lewis tried frequently to tame the fans' high expectations in a young, untested squad. Should it sputter at the beginning of the season, he wanted the fans to be prepared. The coach fretted that the season would not initially meet everyone's expectations, and discontent would rise quickly as it had with football.

Although it is not certain that the integrated squad fueled those concerns, we can assert that the presence of the black athletes did not help the situation. Elvin Hayes and Don Chaney were supposed to revolutionize the basketball world, and supporters of the program had agreed to accept them primarily for that reason. They traded in segregated teams for victories. If the African American athletes and their coach could not demonstrate dramatic results, exponentially hostile crowds would greet them. The fans would have sacrificed their traditionally-white teams for nothing. It is further possible that Lewis's irritability was heightened because of the harsh press Yeoman received less than three months before. He saw the aggressive treatment the football team was subjected to and probably feared that he and his men would fall into the same situation.

With everything riding on the line, the Cougars began their first integrated season on 1 December 1965. Just as Lewis feared, the season began inauspiciously with a loss to the University of San Francisco by a score of 75–67.[75] After that opener, the press began questioning the team's talent and its ability to perform better than previous squads. The crowds, already protective of all-white teams, turned a critical eye toward Hayes, and the loss did not facilitate acceptance. Lewis, understanding all that was as stake, publicly defended his decisions in regard to the team. He let the media know that his talented players would eventually produce victories saying, "I'm convinced we're going to have a good basketball team.... We [just] need to get together and become a team." The intense criticism grated on Lewis, and, as the *Houston Post* reported, "[His] voice, even over 1,600 miles of telephone wire still crackled with the tension and frustration of a coach who had just seen his team lose its basketball opener." He went on to snap at reporters, "I can see some sunshine in a loss.... Our kids didn't quit out there."[76]

The Cougars did not have much time to rebound from the loss as Brigham Young University awaited its chance at Houston only a few days later. The result did not come out much different as the team fell by nearly thirty points, 111–82. Lewis had to face the press again and had little patience for its questions. "Counting his blessings like a pauper searching for an overlooked coin," the coach said the only bright side of the game was, "We don't have to play them again tomorrow night, because they'd probably whip us again."[77] Lewis and his team headed back to Texas with two losses and much apprehension. With one more away game remaining, they could at least avoid the home crowds for a bit longer.

The last game of the three game road stand came on 9 December against the Aggies of Texas A&M. Team members and coaches hoped that the Cougars would finally walk away with a victory and noted reasons for hope. Joe Hamood, team co-captain, told reporters that the Cougars were beginning to function as a group rather than as a disjointed collection of individuals. He said prior to the previous game, "There had been no closeness on [the] team-not like last year. The locker room was as silent as a tomb, no spark. We talked about it and ... [since then] we played like a team."[78] These athletes believed they had worked out the kinks and would overcome their losing ways. Apparently they were wrong. Referred to by the press as "Jekyll and Hyde," the Cougars once again found themselves on the low side of the 93–88 score.[79] The season had started out dismally, and now the team had to own up to the losses.

Hayes shouldered the negativity focused toward the team because he, as the standout, supposedly dictated the game's final outcomes. Success or

Lewis always found just the right words to spur his team to victory. When he retired in 1986, he had amassed 27 straight winning seasons (1966).

117

defeat depended on him, and the media promoted that concept to the public. Even though Hayes averaged 22 points and 14.5 rebounds, his deficiencies such as his struggles on the free throw line and trouble with goal tending were highlighted. Lewis did not leave his star athlete to fend for himself and often warded off the criticism. His comments included sentiments such as, "Hayes held up real well, better, even than I though he would out here," and he barked at the press when they asked about Hayes's goal tending tendencies, saying, "Charge those to me, I'm telling him to go for that ball.... He blocked a lot of shots too."[80] He also went so far as to excuse Hayes from any blame for the early losses insisting that "outside of [him], I don't think anyone played up to [their] potential ... and I know Hayes is going to get better."[81] Chaney did receive some level of criticism but not nearly on the level of Hayes and even still Lewis defended his second black athlete. On one particular instance he said to those questioning Chaney's role on the team, "Don didn't play badly at all in the first half at A&M. He stole the ball twice, scored seven points and had five rebounds. He deserves a chance. Everybody knows he's an outstanding player."[82] Hayes knew from the beginning of his Houston career that he and Chaney would be judged by different, harsher standards, and the reaction of the press only validated his thoughts. He understood that to earn the acceptance of the fans he "couldn't be just as good as everyone else, [he] had to be better," and now he had to step forward and make something happen.[83] That duplicity would not change as Hayes remarked during his senior year, "When we had an off night, the crowds got on us more than the other players ... and that's still the case."[84] For that reason, Lewis wanted all to know Hayes was not responsible for the zero and three start.

Interestingly enough, the Associated Press reports presented balanced coverage of the game and did not single out the African American athletes. Their reports even praised Hayes when the team was losing writing, "[Hayes] is a potential All-American ... [who] threw a scare into the Dons ... [and] 'is going to be a great one.'"[85] The UH student newspaper followed suit as they tried to support Hayes and Chaney writing during those first games, "Although it was a tough loss to swallow for the touring Cougars, [Hayes's and Chaney's play showed] some consolation is in store."[86] Both of these news outlets believed the struggling Cougars and their highly visible black athletes would make a go of it yet.

Amidst the season's disastrous start, the home crowds never attacked Lewis the way they did Coach Yeoman during his early struggles. The press questioned him intensely about the lack of wins and fans were not happy with the situation, but they never suggested that he stood on the edge of being fired. Students did not hang him in effigy, and alumni did not, as far as the records indicate, call for his removal. Dena Lewis, wife of Guy Lewis, confirmed that neither she nor her husband could recall "one single incident ... [where they] received any hate mail or any phone calls that were bad."[87] It came down to basketball's secondary position in Texas' athletic hierarchy. Basketball did not stir up the same response from Texans and southerners because it did not have the same ties to southern culture. Football remained king. Basketball, for at least a little while longer, played second fiddle and did not mean as much to the southern audiences. Fortunately for the Cagers, the adverse reactions remained more tempered.

The Cougars returned home battered from their road trip and readied for their first chance to play in front of the home crowd. They had not intended to go before them winless, but they had no choice, and in order to salvage the season and integration they would have to come out on fire. So, "the road weary mass of misfits with ambitions ... [and] three large lumps on their collective noggins," took on the University of Wisconsin Badgers.[88] A near sellout crowd of 5,100 fans filled Del Mar Gym to get the first view of the team, and, for the first time that season, the Cougars did not disappoint. That first win, which came by a score of 82–57, showed the fans "what all the shouting [had] been about," and brought a renewed hope that a good season was in store.[89] One wrote, "The first win was a while coming but if the rest can be that easy, Coach Guy Lewis and his Cagers [didn't] mind the wait."[90] The situation only improved as Houston won its next five games against Texas Christian University, Texas A&M University, Auburn University, and ninth ranked Providence University by a combined point margin of 517 to 441. Included among those numbers was an incredible 93 point half by Houston.

With the team delivering the promised wins, local sports fans, or at least "the lucky ones who could get inside the hall," showed up in impressive numbers and consistently bought out the various venues the team occupied.[91] The support of the fans rose quickly as students and alumni, all possessing ownership in the school, relished the team's rise to ascendancy. It did not hurt that the Cougar squad won consistently throughout the rest of that season and into the 1966 season. By the end of that next season, Hayes and the Cougars had convinced the city that they could defeat the toughest opponents in dramatic fashion. In one game, Hayes had 55 points and 30 rebounds leading the team to a total of 140 points. Hayes's fame rose quickly as fans clamored to see him, and soon, expressed displeasure when he did not play entire games. Lewis commented one night during which his star athlete scored thirty-five points by halftime, "If I had taken him out of there the fans would have run me out of the [gym]."[92] Cougar fans wanted to win and knew that Hayes could fulfill that wish. On-court success was most important to them, and they therefore embraced the black athletes. Once Chaney and Hayes began to play on the varsity, people who had not previously cheered for a black athlete became a part of the frenzy and then accepted them as individuals. The level of fan support increased so dramatically during that season that at its conclusion, the administration announced its intent to build a gymnasium especially for the Cougars to call home. The Houston yearbook, aptly entitled *The Houstonian*, described the excited environment writing, "Rabid fans supported the team throughout the season. Swelling attendance forced many fans to be turned away from games at the ticket gate. As the year progressed, cheers of "E," "E," "E," turned into "We want a field house," when the fans sensed victory."[93] These men had made a clear statement about their undeniable talent and ability to win and part of their reward was a broad level of acceptance.

Even still, all of the press did not fully embrace Hayes as some emphasized his faults in the same breath as they complimented his point production. They wrote of him after the Cougars' first win, "He might've had even more points but for the fact he missed nine straight shots from the foul line."[94] Opposing coaches made remarks such as "Houston is a good ball club, no question about it. I was a little disappointed [that] ... Hayes didn't show me a fall-away or a hook."[95] Despite his excellent on-court performances, articles still never openly embraced the change. Sports writers continued their criticism when the team struggled and stuck to statistics when it flourished.

For some unstated reason, select writers did not even try to disguise their disdain for Houston and its black athletes. *Sports Illustrated* hammered Elvin Hayes and the Cougars' other black athletes in a featured article. The author wrote that Hayes "loafs much of the time" "beat bloody one teammate" and the blacks participated in only three central activities: basketball, eating, and cartoons.[96] The article poked fun at Hayes's distinct Louisiana accent emphasizing his trouble articulating words correctly and said of his playing ability, "[When] you put the nicknames [of Hayes, the Big E, and Oscar Robertson, the Big O] together [and] say them quickly a few times, it sounds like a jackass, which also, is the way the Houston team usually plays defense."[97] Although the writer included the whole team in his last disparaging remark, he clearly alluded to just the play of Hayes. Not everyone was pleased with Houston or its black athletes.

Still, Hayes maintained a friendly relationship with the media by remaining cordial and obliging at all times. *The Daily Cougar* continued its positive reporting in defense of Hayes's friendly attitude: "In the dressing room after each game Hayes is always willing to talk, pausing obligingly to spend a few minutes with a sports writer for one more question."[98] He tried to pacify everyone he came in contact with and welcomed the attention, whether negative or positive, gained through the media. For him, the tone of the reports did not matter as just seeing his name in print thrilled him. Growing up in Louisiana, his name, or the names of any other African American individuals, never appeared in print and even the smallest mention meant something to him.[99]

Strangely, the black press kept mum on the integrated Cougars. Although the team challenged the color barrier and highly publicized the talents of African American athletes, the press covered the team with little fanfare and limited coverage to a simple recounting of game details. This lack of media attention, although curious, was not unique to the Houston situation. When Texas Western University, with an all black starting line-up, defeated the all white University of Kentucky in 1966, the national media refused to report on the racial aspects of the game and went out of their way to avoid it. [100] Yet, one would think the African American community would want to promote the successes of Hayes and Chaney. They were demonstrating that the black athlete could make it in Texas and in the South but they nevertheless remained surprisingly silent.

The minimal racial discussion would dramatically change following the "Game of the Century."

Throughout the first two integrated varsity seasons, Lewis and company had more to deal with than just final scores and keeping the fans and press happy; they, like the football team, had to go into areas of the South not so friendly toward integration and play. They faced southern universities that looked down on Houston's integration and traveled into states which had violently protested collegiate integration less than two years earlier. Moving through the South proved difficult because hotels, restaurants, and other venues were yet segregated. The team could not go to places together even though they saw themselves as a family. Although the racial restrictions did not directly affect the white members of the team, they too had to deal with the racism directed toward their teammates. They had to bring Hayes and Chaney food from segregated restaurants, had to hear the verbal abuse of opposing fans, and had to leave segregated facilities when they tried to enter as a team.[101] Lewis understood the situation all his athletes faced and instructed everyone to ignore their surroundings. He recalled, "Some of [the southerners] had really strong words, but I told [them] don't pay any attention to them, just forget them and play."[102] Facing these hardships forged together the team and tied the Cougar men together and made them like a family.[103]

While the Cougars' wins led to the acceptance of the two black athletes among many sports fans and the team members, certain historians insist that the racial acceptance would not have materialized if the team had consistently lost.[104] Hayes, perhaps without recognizing the insight of his comment, confirmed the argument as he said, "Sure at first they came out and stared at us because we were Negroes, but they've kept coming out to see us play because we win games and play exciting basketball, not because of race."[105] Fortunately for Hayes and those who supported the integration, the team did produce on the court. During the 1965-66 season, the Cougars finished the regular season with an 18-8 record and the following season posted a stellar 21-5 record. Over those two years, the team would compile a forty-eight game home win streak. The fans demanded successful seasons, and Lewis's Cougars delivered.

The Cougars also had to deal with a rapidly shrinking schedule. Following the 1965-66 season, several southern schools, namely Baylor

University, Texas A&M University, Texas Christian University, and the University of Tulsa, announced that they would no longer place Houston on their schedules. A&M did not stop with basketball as it also refused to play football games against the Cougars. These schools had been increasing their win columns by playing Houston, and the Aggies had won ten out of eleven matches, yet mysteriously they no longer had time for the Cougars. They insisted that the scheduling changes signified nothing more than a full season due to the inclusion of more established programs. Yet, Houston's integrated status clearly played a role in the alterations.[106] Gene Stalling, football coach of the Aggies, betrayed his true feelings about desegregated teams as he said in 1965, "What [A&M] needs is a team that will work, pull, and fight together and really get a feeling of oneness.... I don't believe we could accomplish this with a Negro on the squad."[107] Harold Bradley, the University of Texas basketball coach, was not much better as he said that the Southwest Conference "shouldn't have scheduled Houston in the first place. I won't schedule schools that can out–recruit us simply because of different standards."[108] An editorial in the *Austin American* wrote of the Cougars sudden rise to success, "We are highly indignant that the Southwest Conference champion stands a good chance of having to play an 'outlaw' for the right to play in the [NCAA] Midwest Regional tourney."[109]

As news sources had originally speculated in 1964, Houston began encountering problems with shrinking fields of competition. Lewis, although "expressing keen regret" over the course of events, promised his fans that the decisions of those schools would not impact his team. "We're not folding our tent" was his assurance that he would successfully locate bigger and better teams willing to play his Cougars.[110] Athletic Director Harry Fouke also defended the basketball program saying, "'I am shocked and dismayed by some irrational statements from [Texas's] coach' ... and wryly noted that criticism of Houston's basketball team [had] increased noticeably since the Cougars started winning regularly."[111] Both men promised that the basketball program would continue to move forward regardless of the racial objections of the other Texas schools. They aggressively scheduled top-tier programs to replace those that pulled out of long-standing agreements. The Cougars would move on to bigger competition.

With all the on-court success, the Cougars' African American basketball players had to renegotiate their off court relationships. During their first year with the team, Hayes and Chaney did not draw an immense amount of attention to themselves and could disappear into the larger black population on the UH campus. After the start of that year, however, the two starters became focal points and had to interact with students in a different manner. They became the public face of integration and as such had to deal with those still upset over the process. Not by any means the majority, a few students did make derogatory remarks about the black athletes and express concern over sharing classrooms with them. McVea did not have that period of transition because he never had the anonymity necessary to fade into the background. During his freshman season, his games drew thousands of fans, and he was well known from the first minute he stepped onto the UH campus. Hayes and Chaney did not have to deal with that level of recognition until the 1965 season.

That treatment by classmates only made Chaney and Hayes more determined to show all around them that such fears had no merit, and, because of that perseverance, they and their schoolmates came to at least respect each other. That learning process did not end with classroom interaction as off-campus fraternizing became increasingly common. Both students and alumni invited the African American athletes into the larger university culture and included them in their extra-curricular activities and gatherings. Like McVea, the basketball players saw increased inclusion into white society as time passed. They were invited into the homes and lives of the students, fans, and alumni.

The University's administration tried its best to assist the transition and found ways to continue caring for its growing black population. Hayes found the institution more than willing to support the athletes, alongside the other black students, in whatever manner possible. "The school's officials," he remembered, "were always cooperative, much more than you would have expected at that time in a Southern city."[112] UH was willing to accommodate the needs of the black population and felt that the school truly had its best interest at heart. He and his fellow black schoolmates even petitioned for, and received, courses in African American history. For all of those reasons, the black athletes always refused to participate in any of the growing racial protests. In their opinion, the system had adequately supported them and other black students and visible displays of dissent would only undermine the positive process of integration already under-way.[113] Such a stance speaks to the true situation at Houston. If life at UH had not promoted inclusion and acceptance, racial demonstrations would have provided the black athletes the perfect outlet to let the public know of the discrepancies between reality and the image presented.[114] That these men did not do so allows us to assume that the integration was proceeding as smoothly as possible.

Even with the acceptance they found from their peers, Chaney and Hayes never lost sight of the reality of their situation. They were still black athletes playing in a white world and understood that the larger community scrutinized their every action. Under such a critical eye, they had to monitor all actions closely. Whether on or off the court, their behavior reflected on the entire race, and they had a responsibility to represent it well. That burden made them guard each move made. Hayes said in 1968, "The pressure was on us, and ... [we] knew everything [we] did reflected on the Negro people, so how [we] acted was important."[115]

Throughout those first two varsity seasons, the black athletes on the basketball team maintained an easy-going public persona and appeared unaffected by the mounting pressures. That public face did not communicate the intense pressure they felt from all sides. It was particularly applicable to Hayes as he had to lead the team to victory, apologize when the final score did not go in its favor, and make sure his own personal production lifted him to the top of the All-American lists. He had to keep his academics above the passing line, had a wife and child to care for, and the hopes of his race, his city, and his University all on his shoulders.[116] Those responsibilities, which Hayes felt intensely, placed tremendous stress upon him. Nevertheless, the two persevered and did what was necessary to win. That strain would wane as the years passed, and, by the 1967-68 season, Hayes and Chaney would not feel so burdened by the race issue. That season they would reap the full fruits of their labor as they would rise to the top of the basketball world.

The 1965-66 seasons certainly validated the athletic integration at the University of Houston. Integration was not without its problems and not without its anxiety, however, Hayes, Chaney, and McVea did what was necessary to make the situation work and were committed to achieving success. While neither team did overwhelmingly well that first year, with the football team falling just short of securing a bowl game and the basketball team losing in the NCAA tournament, they did well enough to ease tensions about the process. During their junior seasons, the three athletes improved on that first varsity showing and collected significantly more victories. Throughout the process, Houston fans supported the black and white athletes on a surface level and generally backed the team, although a select group never stopped expecting a disproportionate level of production from the African American athletes. The dislike and distrust of integrated teams still existed to an extent, and Houston still received a recognizable level of unflattering attention from the media, but the Cougars at least commanded respect for their athletic abilities. Lewis and Yeoman stepped out on a limb, and, by the end of the next year, observers understood the benefits of integration. The wisdom of their decision grew increasingly apparent to sports observers throughout the South.

7

Losing the Battle but Winning the War

The integrated teams of the University of Houston made incredible strides during their first two years of varsity competition. They finally realized the original dream of winning on a consistent basis. In those two seasons, the UH athletic program also increased its value in the world of collegiate sports as it held its own against many of the best programs, and, even though still an independent without any conference affiliation, it slowly gained the recognition it had long sought from its peers. A national title would not come to either program in that final year, but both teams struck fear in the hearts of opponents on any given game day. The integration situation had finally calmed down as fans grew accustomed to the black members of the squads, and the athletes had settled into a routine. For all those reasons, the seniors expected to cruise through the last year of their four year stint with the Cougars accumulating wins and accolades without the negativity experienced in previous years. Those expectations would not be met.

The 1967-68 football and basketball seasons would upset the status quo in several regards. Those years proved that integrated teams were superior to those still segregated by virtue of an expanded talent pool. Houston forced other collegiate programs to re-evaluate their stance on the issue. UH wasted no time recruiting more minority athletes and increased that number to eight on the combined varsity teams. Looking at the sidelines, it was apparent that Houston was indiscriminately recruiting players of all races.

Neither team would leave any question as to their prominence or place on the national scene. The Cougars were no longer subordinate to any teams, in the South or otherwise, and, although teams from the Southwest Conference still refused to schedule Houston and looked upon its programs as inferior, no one could seriously question the Cougars' place in the sports world. The squads were maturing into powerhouses as Lewis and Yeoman had hoped all along, and soon Houston would command the respect that it had craved since the formation of the athletic program twenty years earlier. It would be from that vantage point that Houston began the seasons. Don, Elvin, and Warren had one last chance to prove their point. The 67-68 football and basketball teams contained the hopes of the Houston faithful. Supporters were expecting a big payoff in the form of winning seasons.

Not all components of that last year were positive. During the season, serious cracks in the integration arose. On the surface, Houston presented an image of acceptance and tolerance as fans cheered for the athletes, black or white, and apparently had no problems with the racially mixed status of the program. That last year shamefully exposed an ugly truth. Not all observers of the Cougars accepted or even forgot about the racial differences and clearly communicated that the African American athletes should not forget their place in the racial hierarchy. Anticipation hung in the air but something else was about to challenge the efforts of the coaches and players alike.

Warren McVea and the Houston Cougar football team faced a tough schedule during the 1967 season. They had to line-up across from Florida State University, Wake Forest University, North Carolina State University, Mississippi State University, University of Mississippi (Ole Miss), the University of Georgia, the University of Memphis, University of Idaho, the University of Tulsa, and Coach Yeoman's former employer Michigan State University. From the onset of the pre-season, the national media dismissed Houston's ability to compete on the large stage and ranked the program in the lower portion of the top twenty rankings. Only one preseason poll even mentioned McVea as a potential All-American, and he remained well below the radar.[1] Regardless of those slights, Houston would have to find success that year. Because of the NCAA suspension, there would be no bowl game and no national title, but if the Cougars were ever going to become a well-established, highly regarded program, this was the season for them to dominate their opponents. This was McVea's final opportunity to show the benefits of integration and cement his legacy.[2]

The team began with games against two top-tier programs, Florida State and Michigan State. Houston, although a solid team by this point, was not expected to come out with wins over either team; the program according to the media did not have the athletic ability necessary to over-power the truly great teams. Against all predictions, the Cougars jumped out to a quick start defeating the highly ranked Seminoles of FSU 33–13 in a manner that "shocked friend and foe."[3] In front of a record opening

Five thousand Cougar fans await the team plane at Hobby Airport following their 37–7 win over Michigan State. As the team disembarked, the fans chanted, "We're number one, we're number one" (1967).

crowd of 40,336 fans, Houston took a commanding 30–0 lead before sending in the second and third string athletes. The media and elated crowds were shocked at the upset and would grow increasingly surprised the following week. Before an enormous crowd of 75,833, the second largest opening day crowd for Michigan State up to that point, the Cougars played flawlessly and came away with a 37–7 point victory. In what should have been a routing of the Cougars, Houston brought down the mighty Spartans in dramatic fashion. Those two games afforded Houston a place among the big leagues and a third place national ranking. The Cougars were finally living up to, and far exceeding, everyone's expectations.

The last reluctant fans jumped on the Cougar bandwagon with remarkable speed. After victories, "the Cougars' dressing rooms were a scene of mass confusion and exuberance [as] alumni ... [and] fans swarmed among the varsity players who had minutes before defeated [their opponents]."[4] When the team plane returned from East Lansing following the Michigan State victory, five thousand excited supporters awaited it at the airport to welcome their athletes and coaches home. The sight was something officials had "never seen anything like in [their] lives," as the "crowd personified the feelings that UH and all of Houston [felt] for their team."[5] The athletic department received hundreds of letters and telegrams containing well-wishes for the "Cinderella Cougars" and requests for information about the athletes.[6] Even opposing teams applauded the Cougars' skill writing to the *Daily Cougar* staff prior to the start of one game, "Since our team [Wake Forest Demon Deacons] will very likely be undone by your Cougars ... we wish to congratulate you people on your fine team and wish you the best of luck."[7] The letter of well-wishes also included a request for photographs of McVea in the midst of some athletic feat. Yeoman's team was finally making spectators stand up and take notice.

The successive victories surprised even the staunchest detractors. Houston, behind the talent of McVea, had not merely eked out wins but convincingly defeated what most considered the top teams. As all had come to expect, McVea found himself at the center of the media's focus. Although he had spent the past three years as the scapegoat for the Cougars' missteps, McVea because the poster child for one of the fastest rising teams. He had finally "wiped out his previous national press exposure in the Tulsa UH game where his numerous fumbles damaged his image across the country," and he "was no longer a flash in the pan runner to 49 states in the union ... [but] a genuine All-America."[8] He "ran through and around," "snaked around [and] over," and "did ballet steps as he slithered easily through the defense[s]."[9] Even *Sports Illustrated*, which had been overly critical of the runner at times, wrote, "McVea, who runs like a blinking light, like a Zip Code, like a ... a ... oh, where are you, Roget's Thesaurus, now that a man really needs you?"[10] The adjectives used to describe "our boy" could fill volumes, but they all communicated one point.[11] McVea was the reason why the Cougars had "moved up to march with the with gridiron giants," and the media and fans embraced him as a hero.[12] His race, once a significant issue among the hometown crowds, no longer seemed to matter as he dazzled his way into their hearts. Cougar spectators relished in the runner's exploits and took pride in his accomplishments saying things such as "The gasps of amazement ... from Midwest press writers as Warren McVea danced 50 yards through three solid MSU tacklers ... are still music to the ears."[13] Another wrote, "After all the rocks and clods the Cougars have received from newspapers and sports magazines throughout the past two years, the plaudits were too rich to digest."[14]

Almost overnight, McVea became the superstar and team saviour that everyone had impatiently awaited for three years. Yes, the team had helped with the general effort, and the press did recognize their efforts but, even in that, McVea was still the central reason for the Cougars' rise in football fortune. One source pointedly wrote, "The main reason for the ... win can be summed up in one word — McVea. This isn't to say that the Cougars are a one-man team ... [but] it become obvious ... [all] at the Cougars' disposal would be useless if [McVea] was not there to take advantage of these assets."[15] Others stated it more bluntly: "Although he won't admit it, McVea, [is the player] upon whose muscled legs rest most of the Cougars' hopes."[16] At least for the moment, McVea could do no wrong, and he relished the accolades as much as possible.

Even with all the praise heaped upon him, McVea, like his basketball counterparts, never allowed himself to forget the reality of the situation. He was accepted at that point because he produced on the field. When he performed poorly, few stood by him, and when he showed up in dramatic fashion everyone returned to his side. Acceptance from the fans and media lasted only as long as the wins continued, and there were

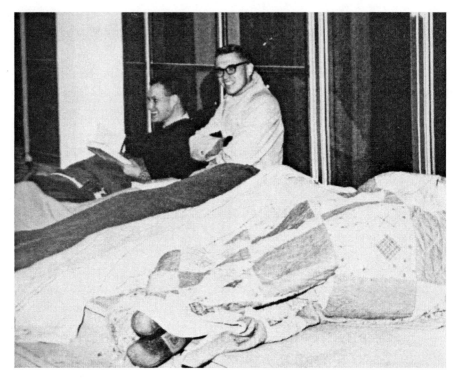

Cougar fever reached an all-time high during the 1967 season. Here, fans sleep outside the athletic complex to purchase football tickets.

groups always anxiously awaiting his fall. McVea expressed this reality: "I realize now that I'm a marked man each time I play. I've gotten used to it though and now I accept it as a personal challenge."[17] McVea's assessment of the situation was very near the truth. In all the excitement of the start of the season, hints of displeasure existed right below the surface. Reporters forced to praise the athlete still played up the racial stereotypes saying things such as "And there was shave-headed, broad-smiling McVea," telling the press how he "[patronizes] a custom tailor ... [gets] his head barbered to the skin every Thursday ... [and] leaves the belt on his football pants unbuckled."[18] Other observers wrote more negative articles which claimed that "he [liked] fast cars and women," and, in a show of bad citizenship, "[had] been known to collect a few parking tickets ... and forget to pay them."[19] Some within the press did not want anyone to forget that McVea was an African American athlete who fulfilled the typical African American stereotypes. He was reckless, defied society's standards, and could not be trusted around young, innocent white women.

As it had since the beginning, and as the basketball team would also do later that year, the team remained focused on the team effort. With the contributions of all members, the team had "put all [opponents] to the sword and [taken] no prisoners," and McVea, as the spotlight athlete, always promoted that outlook to those watching.[20] From the start of the season, he told the media that "togetherness [is] what I'm hoping for. We have a lot of good players this year and if we play together, we're gonna win."[21] After the incredibly successful beginning of the season, McVea again credited the group effort saying, "We're more together this year from the start.... We know each other better. There's more leadership on both the offense and defense."[22] He always mentioned that his spectacular displays of athleticism would not have been possible without the efforts of the other excellent athletes lined-up alongside him. He said after the Michigan State win, "Rich Stotter has got to be the best offensive guard in the country. He was always out there with a block."[23] In addition, McVea never shied away from filling support roles when needed. He was known to throw blocks and make tackles allowing others to run, pass, and catch their way into the endzone. Yeoman, as would Lewis, tried to refocus the attention toward the entire team. He said, "I'm so happy for these kids and the school.... [They] have been kicked around. They have lined up against some pretty good people."[24] For the moment, McVea, who earned the Associated Press Back of the Week during those early games, and his Cougar team mates were at the top of the football world untouched by race or prejudice. That widespread acceptance would change quickly.

During the game against the Wake Forest Demon Deacons during the third week of the season, a brief scuttlebutt between McVea and white team mate Ken Hebert broke out on the sidelines. Although amounting to little more than an insignificant verbal dispute quite common among players throughout the country, the event would betray the true sentiments of many within the Houston following and bring the race issue back to the forefront for the remainder of McVea's college career. The occurrence happened midway through the second quarter when a blown play, caused by a miscommunication between McVea, Hebert, and quarterback Dick Woodall, led to a sack. Following the infamous play, Hebert, who roomed with Woodall and was the team's leading scorer, came up to McVea and said, "You might be good, but you ain't that gosh-darn good."[25] McVea, upset about the confusion and the subsequent sack, responded to him saying, "Get out of my face, just get out of my face." That was the end of the conversation, and both men headed back to the sidelines. By coincidence, McVea did not return to the game again following the verbal encounter. With the team winning by a significant margin, and McVea still nursing an injury, Yeoman kept him on the sidelines for the remaining portion of the second half.[26] The incident, which ended almost as quickly as it began, was nothing more than a minor set to, the likes of which happened between athletes with considerable frequency.

When the team retreated to the locker room following the win, everyone tried to let the press know there was no tension between the athletes and the dispute was not even worthy of a story. McVea explained that "it was not really a big deal.... [Hebert] was upset because I didn't [block], and I was upset because he got in my face. It really was just two misunderstandings."[27] Hebert concurred with McVea saying immediately afterward, "As far as I'm concerned, it's over with.... There's no problem. Warren is still the greatest."[28] Yeoman refused to make an issue out of the event and let reporters know that nothing out of the ordinary had occurred either between Hebert and McVea or McVea and himself. It was only a small argument between two keyed-up athletes. Just about every member of the team repeatedly explained that the situation was not significant, and Hebert even asked, "Does this have to get in the paper?"[29] Their appeals fell on deaf ears.

The facade of acceptance so many had hoped to be a solid wall began to crumble. The UH athletic department had struggled for years to produce a scenario which would demonstrate that black men and white men could join hands and achieve great things. They could do so not as "separate but equals," but rather as human beings working towards a common goal. For a group of dyed in the wool racist fans and journalists this was the last straw. They could no longer mask their bias. Cowardly and hiding behind their printed words, those sports writers made no secret of their contempt towards the successfully integrated UH program and more directly its black athletes. Winners were hard to discredit, but creating false controversy could effectively dismantle the positive attitudes heaped on a reigning sports figure. Hometown antagonists had seized the opportunity to incite a mob mentality in an effort to finally suppress public approval of desegregated sports.

Ignoring the explanation of the team, the fans and the media did not react to the situation so nonchalantly. According to reports, McVea initiated the fight, refused to shake hands with Hebert afterward, pulled away from Yeoman on the sideline, and had been benched for the remainder of the game because of his appalling behaviour. Reporters commented that the event was "a shocking experience like catching your business partner with his hand in the till" and wrote that the fans' "eyes popped like champagne corks, [and] there was this concerted gasp, then a queasy hush."[30] The black running back had fought with a white, All-American calibre, athlete and that was completely unacceptable to most within southern society. Writers insisted that the athlete, who they commented wore "nattily tailored gold [suits]" was "certainly the only All-America candidate ... who has had a near fight with a teammate — a white teammate, at that — in plain view of a Dome full of spectators," and that Yeoman allowed the event to go unchecked because "he is lenient with his Wondrous One."[31] Other reporters, while avoiding any direct comment on race, sounded incredulous that a black athlete would even dream of physically responding to a white team mate. The fans communicated the same sentiments as "Mac the Knife, who received a thunderous ovation when he stepped onto the field for the game opening coin toss, was pelted with a round of booes [after the fight]."[32] An African American athlete could play alongside the whites, but he had better know his place. The "curious thing [which] happen[ed] at the Astrodome" remained in the news throughout the season and changed spectators' perceptions of McVea and the Houston integration.[33]

The situation only worsened with the 16–6 loss to North Carolina State University the following week.[34] Now, the Cougars had a black athlete who did not know his place and a team that did not win. From the moment of his scrap with Hebert, McVea lost much of the goodwill he had cultivated over the past three years. Fans began questioning his ability to get along with the team, to work hard during practice, and his on-field performances. They also questioned whether his injuries, which were known to limit his practice and game time, were severe enough to keep him on the reserve list or whether he was a spoiled athlete simply refusing to participate when he did not desire to. The acceptance of McVea, which had reached a fever pitch just a few days prior to the incident, had mutated into rejection by many as they "booed him when he was sent back in [the games] ... and cheered when [he] was removed."[35] Fans who had once seen McVea as the centerpiece of the Cougars downgraded his importance; they said they would "continue to support the Cougars ... long after the 'moving on' of Warren McVea."[36] Sports writer Paul Orseck, who insultingly referred to the University of Houston as "Cougar High," walked into a room which McVea occupied and, although writing an article on his injuries, refused to even acknowledge his presence.[37] Rumours "began to be circulated by team supporters apparently seeking scapegoats for the UH fall ... [that told] of a team fight at halftime ... and dissension of the squad because halfback Warren McVea was not required to practice with the team."[38]

McVea was no longer the golden child, and it was uncertain if he could regain all that was lost. He paid dearly for challenging a white athlete in front of a huge audience and commented, "It's funny how fickle the fans can be. They were down on me bad in 1965 and some are starting to do the same now."[39] Yeoman became "philosophical about the fact that the Cougar fans [had] begun to turn both on the team and McVea [and said] 'most of those people are fair-weather friends. We'll live without them."[40] Hebert tried to refocus on the team aspect of the game saying, "If [the team] gets together from now till the end of the season, we'll still be up there near the top. If we don't let [the disruptions] affect us."[41]

Despite any claims to the contrary, the team was not at odds. They interacted on a regular basis as teammate George Nordgren cut McVea's hair every Thursday, Tom Paciorek, who was drafted by the Los Angeles Dodgers in 1968, told the school newspaper of how he and McVea spent time together, and UH students had grown so accustomed to seeing the football athletes together that when some members were missing from the group a reporter questioned, "I wonder what happened to Mac (McVea), Don (Bean), and Little Kenny (Hebert)?"[42] For the athletes and coaches, nothing had changed. They still accepted not only McVea but the other black athletes that had joined him during the past two seasons and continued on as normal. The negative reaction of the crowds would not dampen their friendships or camaraderie. On the inside at least, the team remained on good terms as it had for the previous three years. They continued to live what they preached.

Not all fans and alumni turned to vitriolics attack as many ardently defended the Cougars. UH loyalists attacked the negative fans and the

McVea participates in Homecoming activities with two Cougar co-eds (1967).

McVea rumbles 20 yards to the endzone in the 1966 34–14 defeat of Utah. Although injured, McVea still scored the go-ahead touchdown here in the 3rd quarter.

negative press which had picked apart their team and heightened positive awareness of the racial issue once again. The proponents of McVea did not leave him to defend himself and spoke up for him so Cougar audiences would realize that "no matter [how] this athlete is doing now, UH fans should have enough respect to cheer him for what he's done for UH in the past. He deserves that much."[43] Further, certain fans pointed out the unfair expectations placed on the injured McVea writing, "No one seems to have the ability to understand that an injured runner is not going to turn in the same performance that he did before being injured.... If [he] never plays another set of downs, he will still go down as a great player."[44] The *Daily Cougar* staff attacked the *Sports Illustrated* for its treatment of McVea saying the piece, which had been advanced billed to the school "an in-depth study of Warren and the wonders he has wrought," ended up printing what "most UH students [found] less than above board."[45] Some fans even threatened to stop attending games if McVea remained on the sidelines, as he often did after the Wake Forest game. After all, they "came to the games hoping to watch McVea razzle, dazzle the opposition."[46]

The *Daily Cougar*, as it had done many times before, stepped forward to defend one of its own. It refused to accept the notion that McVea's treatment was the result of "the fickleness of all sports fans," and filled its opinion pages with letters of outrage over the behaviour of certain fans.[47] A student wondered whether the treatment of McVea was an innocent occurrence or whether the "black athletes' abilities [were] being suppressed by the white power structure of Houston and the bigots of the UH community."[48] In a point of view that mirrored the ideology behind the 1968 Olympic Boycott, some questioned whether McVea and the other black athletes were little more than pawns in the larger white power system.[49] Regardless of the argument used, the Cougars had a group of supporters which accepted the team as they were, even with its racially mixed and sometimes hot tempered team members, and tried to get the rest of the fans to do the same.

As much racial hypocrisy as that season showed from both fans and foes, it was not completely without racial merit. During the 1965 and 1966 seasons, the Cougar gridders experienced discrimination and prejudice first hand and with great regularity when facing southern opponents. They frequently traveled through the South and dealt with death threats, racial slurs, and openly hostile crowds. For them, the games they played in Starksville and Oxford, Mississippi during the 1967 season were nothing unusual.[50] Although the game in Oxford would be the first integrated match-up there, the Cougars were prepared for anything they faced. That acclimation, however, did not apply to the fans which opted to follow the team. With the Cougars on the top of the football rankings, students and alumni followed their team on the road in larger numbers, and their experiences heightened their awareness of the reality of Southern life and the prevailing attitudes within it. While visiting Mississippi, they noted that "under [the surface] ran a mood of tension-an inflection in a voice or perhaps a passing glance from a bystander which seemed to convey something more than sheer curiosity ... [and] one could hear State fans speaking favourably about a mutual admiration society known as the Klu Klux Klan."[51] That tension turned into open hostility inside the stadium walls. Students saw black spectators placed in "the nigger section," heard state troopers telling blacks cheering for UH, "You might get hung for that, boy," and those seen encouraging the black UH supporters were threatened with bodily harm.[52] Cougar fans became by extension black and they experienced, at least to a degree, the brunt of racism. Many among those road warriors began questioning why such repressiveness had been allowed to continue unchecked for so long and why that "area of the country ... [had] refused to react to changing human relationships with anything other than blind resentment."[53] Football allowed many supporters to understand first hand the harsh reality of racism.

When the students returned from that game, they recognized that football represented more than just a sport; it represented the struggle between equality and prejudice. McVea and the other black athletes, in playing with white athletes, were openly challenging the southern way of life and many fans finally realized the larger impact of integration. Those that went into Mississippi learned that "the spirit of Jim Crow [was] present in the stands at game time ... but [through the Cougar victory] it suffered a quick, shattering demise on the playing field."[54] That experience made many students conscious of the pioneer Houston had become. Much of the Cougar fan base began by accepting only the African American athletes that joined the program and somewhere along the way no longer saw race and embraced them as fellow Cougars rather than just as black athletes. When other schools challenged the presence of McVea and his fellow African American athletes, they became defensive of their athletes and, at the same time, proud of UH's racial accomplishments over the preceding four years. They heralded the strides UH had taken in "accept[ing] the Negro in athletics ... which reaches from the football field and the basketball court to the highest level of student organization."[55] Houston's athletic integration was impacting more than just athletics as it made students recognize the reality of southern life and label it as unacceptable.

This reaction demonstrated that the general attitudes of the student population were changing. In 1962, two years before McVea joined the team, the Cougars were scheduled to play Ole Miss in Oxford, Mississippi, but the unrest surrounding the enrolment of James Meredith threatened to cancel the game.[56] An editorial in the *Daily Cougar* suggested that the Cougars withdraw from the competition because any school that displayed such violent racial reactions was an "unsuitable opponent."[57] The responses that opinion evoked displayed how southern the attitudes of the Houston students remained despite the integrated status of the University. Students wrote in siding with Ole Miss; one said, "It seems to me far more 'unfit' for a power mad dictator to ... force the decisions of a socialistic administration upon the people" and further that "it would be an honor for our Houston Cougars to play Mississippi's Rebels (a group that will still fight for its beliefs)."[58] Others stated more directly that the editorial was a "vile, vicious, and irresponsible attack on the fine people of Mississippi and their great university" and "[UH students are] blushing with shame — shame that [the *Daily Cougar*] has brought on the University of Houston with [its] unkind words regarding the University of Mississippi and its students."[59] These comments show that within five year's time, the opinions of the UH student population had changed drastically. They went from ardently supporting the segregationist practices of the South to openly decrying their treatment of African Americans on and off the field. Clearly, athletics made a difference in people's racial perceptions and attitudes.

The impact of McVea and the Cougars went beyond the alterations of students' racial attitudes and affected change in southern programs. Those men showed schools in the South that integration was in their best interest and convinced many fans that black athletes were a necessity. In Mississippi in 1967, fans were overheard saying, "Just wait for a few years. Then we'll have our own [Don] Beans and McVeas."[60] Yeoman drew a direct connection between the Cougars' success and further integration: "The Mississippians can stand everything but losing. Obviously they were not going to win without black kids."[61] The performances of McVea also made an impact on Florida State University. Following the 1966 match-up between the two teams, in which McVea ran back a kickoff for 92 yards and a game tying touchdown, the members of the all-white Seminole team, including current FSU President T.K. Wetherell, were "left awed by speed they had never seen before ... [and wondering] when would blacks be accepted by [programs] in the Deep South."[62] As the first African American to play on the field in Tallahassee, McVea unquestionably demonstrated to the Seminoles the benefits of integration.[63] Team member Pat Pryor summed up the impact of the Cougars' black athletes saying of southern fans, "[They] probably thought the grass on the field would die if a black kid sweated on it.... [They] could not have gone home without respecting, even though grudgingly, the talent and grit of our black players."[64] Even with all the turmoil of the 1967 season, the integrated Cougars were making a difference in perception of race.

The 1967 football season ended without much resolution. The team finished up the season with seven wins, three losses, and, for the third year in a row, attended no bowl game. The polarization of the fans did not decline as some remained ardent defenders while others kept second-guessing the on and off field actions of McVea through the end of the season. The Cougar athletes, especially the seniors who had been together since the days of the freshman squad, did not allow the outside negativity to dampen their sense of accomplishment. After their last game in the Astrodome which they inaugurated in 1965, the athletes' "dressing room was alive with a carefree, jovial atmosphere infecting everyone present."[65] It had been a gruelling season, filled with tremendous highs and equally deep lows, but the team had learned that race relations did not have to be "a hate/love relationship," and they exited the locker room not only as team mates but as friends.[66] His days at Houston had given him the tools he needed to succeed at the next level, and it was time for him to leave the city and the school behind. McVea left Houston as a solid athletic prospect for professional ball and would walk into the NFL as a highly drafted athlete.[67] As he parted ways with the program, Warren McVea let the nation know that he had made the correct choice in moving to Houston. He had received everything promised by Yeoman and informed the public "if I had it to do all over again, I'd still come to Houston. The only thing about it is [now] I'm more sure."[68] The door closed on McVea's Cougar career, and everyone that truly mattered was satisfied with the results.

8

Game of the Century

Lewis's Cougars, over the first two varsity seasons, compiled an impressive number of wins. They had been invited to the NCAA tournament twice, Hayes had been named to the All-American list twice, and by 1967 four of the five starters were African American athletes.[1] Even with all of that, Houston was not placed among the game's elites, and neither the team nor the pioneering athletes received more than standard attention from the mainstream press. The school's newspaper ranted and raved about the exploits of the men in red uniforms, but, in the public's view, Lewis's men did not stack up when compared to the greats like the University of California at Los Angeles Bruins coached by the legendary John Wooden.[2]

That perception would change overnight on 20 January 1968. The game which occurred on that evening not only marked what many consider the birth of modern basketball, but it exalted the University of Houston and Hayes as a beacon of integration. It showed a national audience that southern teams, loaded with black talent, would dominate the NCAA and would do so consistently.[3] The South and everyone within it would have to face the issue of integration whether or not they supported it. Although the entire year was record-breaking and the Cougars finished the regular season with a 28-0 record and a number one ranking, that single game defined the 1967-68 season for the Houston Cougars and remains to the present day the most lasting legacy of the integrated Cougar squad. Because of that, we must explore what will forever be known as the "Game of the Century."

The match-up began as the brain child of Lewis, who believed that basketball could draw in huge audiences. He believed that if done in a

Don Chaney, known for his strong defensive abilities, guards against the University of Miami during a 111–96 victory (1966).

larger than life fashion, fans would flock to see collegiate basketball games. The best place to hold such a grand event was the Houston Astrodome where Yeoman's team had played for the last three years. Many feared that the venue's size and configuration would not support basketball, but Lewis resolutely defended his plan. He argued that if spectators could follow a baseball from the upper decks, they could certainly follow a ball over three times as large.[4] Furthermore, the seating capacity of the Dome would allow everyone interested to view the two teams in person. Lewis would invite the nation to watch the game via network television for the first ever nationally televised collegiate basketball game and would cement Houston's place in history.[5]

The opponent was easily selected. UCLA, the reigning NCAA champion, had already agreed to play UH in Houston that season and apparently agreed to the change of venue. As an added level of interest, the Cougars, which had lost in the NCAA tournament semi-finals to the UCLA Bruins led by Lew Alcindor (Kareem Abdul-Jabbar) the previous season, were ranked just behind the Bruins in the polls. A rematch between the number one and number two teams in the nation excited even the most casual basketball fan. The Bruins, riding an incredible forty-seven game winning streak lasting over two seasons, would take on the undefeated Cougars in the Astrodome in late January 1968. With the date of the meeting set, and the tickets on sale, the two teams prepared themselves for the match-up.

Even though the media had covered Hayes and the Cougars for nearly four years and were accustomed to their success, the impending game had a divisive effect. On one side were reporters excited about the game who wrote about its historic significance and the excellent opportunity it presented Houston to claim a top spot in the national polls. Those writers gushed: "This is it, the game all of Texas and several other portions of the civilized world have long awaited," and "the college basketball game against which all future games will be measured tips off ... amidst the carnival atmosphere that only the Astrodome can provide."[6] Others called the meeting a "dream game" for Houston and discussed the best strategy the Cougars could adopt to hand the Bruins a loss.[7] Even *Time*, not normally interested in covering athletic events, marveled at the game: "Folks go first class in Texas, and first of all is that bubble-topped monument to ... plastic grass ... [where] the unbeaten, second-ranked Houston [takes on] ... the unbeaten, top-ranked U.C.L.A."[8] This game would be legendary, and these reporters let the public know they were stoked about it.

As Houston stood on the edge of greatness, many members of the press went on the attack. The possibility of Houston, with its four African American starters, achieving such success was unacceptable to certain media outlets. One method used to create divisiveness was to emphasize the Cougars' negative characteristics. The team, but more particularly the black players, was lazy, undisciplined, and unconcerned with the upcoming task. A reporter out of Dallas wrote of Hayes, "On the eve of the University of Houston's magnetic game with UCLA ... Big E looked sleepy, all right ... unconcerned. Big E might have gone fishin'." The article ended by commenting, "It's hard to talk to the Cougar players in the dressing room.... It's just that the radio is blaring so loudly you can't hear anything.... [and] one of the players muttered, dancing past, 'soul music, man.'"[9] Another newspaper hinted that Hayes's mind was not on the game but on the parties he could attend with members of the UCLA squad. It

Elvin enjoys a post game chat after 158–81 win over Valparaiso (1968).

"Big E" grabs a rebound against Virginia Tech (1968). UH wins 120–79.

said, "Elvin hopes to take Lew with him to some fraternity parties after the game."[10] Most detractors tried convincing readers that Houston was "not quite good enough to cope with what may be the best college team of all time."[11]

On the surface, objections to the integrated team appear illogical because it had played together for nearly four years and was matching up against another integrated squad. Whether the Bruins or the Cougars came out on top, an inter-racial team would be the victor. On a deeper level though, a difference did exist. African American athletes belonged in certain locales, particularly in northern and western regions. They could play in these areas and not threaten the traditional way of life within the South. Houston was part of the South, and therefore black athletes did not belong. Basketball was quickly catching up to football in southern popularity and was subsequently receiving the criticism usually reserved for the gridiron goings on. For that reason, the number of spectators hounding Houston and hoping it would fall increased.

The game, which drew in a record breaking crowd of 52,693, lived up to all the hype that surrounded it.[12] The standing-room-only crowd, which included members of the U.S. Information Agency producing a film for international distribution, packed the Astrodome, armed with binoculars, to see the Cougars come away with a spectacular 71–69 victory.[13] Hayes scored 39 points, brought down 15 rebounds, 5 blocks, and 2 steals while Chaney accumulated 11 points and 6 rebounds. Furthermore, the two other black athletes totaled 17 points, meaning that the white members of the team only scored 4 of the 71 total points. The Cougars battled their way to a victory, and, for most of the fans that night, the color of the athletes was irrelevant. When the final second ticked off the clock, the "screaming partisan crowd poured out of the stands at the finish and carried [Hayes] off on their shoulders chanting, 'We're Number 1, We're Number 1.'"[14] Dick Enberg, who broadcast the game for CBS, recalled the sight of the elated fans rushing court saying, "We could hear the sound of the fans running. It was like the charge of the Alamo. They were leaping over our foxholes to get onto the floor to celebrate."[15] *Sports Illustrated* said of the celebration, "It appeared that the entire city of Houston was having an impromptu jamboree at center court, with Hayes the focus."[16] It did not matter that the winning effort was led by a black player or that only a single white athlete started, all that mattered was their Cougars had done the impossible. This colossal victory hit the newspapers almost instantaneously and filled the headlines of every major local and national press. The Cinderella Cougars had pulled off the impossible while the world watched.

The Hayes-led Cougars had racked up numerous victories since 1965, yet, never did the star receive the type of attention he did following that win. Sports writers pinned a variety of accolades on him saying of Hayes, "The Big E ... is something to behold.... He was more fun than a national park ... and you doubt that there is a more complete player in all of college basketball."[17] To others, Hayes "was the man of the hour in the game of the century," and "the most versatile big man in college basketball."[18] The *Daily Cougar* referred to him as the "guiding spirit behind the UH

As they did with McVea that same year, fans carry a victorious Hayes off the court following the Game of the Century (1968).

win ... [as] he brought the UH bench and the entire stadium to their feet with an indescribable series of basketball feats."[19] His image flooded the media and suddenly much of the school, the city, and the nation embraced him, and his fellow teammates, as their darlings. He had "emerged as the gold-plated hero of a game as spectacular as the surroundings in which it unfolded."[20] Previously, Hayes had been faulted for the team's losses, but now he received almost sole credit for its win as evidenced by the *Houston Post* headline which proclaimed, "Elvin's 39 Leaves Bruins in Ruins" and "Who's Number 1? Hayes, Houston, That's Who!"[21] Hayes and his teammates had come a long way since the 1964 season, and now many in the sports community, even within the South, could accept the role of the black athlete. Finally, the Cougars received the "much-deserved credit" they had been waiting for since they first became a team.[22]

To no one's surprise those displeased with the role of black athletes made their sentiments perfectly clear. Some accounts of the game treated Hayes with a certain amount of disrespect. The *Houston Chronicle* ended a piece on the game, entitled "Hays [sic] Took Alcindor Partying After Game," with a quote full of typographical errors in an otherwise flawless piece of journalism. It read, "For the Big E and the Bigd a [sic], it will be a talkathon into the wee hours as they went fraternity hopping after the game. 'That's ritht [sic] ... I'm goint [sic] to pick up Lew and we're going to party.'"[23] Perhaps these mistakes signify nothing; however, the errors appear as more than innocent oversights. Hayes's physical characteristics were also exaggerated and emphasized pointing out his big grin, a characteristic of the stereotypical African American man, and wrote comments such as, "[Hayes] was as cheery as a 6–9 giant cricket," and "as strong as a water buffalo."[24] Hayes was a grown man with a wife and child who had just played one of the greatest games of its time, yet, he was compared to an insect and a large animal. While it would be three years until *Sports Illustrated* would articulate the theory that black athletes were genetically engineered to play sports, the media already concentrated on the black athletes' physical abilities rather than any mental ability.[25] A columnist for the *Daily Cougar* hinted at this writing that he would avoid using "weak adjectives [to] partially cover E's performance."[26]

Attention seeking journalists tried their hardest to create a wedge of dissention between team members, even dredging up recycled stories.

Ken Spain and Elvin Hayes join forces to block the shot of a Michigan player during the 1967-68 season. UH wins with 91–65 final score.

During the previous season, following a loss to UCLA in the NCAA quarterfinals, reports surfaced that claimed Hayes had "read the riot act" to those who had not adequately contributed to the Cougar effort. When Houston won the rematch, the headlines read, "Hayes' Mates Not Chokers," and commented that this time around Hayes would have no need to castigate any other player.[27] Although Hayes adamantly denied any such event, and the alleged issue occurred the previous year, the reports resurfaced following the win. This time around, they asserted, Hayes could not verbally harass the others.

Some of the disapproval was not as obvious to the casual reader as it praised the white and denigrated the black athletes with great subtlety. In multiple reports, the Cougars' black athletes were many times treated in stereotypical, caricature-like fashion. Ken Spain, the lone white starter, however, was portrayed as a "6–9 blond ... [who spoke] matter-of-factly in the noisy din that was the Cougar dressing room.... [and] didn't shoot the ball [enough]."[28] While the African Americans celebrated to the sound of soul music, Spain articulately answered questions for surrounding reporters. Although it could be argued that the comments harbored no ill will but were simply colorful journalists creating unique accounts of the events, it is difficult to ignore the reaction their crafted reports caused. In the eyes of the press and its readers, Hayes and his fellow black athletes were the typical undisciplined bunch while the blue-eyed, blond haired, light skinned Spain was a well-spoken, disciplined athlete.

The Cougar squad fully recognized the attack they were often under and, as they had in all along, closed ranks. Hayes was unquestionably the star of the game, but everyone played their role, and the team let the press know that success depended on the contributions of each member. Coach Lewis, who once emphasized the incredible production of Hayes, now turned his focus toward the team effort saying, "Elvin was fantastic out there, but it was a great team effort."[29] Hayes said of George Reynolds, affectionately known by his teammates as "Dr. Soul," "Man alive did he do a great job handling the ball against the press and on defense out front," and of Ken Spain, "[he] did a fine job." In almost every statement he made sure to "credit togetherness for the victory."[30] The white players, whose playing time was severely reduced, expressed just how hard of a job the starting five had, and how they did not resent their limited minutes. One of them said "Man, there was a lot of pressure. I'll admit I felt it.... It was a great thrill to get into the game, but I was scared."[31] The *Houston Post* tuned into the theme of the game: "In the end, the basic factor on which the UH won this victory was as old as team games themselves."[32] Without question, the Cougars worked and played as a team regardless of their different races, and the press was finally pointing to the sense of unity among the black and white athletes.

Although clearly a group victory, the team did not resent the level of attention Hayes received and did not mind hyping him as the best player in college basketball. Chaney and his fellow Cougars had "no doubt in [their] minds [that Hayes] was the best player on the court."[33] Spectators noted, "It is a measure of the team's unity that [the team] kids Spain about being the only Caucasian in the usual starting lineup ... [and] the White Hope.... You conclude that these ... Houston Cougars are quite a group, tough but loose, one for all and all for Elvin."[34] Jerry Wizig wrote metaphorically of the relationship among teammates, "Hayes built the coffin and the University of Houston [team] barely nudged UCLA's fantastic Bruins into a grave."[35] For the family-like team, the success of Hayes was shared by each and every member, and no one minded the praise sent his way.

Portions of the black press continued their silence on the integration issue, but the *Forward Times*, quickly picked up the story. After almost four years of muteness, the black newspapers began calling for the black community to recognize the contributions of the Houston athletes that had desegregated the University's athletic programs. One writer commented,

> The Cougars ... have been a good winning team all season, but few
> Negroes have really given them the consideration that they really deserve
> ... I feel at this time we should give an ovation to all the Negro stars who
> have been keys in pushing both the football and basketball team through
> key seasons with top wins.... There is little doubt that [those wins] took
> "Soul."[36]

When Hayes and Chaney initially walked onto the campus, the black press granted little recognition to the pioneering move. Now that Houston had made its way to the top of the NCAA, the African American community was ready to embrace the large number of black athletes filling the Cougars' rosters. *The New Courier* wrote, "One could not help remembering ... eight of the ten starters [on both Cougar teams] were handpicked Negroes ... [who are] another galaxy of dazzlers."[37] At long last, the black press decided to discuss the importance of the UH integration only after the athletic program made national headlines.

Interestingly, the "Game of the Century" created a bond between the University and the larger African American community. The University was no longer just a white college with a few black athletes; it was an institution that was as much black as white. "Since the Cougars won," a reporter commented, "the Houston Negro feels closer to the University of Houston than he has ever felt since they first integrated [athletically] four years ago."[38] The school also had a head coach who "treats everyone the same regardless of his ability or position ... [and] is a very understanding person, one you can take your problems to."[39] *The Dallas Morning News* praised Lewis's landmark decision more directly saying of him, "The resident genius, who broke the color line in athletics ... was not afraid to desert tradition. [He] is a resolute man and he has made democracy work. He has molded the black and the white into a team."[40]

Clearly, the UCLA-Houston match-up brought long overdue recognition from the black community to Lewis, his players, and the University for the color barrier they challenged. It served as an "ambassador of interracial goodwill" as, with that one win, Houston's basketball team provided common ground on which both the black and white community could stand.[41] The Cougars had one foot in each community and welcomed all fans to stand behind them. Only one critical account surfaced when a black reporter sounded off against Hayes and Chaney. He argued that these athletes were no longer black because they had sold out to the white man and lost all remnants of their ethnicity. "When our kind become superstars, in any sport," he wrote, "they transcend 'Negro' and become, in fact, temporary whites-with all the notices and plugs that a daily press, the radio or television media can provide."[42] Outside of the few detractors, the majority of the black community was accepting the Cougars invitation.

The African American media outlets were not alone in their notice of the racial change transpiring in Houston. Mainstream publications suddenly emphasized the UH integration and highlighted what should have been noted four years earlier. The "Game of the Century," and the intense publicity it brought to the Cougar program, drew attention to the issue of desegregation and turned Houston into a symbol of progress in the struggle for racial equality. Chaney, Hayes, and McVea were suddenly promoted as pioneers who made sacrifices and took risks to change the nature of athletics within the South. The *Washington Post* even printed an article extolling the role the three of them played in changing the nature of the southern sports world. The "Game of the Century" indelibly changed southerners' perception of black athletes for the better. They were now seen as valuable additions to any team.

Chaney and Hayes bolstered the positive awareness by telling the press that the situation was as good as advertised. Although black athletes throughout the nation were beginning agitate for change and the boycott of the 1968 Olympics was gearing up, the Houston athletes did not utter a single negative word about either the school or the basketball program. Hayes had nothing but praise for UH, the coaches, and the team and maintained that Houston's integration was thriving: "Everybody's been just great to us."[43] In that same interview, he insisted that the Cougars had moved past the race issue altogether, remarking, "I don't think anyone worries about which players on our team are white and which one's aren't. That's the way it should be."[44] Chaney also shrugged off the inquiries and lauded his alma mater for they way he and his fellow black athletes were embraced on campus.[45] Neither of these men even hinted that Houston had mistreated them or shown them anything other than respect and equality. Soon, an ever increasing number of coaches began seriously examining the issue. They looked at Houston and slowly came to the realization that segregated teams were a dying breed.

The Cougars, with a team full of African American athletes, completely surpassed the schools in the Southwest Conference as they now filled the subordinate position long held by Houston. Reporter Mickey Herskowitz pointed out what many were rapidly coming to understand writing,

> It would be tiresome and trite to say that basketball in Texas came of age Saturday night. It would also be untrue. Some Southwest Conference schools will continue to struggle to draw in a season what the Cougars ... attracted in one evening.... The Cougars are plainly heading for high

places ... and the SWC schools are beginning to feel the pinch.... I don't know about the SWC but if it was me, and I belonged to a union, and my business was getting hurt by a guy who didn't [belong to the union], I'd work like the dickens to get him into the union. Then you could quit complaining, and just compete.[46]

One by one, the SWC and other southern conferences began questioning their own segregation policies. The member schools reevaluated their policies not because of any newly developed concern for racial equality but because they could not stand consistently losing to what they had deemed the lesser schools. For example, the supporters of the University of Texas, which would win the last national title with an all-white football team, began questioning why it had not yet made the change.[47] As an observer stated, "Once their fans saw Warren, they [urged] their coaches to recruit one or two [blacks]."[48] One sports writer stated the day after Houston's victory over UCLA, "The UT obviously needs a more enlightened admissions system in judging its Negro ... applicants.... In not doing something other than adhering to an artificial measuring standard for the underprivileged types, whether athlete or not, the UT seems to be among the unenlightened schools of the nation."[49] Regardless of the motivation behind the changes, the athletic segregation would not last much longer. Although some integration appeared shortly after the Cougars' initial decision to desegregate, the period after the 1968 season saw the most significant change in the landscape of southern athletics.[50] In a domino effect, one southern program after another invited the black athlete to join their previously all-white rosters.

Change was happening in more places than the hardwood, and it was becoming noticeable even in intensely segregated places like Louisiana. Hayes had not been recognized by the media before leaving for Houston, yet the local and state presses changed their opinion following Hayes's remarkable UH career. The week following the UCLA game, he earned the honor of amateur athlete of the year for the state of Louisiana, the first time an African American athlete had ever won the award.[51] Houston's Cougars were changing perceptions of race even in the areas where changed seemed impossible, and Hayes recognized it.[52] He found validation in the award saying that he always "wanted to be 'a somebody' and surely that ambition was fulfilled [with the award]."[53] Because of his athletic accomplishments with Houston, Hayes became accepted by much of the intensely prejudiced white community of Louisiana despite his skin color.

That season, in which the Cougars finished the regular season with a 28-0 record and a first place national ranking, ended ironically with a loss to UCLA in the NCAA tournament which served as the capstone for Chaney's and Hayes's careers at the University of Houston. In the three varsity years they played under Lewis, they compiled an overall record of 81 wins and 12 losses, and Hayes received three All-American nominations and was named the 1968 National Player of the Year.[54] They had made "their final appearance before the hometown folks they [had] come to love and respect," and, at the conclusion of that basketball season, they left behind the program which lifted them from obscurity and gave them an opportunity to seize the benefits which previously belonged only to whites.[55] The fans recognized the just how special those years had been. The yearbook wrote at the end of the 1968 spring semester, "[Hayes] started Houston's basketball sparks, a spark that led to a roaring flame of 'round-ball fever' [and] you can bet UH basketball will never be the same. 'E,' thanks for the memories."[56] Both athletes entered the National Basketball Association's draft and were selected in the first round. Hayes went to the San Diego Rockets as the number one overall pick, and Chaney went to the Boston Celtics as the twelfth pick. With their departure, the school's integration was complete. The younger black athletes who remained, and the many others that would join in subsequent seasons, would continue to represent the black community. Integration at Houston and elsewhere throughout the South would not disappear.

The conclusion of the 1967-68 seasons brought an end to the first major athletic integration, and it fulfilled the majority of its original goals. Lewis's and Yeoman's assessment of the situation proved correct as integration turned a "school that only began playing major college sports in 1946 ... [into] a program that produced championship-caliber teams."[57] Suddenly, the elusive Southwest Conference could not match up against the independent Cougars, and the press began noticing the discrepancies between the two. They wrote, "The Cougars are finally at the top, after 21 years of climbing, and there is fear in the hearts of future Houston opponents.... [They] will never get into a conference again ... certainly not the Southwest Conference."[58] Houston's position changed drastically in four years, and it no longer felt the need to plead for entrance into the SWC. If the SWC wanted Houston to join, it would have to treat the Cougars as a welcomed equal. Harry Fouke communicated Houston's perspective on the issue as he informed the media: "We are not going begging.... If the conference wanted to expand we would be interested. But, Houston would have to be wanted, rather than the other way around."[59] Fouke, with all the bargaining chips in his corner, would wait until the school's conditions were met.

The long sought after admission to the SWC finally came in 1971. Although the school had to agree to a five year probation period during which it could not compete for conference titles the Cougars had finally achieved membership in a nationally significant conference. They received all the monetary benefits and publicity the charter schools were privilege to and flourished in the new system. Integration fulfilled its mission as Houston successfully transitioned from a mid-major institution into a powerhouse program capable of standing with any other program in less that a decade's time. When the Cougars were finally able to compete for the SWC title, they came out ready to prove they belonged there. The football team, on which former UH football coach Art Briles was a member, won ten games on its way to the conference championship in 1976, the first year it was eligible to compete for the title. It would be the first but certainly not the only title for Houston. Finally, the Cougars' quest for athletic legitimacy had been fulfilled.

The success of the integration applied to the athletes as well. Chaney, Hayes, and McVea came to the UH campus under controversial circumstances and left, to most at least, as athletic heroes. The three athletes received the education and nurturing promised from the beginning and expanded their athletic prospects in the process. They matured into nationally-recognized athletes desired by professional teams and received the fulfilled promises made by the University and the coaches. At the conclusion of the 1967-68 seasons, the tenure of the first three African American athletes came to an end. Both parties managed to pull off the ultimate victory; they found a true win win situation for themselves and ultimately other southern universities.

9

A Cruel Deception Indeed

With the exit of Chaney, Hayes, and McVea, Houston's foray into athletic integration was finished. The three African American athletes had started in the program as eighteen year old freshman and matured into men ready to join the professional ranks in their respective sports. They had the education and the experience necessary to thrive under any circumstance and, the University of Houston had provided them the opportunity to leave the segregated environment of their youths behind. The three athletes helped promote this perception. They had only kind words for the school as they headed off in new directions and cashed in on the athletic talent perfected and displayed at Houston. Yeoman's and Lewis's grand plan had been successfully implemented, and many other African American men followed in the footsteps of those first athletes. But Houston and its faithful fans would not have long to triumph in the Cougars' accomplishments. Just as the media had done time and time again, one reporter stepped forward to try and tear down the solid reputation UH had spent so long building up.

In the summer of 1968, *Sports Illustrated*, the magazine which wrote so many harsh things about Houston and its black athletes over the previous four years, published an exposé on what it claimed was the true reality of life for the African American Cougars. "The Black Athlete: A Shameful Story," Jack Olson's five part work, appeared at the height of the Black Power movement and the African American boycott of the 1968 Olympics in Mexico City and aggressively attacked the image of racial acceptance and harmony that Lewis, Yeoman, and their athletes had been promoting. Olson wrote instead that the first three black Cougar athletes were shamelessly mistreated and used for the benefit of the school and then tossed aside when their eligibility expired.[1] Neither the coaches nor the administration, according to the articles, cared about the athletes well being or education but only about developing their own reputations and increasing the program's number of wins. Those athletes were seen as little more than hired guns and were certainly not student athletes on campus to receive an education. The articles, which prominently displayed Chaney, McVea, and Hayes, "explored the roots and validity of the black athlete's unrest — and [discovered] them well founded."[2] It raised serious concerns about the reality of sports integration and about the real legacy of Houston's integration. Had, as Olson claimed, the Cougars' picture of racial harmony really been a sham? Had they only perpetuated the existing racial system? Or, were the Cougars once again victims of acidic attacks by a biased reporter looking to make a name for himself and a magazine looking for its next dollar?[3] As will soon become obvious, it was the latter.

The first two installments of the article, respectively entitled "The Cruel Deception" and "Pride and Prejudice," dealt with what the author claimed was the cruel reality of collegiate athletics. He argued that colleges and universities throughout the south used the black athlete for their own gain, both in reputation and in finances, and yet never viewed or treated them as equals. African American athletes were little more than hired performers, and programs only allowed them onto their campuses and onto their squads because of an insatiable desire to win. Administrators and coaches cared not about the athletes themselves or their education or futures but only about marks in the win column and "held [them] in rigid social check at [most] U.S. colleges."[4] Blacks could not socialize with the whites on campus, could not interact with white team mates outside of the sports arenas, and were forced to serve as work horses day in and day out. They had no true white friends either on or off campus, had to play through serious injuries that would sideline any other athlete, and had to consistently perform at a higher level than all the others. Olson contended that as a result these men "were dissatisfied, disgruntled and disillusioned ... [and] say they [were] dehumanized, exploited and discarded."[5] Ultimately, the claim that sports brought blacks out of the repression and into white society was just an illusion. The athletes did more for the world of sports than it did for them, and collegiate and professional programs throughout the nation should be shamed because of that reality.

The University of Houston felt the brunt of Olson's diatribe on athletic inequality. In the articles, the Cougars, along with Texas Western (UTEP), were highlighted as particularly blatant abusers of black athletes and told audiences that they should be appalled at what was going on behind closed doors. Olson included quotes from Houston's black athletes and painted a vivid picture of these men living in a system of racial repression. They had just made sports fans across the nation sit up and take notice of the UH program, yet were unable to live with the same rights and privileges as their white counterparts.

The series minimized the role Houston played in the lives of these three athletes. Olson wanted to make certain his readers knew that Yeoman and Lewis had not done these men any favors by offering them spots on the Cougars' roster. Houston had not rescued Elvin Hayes from the racially backward Rayville or given him his only chance at a prosperous future because he was a determined individual who navigated his own way through an exclusionary white society. His strong-willed mother, and equally hard-headed late father, made certain that Hayes made something of himself and refused to let him perpetuate the cycle of repression. Houston provided him an outlet to accomplish that goal but if it had not been UH, it would have been another institution and another path to greatness. Olson insisted that the Cougars had no right to say they helped him along the way. Elvin had done Houston the favor, not the other way around.

According to Olson, the McVea was no different. McVea supposedly said he was not blind to the exploitive nature of the relationship. He purportedly came to that realization after a brief conversation with an assistant coach in which he was told that he should be grateful for the opportunity Houston had provided and not question any treatment he received. Olson retold how McVea, "a short, black artillery shell of a man, snapped back, 'I think I've been pretty darn good to this university. I want you to remember one thing: you came to me, I didn't come to you.'"[6] McVea allegedly let the staff know that the school did not make his career, and Olson wanted his readers to know the same thing. Houston was not the great liberator it claimed to be.

But Olson was missing the point here. UH knew it was lucky to sign these highly talented athletes and never claimed full responsibility for their rise into athletic stardom. McVea, Hayes, and Chaney had numerous offers from big name schools and all involved from the administration down the students knew Houston had scored a major coup by signing them. What the school did do was give these athletes a chance to confront the southern attitudes and force racially backward individuals to at least acknowledge their abilities and accomplishments. It gave them a chance to play in the South where their families and friends could watch and allowed them to develop friendships and camaraderie with white players and fans. For Hayes, that shot meant everything. He expressed the role Houston played in his personal growth saying, "I'm not bitter today about the prejudice [of my hometown].... I guess I would be bitter if I had been denied the opportunity to work my way out [but] ... I was offered all the opportunity in the world thanks to the University of Houston and ... Guy V. Lewis."[7] For Chaney too, the campus provided a chance for him to learn how to interact with the whites he had feared and resented during his youth in Louisiana. Houston provided an atmosphere where he could interact with whites and facilitate understanding and acceptance among the races in a way that had not been possible previously. He pointed out that "three years after Elvin and I got there, Houston had its first black homecoming queen. That was amazing to me, that a school that had been all white could have something like that happen in so short a time."[8]

As recently as 2006, Hayes and McVea reiterated that they did not feel exploited by the University. They were not tossed aside at the end of their four year stint without an education or a future. McVea never completed his degree and Hayes obtained his diploma seventeen years after his last athletic semester, but they both insisted they received everything promised.[9] Hayes was perfectly clear about the situation commenting that whether or not the athletes graduated, they were nevertheless presented with the opportunity. "In exchange for tuition and books," he stated, "I [had] an opportunity to get a good degree and play basketball in return.... It was a fair and even trade."[10] He re-emphasized the point: "I don't agree with most blacks who say a school used them.... If you don't go to class, there's nothing they can do for you."[11]

McVea stood right alongside Hayes on that point and wanted to state for the record that Olson did not accurately represent the athletic department's attitude toward the black athletes. He remarked that the argument between him and the assistant coach that Olson centered his argument around was nothing more than a miscommunication. He clarified the incident: "We didn't really clash, we just had a misunderstanding.... I don't think he meant anything by it, it just came out that way."[12] As far as the claim that Yeoman ignored McVea's injuries and risked the athlete's entire career for the sake of the team, McVea discounts that as well. He pointed out that the team trainer, Tom Wilson, always informed the coach when he could or could not play and believed that he never took chances with his health. Wilson, said McVea, "was the best in the business, the best.... Tom Wilson never lied to me about any [injury]."[13] For whatever abuses might have occurred in other programs, these men do not believe Houston guilty of any of them. They have consistently maintained that for the program's part, everything proceeded just as it should have. All these years later, the athletes defend the University of Houston and its athletic department and laud it for allowing them to confront the racial issues which were polarizing the lower U.S.

Olson's next accusation involved the lack of interracial interaction. He stated that Houston kept the black athletes in isolation, always separated from the larger campus community, and acceptance among the athletic community never fully occurred. Blacks and whites played together but very little else. Chaney reportedly told of the racism that exuded from the team and of the awkward situations blacks often found themselves in. He shared one instance where a group of team mates were "chortling about the blacks on Tarzan [and] they'd be saying things like, 'Get that nigger,' 'Stupid nigger,' ... and they would giggle and laugh. Then they looked back at me and shut up."[14] Hayes was no different. In the article, he spoke of spending most of his time in the "black ghetto, jiving around with the poor boys of grammar" rather than his fellow Cougars.[15] The University of Houston did not provide a sense of community or acceptance for the black athletes, and neither they nor their fans truly knew these men. Olson wrote, "What does the white man cheering in the grandstand know of ... Elvin Hayes? Not a thing — and that is part of the shame."[16]

McVea, according to the article, claimed that the team never accepted him as anything other than an ignorant second class citizen. "Whatever happens to you out on that field," he said, "the white players are thinking two things about you: that you're some kind of superhuman because you're black, and that you're dumb."[17] McVea spoke of the loneliness he felt on the Houston campus which was heightened by the reality that "off the field, [he and team] were strangers."[18] He supposedly felt as though "in his whole college career [he] only had one real good white friend."[19] Sadly according to Olson, that friend was not even a member of the team or a classmate but rather the head of the campus traffic department who invited McVea to his child's birthday party.[20]

On this count, Olson could not have been further from reality. The men of those teams lived, played, and socialized with each other on a regular basis. They were spotted on and off campus together, visited each others homes for holidays, and developed solid friendships which are still intact. Almost forty years after the end of their years at Houston, the men of those teams remain friends. Roommates Lorch and Hayes as well as Tracy and Chaney still have active friendships and communicate regularly. McVea also stayed in touch with his fellow Cougar gridders. He related that when he was inducted into the University of Houston Hall of Fame in 2004 many of his former team mates showed up to recognize him, and that that act of support touched him.[21] Dick Woodall, the quarterback of the 1967 squad summed it up: "We were all friends. We remained friends."[22] When the 1966 team had its 40th reunion, the members sat and talked like no time had past. If, as Olson contended, these relationships were fleeting and shallow, these men would have long since lost touch. Instead, they cultivated true friendships which have lasted even into the new millennium.

The issue of white young co-eds was an even stronger point of division. Historically, the biggest fear regarding integration was the supposed sexual power that black men possessed. African American men, according to popular belief, would defile any white woman they socialized with and therefore had to be kept away from the innocent young ladies who filled the college campuses. Olson claimed that UH whole-heartedly embraced that racial myth evidenced by Chaney's claim that white athletes reacted negatively to his association with white women. He explained, "If a Negro guy is talking to a white girl, a team mate will ... discourage the girl from talking to him. The white athlete always automatically thinks we're doing something bad with the girls.... They'll cut the white girl socially ... because she talks to us."[23] For Hayes the issue of interracial dating was not important as he had married during college but for Chaney and McVea the issue was a constant concern. According to Olson's writings, the black athlete had to restrict his association with them or face the consequences. Black and white athletes lived in different spheres from the first day to the last, and that applied to the female population as well.

The criticism related to interracial dating was simply ridiculous. It is not doubtful that white women were discouraged from associating with black men and that white men disapproved of such interactions. But that should not reflect badly on the Houston program because southern society did not tolerate interracial dating. The largest fear among whites was that their virtuous daughters would be corrupted by the increasingly brazen community of black men. That irrational belief had been floating through society since well before the Civil War, and the Houston staff would not bring it to an end. Nor should they be expected to. They had a responsibility to win games and teach their athletes how to play sports and get an education not tackle interracial dating. Nevertheless the coaching staffs tried to work through any incidents as judiciously as possible. Chaney admitted in his interview with Olson that after the various scuttlebutts, the coaches would "talk to [the athletes] and bring [them] back together again as a team."[24] Not all racial prejudices could be overcome at one time, but UH certainly did what it could to deal with those that remained in an equitable manner.[25]

Beyond that Olson wrote the coaches and fans never provided support for their black athletes. While Houston had informed the public that Yeoman and Lewis were colorblind coaches who protected their athletes from excess negative attention when possible and ensured that all players had a fair chance at success both athletically and educationally, the reality was much less flattering. These coaches suposedly used their black athletes for personal gain and cared little about them outside of that. They dictated how the three men would conduct themselves in every aspect of their lives. Chaney outlined the situation clearly. He said, "It's like this. You're there to do the job. You're somebody they hired. You're a workhorse. A workhorse isn't supposed to talk back ... is he?"[26] He continued by faulting coaches for implementing a double standard when it came to court time. "A white kid can make five or six mistakes and stay in," Chaney lamented, but "[black athletes] make one and [they're] on the bench."[27] In Olson's world, the three Cougars were living in repressive conditions.

But according to the athletes, this simply was not true. Their coaches were indeed fair men interested in them as individuals rather than just as athletes. Although Olson portrayed the coaching staffs as prejudiced individuals who refused to afford the same privileges to the white and black players, the athletes have consistently viewed them with admiration. They each saw in their coaches men willing to risk everything to grant them a fair chance with the Cougars. Lewis and Yeoman brought them there to win, but they still treated the three with equality and respect. Hayes said of Lewis, "He was a person who changed your perception of reality and the [of] way things ought to be. Here was a man giving you an opportunity when everybody else was just pushing you to the back of the bus."[28] Chaney praised Lewis for taking the chance on not just one but two black athletes at the same time, remarking, "You have to give [him] a lot of credit for bringing in two black athletes at the same time, don't you? That was a bold move at the time, especially in Texas."[29] These two men clearly respected Lewis, and Hayes articulated, "He's been like a father to all of us.... He's quite a person and quite a coach."[30]

Warren McVea had just as many kind words for Yeoman. He praised his coach for putting everything on the line for him and for making certain that he had an equal opportunity. Yeoman's friendship extended beyond the four years he played at Houston. McVea said of Yeoman, "Coaches say anything to get players, but this man said it and actually stuck to it. He's still my friend, [and] I'm most proud of that than anything. He just never got off the wagon, even in down times.... He's a special person in my life."[31] Despite Olson's claims to the contrary, McVea knows that his coach truly cared about him as a person because Yeoman has never stopped looking out for him and still stands beside him even though he is well past his playing days.[32]

Finally Olson ripped Houston apart for its vocal fans. Hayes pointed out to Olson that "the crowds expected us to be terrific every minute. When we weren't they got on us."[33] McVea told how the fans never afforded him an off night even when injured. He commented, "If we say we're hurt, they say we're faking. I played four years with injuries and you hardly even heard a word about it."[34] An unidentified member of the Houston athletic staff concurred confiding in the author, "Mac is no complainer.... He was hurt almost all the time.... Somehow [people] couldn't accept that a

Negro athlete could be hurt."[35] Cougar fans claimed the *Sports Illustrated* author did not change their racial perceptions because of integration but accepted the black athletes only because of their physical capabilities. The situation was in actuality only a variation of the slave/master relationship, for, as long as the African American athletes could perform their assigned duties, their presence was acceptable. The minute they did not accomplish those tasks, the fans dismissed them from their presence. The Cougar supporters clearly communicated the precise nature of that relationship when one of the athletes acted in an unacceptable manner. Olson pointed to the McVea/Hebert incident as an example writing that because "he had stepped out of his place ... he is still known in parts of Houston as the 'smart nigger' who had the effrontery to stand up to a white man in front of 41,000 people."[36] In passage after passage, Olson lambasted the UH fans for being just as racist and prejudiced as they had been four year previously.

To say that Olson spoke completely out of turn would be slightly untrue. A portion of the Cougar following never moved beyond the race issue, and the public perception of the fight between McVea and Hebert undoubtedly demonstrated that. But even then, the point should not be lost that a majority of Cougar fans were not prejudiced Southerners waiting to put the African American athletes in their place. Those UH supporters adamantly defended the athletes from the negative attacks and constantly pointed out all of the success the teams had achieved and all of the positive steps they had taken. Win or lose they stood behind Cougar athletes. Signs of this acceptance by the fans were apparent throughout those years. From white fans carrying Hayes and McVea off the court and field, to white well-wishers flooding the Cougar locker room to the white students decrying the treatment of blacks in southern cities, perceptions of race and integration had unquestionably changed at Houston.[37] The fans no longer saw black or white but simply the red and white of the jersey. Athletes were Cougars first and foremost regardless of skin color. No situation, regardless of how progressive or its geographical location, would demonstrate complete acceptance of integration but to label the entire Cougar nation as a taunting, jeering mass of racially backward fans is simply untrue and unfair to so many loyal supporters.

Olson's report maliciously attacked the Houston Cougars and led the nation to believe that unpardonable transgressions occurred there. It skewed athletes' comments and made inaccurate generalizations about UH athletics to make the situation seem harsh and deplorable. Even though the claims were false, the articles severely damaged Houston's public image. Because of its prominent position in the series, the Cougar program could not put space between itself and the accusations flung at it but had to face the brunt of the controversy. For the public, it became the poster child of programs abusive to black athletes, and a significant portion of the *Sports Illustrated* readership expressed disgust over the situation portrayed by Olson. Letters to the editor flooded into the magazine and decried the existing system.[38] Brent Musburger, now a prominent ABC sports broadcaster, heralded the piece saying it was "a revealing, shocking, and moving look at the Negro in American sports ... [and] one of the most important sports documents written."[39] Readers also wrote in, "Unquestionably the best Negro athletes have within recent years been proselyted [*sic*] and cajoled by major university departments with only one thing in mind-produce on the field or court" and insisted "the sports world has shown that black and white can achieve together; it can credit itself with no more."[40] Certain schools quickly distanced themselves from Houston, telling the public, "Let the American public know of the injustice and where it has taken place, but do not condemn the whole of collegiate athletics because of the actions of the few."[41] Almost all readers believed Olson's depiction of the racially repressive sports culture without question "because it was written for, and printed by, *Sports Illustrated* ... not because it [was] true."[42] In their eyes, a magazine of that reputation would never publish untruthful articles, and so the national image Houston had taken so long to build and the integration it had so painstaking established took a severe beating.

So, which version of Houston's integration is the truth? Was the public image presented throughout the four years merely a facade, or was Olson a yellow dog journalist looking for a story to cement his literary legacy? Were the men really athletic minstrels rather than participating equals? With both views bolstered by supporting quotes, determining the answer to this question is difficult. If this were all the evidence, history would have to call the situation a stalemate. But as they say, we must look at the rest of the story.

First, Houston was not alone in its objections to Olson. Texas Western coach Don Haskins, known for his 1966 NCAA championship victory over the University of Kentucky, took great umbrage with the charges levied about his team and athletes in his memoir *Glory Road:* "That magazine hurt my players and their parents. And it was wrong.... I used to respect that magazine, but like a lot of people through the years, I realized its purpose isn't about telling the truth.... Its goal is to create controversy ... [and] I have never forgiven [it]."[43] As for the Houston athletes, they have stated emphatically that Olson took their statements out of context and misrepresented the situation. Warren McVea said in the summer of 2006 that he did tell Olson about a few instances where disagreements occurred between himself and the staff and teammates but that he went on to explain that those events were simple misunderstandings not evidence of pervasive racism. The remainder of his thoughts were not included. Elvin Hayes joined McVea in pointing out that neither he nor his fellow African American team mates ever participated in protests or demonstrations. If these men were ever going to prove how badly they had been treated surely this would have been their time to do so. And at that point, they would have had the complete freedom to expose any harsh treatment. They had played through their careers and had no reason to sugar coat the truth.

Further evidence of the University's care for its athletes came in the late 1960s during a period rife with unrest.[44] Between the Olympic boycott and the protests in both black and white college athletic programs, the situation was unquestionably tense.[45] At Houston the seeds of that dissention never sprouted and no such movement arose within the athletic department. Even when the Black Panther Party came to campus to organize the athletes, not a single member of the team joined. Yeoman remembered that the group came to UH to try and organize the black athletes and cultivate unrest but could not find students interested in what they were selling. The reason was two fold. First, the athletes were not unhappy with department's treatment, and second the group made the mistake of insulting the white community the black athletes had grown fond of. Many of their team mates and friends were white, and they would not let a group of outsiders, black or not, insult them.[46] They were a family and not even the Black Panthers could break them up.

Despite the futility of such organizations, the school put the needs of the black athlete on the front burner. In 1969, the University formed a special committee to evaluate the condition of the black athletes just to ensure that no dissent was brewing among the ranks. The thirty-one athletes informed the committee, through confidential interviews, that they "did not feel that racial discrimination [was] prevalent on athletic teams ... [and] no unfair treatment ... was observable."[47] They also told the administration that the school was meeting their academic needs and any academic shortcomings came down to personal failure rather than departmental neglect. The only request made was that the committee consider hiring a black coach to which one member responded, "We can do a great deal more."[48] Without question, the University of Houston was committed to its black students. And so, forty years later the true "cruel deception" as printed by *Sports Illustrated* has been exposed.

So how should Houston be remembered? What lasting impact did the integrated Cougars affect? Although Houston athletics did not lead to any civil rights legislation and never had the direct impact of Martin Luther King, Jr., or Rosa Parks, or Malcolm X, it did make a clear dent in the pervasive racism of the South. The Cougars, through their ability to place black and white athletes under a common team cause, demonstrated to its supporters and critics that different races could not only co-exist and co-operate as a team, but that interaction could prove immensely successful to society in general.

Toward the lesser cause, the integrated Cougars demonstrated the financial benefits of integration to the city of Houston.[49] Historians often point out that the boycotts of the mainstream civil rights movement were so effective because they made racial equality economically beneficial to whites. By demonstrating the financial rewards of desegregation, whites were more willing to accept changes. The UH athletic integration worked in much the same way. From sold out football games to the phenomenally successful UCLA/Houston match up, the Cougars increased city revenues and brought national exposure to Houston. The city, understanding the benefits, did not limit integration to the fields as the Astrodome had integrated seating allowing blacks and whites to watch the events together. When the Cougars filled the Astrodome with fans and brought national exposure to the city, Houston stood behind the UH teams, black athletes included.

Beyond the city limits and toward the greater cause, the Houston

Before a crowd of 42,061 exited fans, Houston routed Tulsa 73–14 avenging its nationally televised loss the previous year. Here, Tom Beer gives McVea a much needed block (1966).

teams forced other schools and conferences to re-evaluate the status of integration. As mentioned in the previous chapter, the Southern programs, noting the stellar success of the UH programs, were forced to consider lifting racial bans. The Southwest and Southeast Conferences gradually began lowering the segregation barriers and allowing black athletes to slip onto their courts and fields. While one cannot concretely say that Houston was the sole impetus for the changes, it can be argued that it was responsible for opening the dialogue. Within a few years of the Cougars' move toward athletic equality, the major programs touted their black athletes and began reaping the benefits of integration.[50] Had Houston not taken that first step, the change would have without a doubt been much longer in coming.

But to the greatest cause, the athletic integration helped further the general civil rights cause by positively impacting the number of minorities attending the University. With the athletes' feats visible throughout the nation, African Americans saw the changes at Houston and grew interested in attending the school which gave Chaney, Hayes, and McVea a chance at success. Gene Locke, currently a partner in the Houston law firm Andrews Kurth, LLP, and counsel to the Harris County Houston Sports Authority, attended Houston for just that reason. Although his uncle was the first black professor at the University of Texas and the Austin school seemed the logical choice for him, Locke decided on UH principally because of the three pioneering athletes. He commented, "What turned the tide for me was UH's decision to integrate the athletics program.... That sent a signal: here's an institution that is opening up."[51] Tom Beer, a member of Yeoman's 1965 squad, concurred: "UH's [athletic] desegregation greatly enhanced the school's social structure as a greater number of minorities ... became an integral part of the school's academic and social fabric."[52] Houston's integrated athletics drew in increasing numbers of African American students to the campus where they were provided with a solid education and a welcoming environment.

To conclude, the University of Houston did what few other institutions were willing to do and saw incredible racial gains as a result. Both the city and the Houston campus changed substantially because of the decision to integrate the basketball and football programs. The racial adjustments the team and spectators made changed the racial environment within Houston for the better. While the same cannot be said for every program throughout the nation, sports at the University of Houston broke down racial barriers other activists could not, and all involved should be applauded for their willingness to step forward and put themselves and their careers on the line for the sake of racial equality. The summation of these men's character can be defined as loyal. They were loyal to each other, loyal to their word, and unequivocally loyal to UH. The goal set in 1964 had finally been accomplished: one team, one color. Cougar blood brothers on the field or court, whether black or white, they all bled red.

Conclusion

In the nearly forty years since the Cougars' first three black athletes left the courts and fields of the University of Houston campus, the surrounding landscape has undergone many changes. The young athletes who once stood at the center of collegiate athletics and the coaches who stood by them have retired from the sports scene and have assumed the role of spectator. But their careers were anything but unfruitful.

Elvin Hayes, who was drafted as the number one pick in 1968, enjoyed a long career in the NBA playing for the Washington/Baltimore Bullets (Washington Wizards) and the San Diego Rockets (Houston Rockets). During his time in the NBA, he not only led his team to a championship title but amassed astounding statistics along the way. By the time he retired in 1984, he had become the first individual to play 50,000 minutes (since outdone by only his former foe Kareem Abdul-Jabbar and Karl Malone), rebounded 16,279 loose balls (still the fourth highest), and scored 27,313 points (landing him sixth on the all-time leaders list). For his tremendous accomplishments, he was inducted into the Basketball Hall of Fame in 1990 and was named one of the NBA's 50 Greatest Players in 1996. His college coach is still awed by the amount of talent endowed upon him as he told the *Sporting News* in 2002, "My gosh, Elvin was 6-9 and could outrun anybody on my team forward or backwards and out jump them all."[1] Since retiring from the game, he has not showed any signs of slowing down. He entered the automobile business, purchasing several car dealerships in the Houston area and currently spends his free time overseeing the daily operations and traveling. Always looking for new challenges and adventures, he recently completed training to become a peace officer. Although not looking for a new career, he has fulfilled the lifelong goal of joining law enforcement. Even in retirement, he is pushing himself to grow and develop in new and different ways.

Don Chaney followed Hayes into the NBA in 1968 landing with the Boston Celtics with whom he won two championship rings. He played eleven seasons in the NBA and one in the ABA before retiring from the game. After hanging up his jersey, he tried his hand at coaching and was a NBA head coach for twelve years. After making stops with the LA Clippers, Houston Rockets, Detroit Pistons, and New York Knicks and earning the Coach of the Year Award in 1991, Chaney walked away from the game for good after the 2003-2004 season. He was elected to the University of Houston Hall of Fame in 1981. Like many of his fellow Cougars, he can be seen at UH athletic events on a regular basis.

Guy V. Lewis, known for his colorfully brilliant blazers and polka dotted towels, remained with Houston through the end of his coaching days. After thirty seasons as head coach, Lewis took off his coaching shoes in 1986 leaving behind a long legacy of winning including 592 wins, 27 straight winning seasons, 14 NCAA Tournaments, and 5 Final Four appearances.[2] Although he achieved tremendous success with the teams led by Chaney and Hayes, his later career had just as many moments of excellence. He coached the teams affectionately known as Phi Slama Jama, with famed athletes Clyde "the Glyde" Drexler and Hakeem "the Dream" Olajuwon, to the NCAA Final Four and Title Game in 1983 and 1984 respectively. Despite his demonstrated ability to coach teams to victory, he has been intentionally and unduly ignored by the Basketball Hall of Fame year after year. Lewis's record and the quality of athletes who came out of his program prove to all unbiased observers that he knew how to bring the best out of his athletes and taught them how to win consistently.[3] Hall of Fame bid or no, Lewis's career places him among the coaching elite, and he will long be remembered as one of the coaching greats.

Following his retirement, he and his wife Dena remained in the Houston area and still faithfully attend every Cougar basketball home game, played on the Guy V. Lewis court. Their loyalty to the school, which now has an azalea garden named in their honor, has never wavered, and they are beloved by all Cougar fans. They celebrated their 65th wedding anniversary in 2007.

Warren McVea, who had an all-around remarkable career at Houston, found his way into the NFL as he was drafted fourth by the Cincinnati Bengals in 1968. Within two years, he won a Super Bowl ring with the Kansas City Chiefs. McVea retired from the NFL in 1973 due to the fact that he could never quite shake the injuries which had plagued him since his college days. Accomplishing what most professional athletes dream of but never realize, he walked away from the game with a championship to his name. In 2004, he was inducted into the University of Houston Hall of Honor because of his contributions to the school both on the field and off.[4] Today, he resides in Houston and can still be seen at Cougar football games. In the fall of 2006, he stood beside his teammates at Robertson Stadium and celebrated the 40th anniversary of the 1966 season. Although many gridiron greats have come and gone since his days with UH, most true fans still acknowledge the speedy runner as a one of the greatest athletes to don a football uniform.

As for the coach who brought McVea to Houston, Yeoman finished out his coaching days with the Cougars in 1986, the same year as Guy V. Lewis. The coach who changed the face of football not only through integration but also through the creation of the Veer offense brought spectacular success to the university and carved out a place for the Cougars on the national scene. During his twenty four years as head coach (1962–1986), he compiled a 160-108-8 record, took his teams to eleven bowl games, and won four Southwest Conference titles.[5] He was inducted into the College Football Hall of Fame in 2001 and the Texas Sports Hall of Fame in 2003. He coached 49 All-Americans, 69 future NFL athletes, and stands as the winningest football coach in Cougar history. Currently, he remains on staff with the UH athletic department helping with fundraising, and he is present at all of Houston's home games cheering on the school that he helped put on the map. He and his wife A.J., who accompanies him to Cougar games, still reside in Houston.

The University of Houston has also undergone significant changes. Whereas it was one of the first of its kind to embrace diversity in the 1960s, it is now one of the most racially varied campuses in the nation. Not only black and white students but individuals from every walk of life co-exist and interact with each other as though color and race did not exist. As of the fall of 2004, the student population has expanded to just over thirty-five thousand which includes 39.5 percent white, 18.7

percent Asian/Pacific Islander, 18.1 percent Hispanic, 13 percent African American, 8.1 percent International, 0.4 percent Native American, and 2.2 percent unknown origin.[6] The 2008 *U.S. World News and Report* ranked Houston second on its list of diverse colleges. As these students swarm around the campus throughout the year, it is clear that the days of a primarily white campus have long since passed, and a new international community has assumed its place. Tom Beer, a member of the 1965 football team, feels the racial strides of the Cougar athletes helped set the tone for today's campus saying that Lewis's and Yeoman's decisions "paved the way to UH's great success [with diversity.]"[7]

The University's academic programs have vastly improved since the 1960s as well. Many of its programs can stand up against those offered at the elite colleges, and UH students are being prepared for successful careers in a multitude of professions. Even with all the positive aspects and the excellent education being offered, the rogue reputation of the University of Houston, intensified by the athletic integration, has not diminished over the years. But ultimately, it is a reputation Houston fans and alumni have learned to embrace. They are proud that the University, like the fiercely independent state in which it is located, took its future in its own hands and forced the state and the nation to take notice.

Athletically, Houston has been on an up and down journey since the 1960s. With its admission to the SWC, the Cougar programs flourished winning the conference title in football five times in seventeen seasons and the basketball regular season title twice. Athletes earned national awards and entered the professional leagues with frequency. By the mid–1990s, the Cougars were a constant sight at the top of the national rankings in both sports, and the teams' athletes were on the top awards lists and on the covers of national magazines.[8]

When the SWC folded in 1996, however, Houston once again found itself left out of the inner circle and became a second tier program almost overnight. Through a series of political maneuvers by the state legislature and SWC officials, the University of Texas, Texas A&M University, Texas Tech University, and Baylor University joined the Big VIII, which was renamed the Big XII, at the expense of Houston and the other SWC programs. The remainder of the schools, including Houston, Rice, SMU, and TCU were left to their own devices to find other conferences willing to admit new members. Houston, never able to shake the renegade reputation it earned during its formative years and never fully accepted by its southern counterparts after forcing the issue of integration, joined Conference USA, a solid mid-major conference.

After winning the inaugural football championship in 1996 its fortunes fell. It would not win another championship in either football or basketball until the 2006 season. That season, the football team defeated the Southern Mississippi Golden Eagles to win the conference title and a spot in the Liberty Bowl held in Memphis, TN. That Conference Championship, combined with an appearance at three bowl games in four seasons, has led the program to much the same position it was in before integration. It improves its reputation by scheduling the larger schools from larger conferences in an attempt to bolster national recognition and eventually improve conference affiliation. The Cougar faithful hope a change will come soon and the days of national prominence will find their way back quickly, but, for now, they must sit and wait.

As much as the Cougars' fortunes have fallen in recent years, the losses have done nothing to diminish the presence of the black athletes. Houston's rosters, like those of almost every other professional and amateur team in the nation, have exploded with African American athletes to the point where the white athlete is in the minority. The 2006-2007 Cougar basketball team has only one white member who sees limited minutes while the entire starting five are black.[9] The football team, although a bit more balanced than other Cougar squads, is still majority African American in its composition.[10] Graduation rates, long pointed to as a sign of neglected athletes, are up to over 50 percent, and the University has increased its efforts to see all athletes earn a degree even after they have used all their eligibility.[11] The school recently re-affirmed its commitment to its athletes' education by allowing a permanently injured athlete to keep his scholarship. The life of athletes, of all races, on the Houston campus has clearly improved with time, and these young men are being offered the same benefits as the white athletes. In addition, Houston added another chapter to its landmark history by hiring Kevin Sumlin, the first African American coach in a Division I Football Bowl Subdivision program in Texas.

Even at that, the integration of southern athletics, spurred forward by the Cougars, did not completely alter the racial attitudes of spectators across the nation. Despite all the improvements in race relations, not all aspects of racism have dissipated in the forty plus year time span. Collegiate fans still contain pockets of individuals who have not relinquished their prejudices. Though the day of widespread discrimination and racial oppression have passed, very small pockets of individuals continue to treat white and black athletes differently, to expect more from one group than the other, and refuse to accept complete social interaction between the races.[12] But contrary to the beliefs of Eagles Quarterback Donovan McNabb and others like him, the black and white athletes of this generation are no longer subjugated to different standards of performance.[13] As with any other large group of people, sports spectators will never embrace a homogenous belief system, but that should not lead to the conclusion that the racism and oppression of the 1960s is alive and well in today's sports world. Times have changed and so have the attitudes and perceptions of race.

With the passing of time, the memory of these Cougar teams fades from the campus history. Many students and fans have forgotten the racial inequalities fearlessly torn down during the 1960s and are increasingly unaware of the men who put everything on the line to challenge an exclusionary system of segregation. Time had eroded some of Houston's most vibrant history and so far no conservation efforts have surfaced to reverse the trend. Whereas the larger institutions, with arguably less to commemorate, aggressively promote their former athletes and significant victories, UH allows its landmark integration to quietly fade away. No building bears the names of the pioneering athletes, and no facilities are titled in their honor; they are, outside of the memory of the older alumni and a few token mementos, just names in record books.[14]

But it was not all for naught. If they never receive the deserved recognition and are white-washed from the collective memory, their contributions are not any less real. The landscape of Southern athletics was indelibly changed for the better after the 1964 Cougar integration, and African American athletes were given a real shot at forging their own paths at a university of their choosing regardless of the color of their skin. UH athletes and fans have also reaped the benefits of those years. As the teams once again work their way back to respectability, they have a remarkable history to fall back on. Current players and coaches, as well as the fans that so loyally follow and support them, can look back at the thirty year period when the Cougars stood toe to toe with the big boys and find not only a sense of pride but a reason to hope that soon they will return to the top of the college rankings. For all of that, we can thank the brave athletes and coaches, both black and white, who took the first steps onto the segregated fields and courts and forced the South to deal with its racial issues and reexamine its practices. They risked both their futures and personal safety, and perhaps someday their actions will finally be honored properly.[15] Until that time comes, Chaney, Hayes, and McVea, as well as the team mates who stood resolutely alongside them will remain the unsung heroes of the Houston Cougars.

Chapter Notes

Introduction

1. Alexander Wolff published a work on the integration of southern football programs and completely ignored the role of McVea even though he and the Cougars integrated before any of the other programs featured in the story. See Alexander Wolff, "Ground Breakers," *Sports Illustrated*, 7 November 2005, 58–67.

2. David K. Wiggins, "Edwin Bancroft Henderson, African American Athletes, and the Writing of Sports History," in *Sport and the Color Line*, ed. Patrick B. Miller and David K. Wiggins (New York: Routledge, 2004), 271–288.

3. E.B. Henderson, The Black Athlete: Emergence and Arrival (Cornwells Heights, PA: Publishers Agency, 1979).

4. See Nadine Cohodas, *The Band Played Dixie* (New York: Free Press, 1997), Morgan Preston, *The Edge of Campus* (Fayetteville: University of Arkansas Press, 1990), and Richard Pennington, *Breaking the Ice* (Jefferson, NC: McFarland, 1987).

5. Patrick B. Miller, "The Manly, the Moral, and the Proficient: College Sport in the New South," in *The Sporting World of the Modern South*, ed. Patrick B. Miller (Urbana: University of Illinois Press, 2002), 17–51.

6. Usually, integration came after landmark losses such as the University of Kentucky's loss to Texas Western in the 1966 NCAA championship game. See Frank Fitzpatrick, *And the Walls Came Tumbling Down* (Lincoln: University of Nebraska Press, 2000).

7. Charles H. Martin, "Jim Crow in the Gymnasium," in *Sport and the Color Line*, ed. Patrick B. Miller and David K. Wiggins (New York: Routledge, 2004), 233–250.

8. Jay Coakley, *Sport in Society* (St. Louis: Mosby, 1978).

9. The black community understood the implications of their support of athletics and on occasion used it to their advantage. In Houston, for example, African American leaders would only give their support to the Houston Astros, the newest expansion team, if seating at the Astrodome was desegregated. The city, not wanting to lose revenue, granted their demand. See Thomas Cole, *No Color Is My Kind* (Austin: University of Texas Press, 1997).

10. See David Faulker, *Great Time Coming* (New York: Simon & Schuster, 1995).

11. Black colleges had their own fully functioning intercollegiate league (Central Intercollegiate Athletic Association), which would likely decline if the best athletes opted for white universities.

12. Nelson George, *Elevating the Game* (New York: Harper Collins, 1992).

13. Pamela Grundy, "A Special Type of Discipline," in *Sport and the Color Line*, ed. Patrick B. Miller and David K. Wiggins (New York: Routledge, 2004), 101–125.

14. Karin Shaw Anderson, "Garland ISD Official Inspires with Fairness and Understanding," *Dallas Morning News*, 15 February 2007, via *Dallas Morning News* Online, http://www.dallasnews.com/sharedcontent/dws/news/localnews/stories/DNbhgarsupt_12met.ART.State.Edition1.2963136.html.

15. Randy Roberts and James Olson, *Winning Is the Only Thing* (Baltimore: Johns Hopkins University Press, 1989).

16. Terry White, ed., *Blacks and Whites Meeting in America* (Jefferson, NC: McFarland, 2003), 102.

17. Chuck Cooper integrated the National Basketball Association in 1950.

18. Martin Kane, "An Assessment of Black is Best," *Sports Illustrated*, 18 January 1971, pp. 72–83.

19. Harry Edwards, *Sociology of Sports* (Homewood, Il: Dorsey Press, 1973). Edwards was responsible for organizing the black boycott of the 1968 Olympic Games in Mexico City.

20. Wiggins, "Henderson."

21. Adolph H. Grundman, "The Image of Intercollegiate Sports," in *Fractured Focus*, ed. Richard Lapchick (Lexington: Lexington Books, 1986), 77–84.

22. Richard Lapchick, *Broken Promises: Racism in American Sports* (New York: St. Martin's, 1984).

23. Kareem Abdul-Jabbar and Peter Knobler, *Giant Steps* (New York: Bantam Books, 1983).

24. Bill Russell and Taylor Branch, *Second Wind* (New York: Random House, 1979).

25. Timothy Davis, "The Myth of Superspade: The Persistence of Racism in College Athletics," in *Sports and Inequality*, ed. Michael J. Cozzillo and Robert L. Hayman, Jr. (Durham: Carolina Academic Press, 2005), 276–286.

26. G. Edward White, *Creating the National Pastime: Baseball Transforms Itself* (Princeton: Princeton University Press, 1996).

27. Kenneth L. Shropshire, *In Black and White* (New York: New York University Press, 1996).

28. This position is becoming increasingly difficult to realistically defend as the number of black coaches and black managers is noticeably on the rise. For example, both head coaches in the NFL 2007 Super Bowl (Tony Dungy of Indianapolis and Lovie Smith of Chicago) and one of the two coaches in the NBA Championship series (Avery Johnson of Dallas) were African American.

Chapter 1

1. The mission of the school was to "be a place where any citizen, old or young, is enabled to pursue any type of training for which he is willing and able to pay." Patrick Nicholson, *In Time* (Houston: Pacesetter Press, 1977), 334.

2. Cullen was a wealthy oil man who invested millions into various projects around Houston. His financial support of the University of Houston and the creation of the Cullen Endowment were arguably the most lasting contributions. Elvin Hayes, *They Call Me the "Big E"* (Englewood Cliffs: Prentice Hall, 1978), 33.

3. The form rejection letter reads, "I must report to you that to date no Negro has been admitted to the University of Houston. The subject of desegregation is a matter of active study on the part of our Board of Governors, but no action can be expected immediately. May I suggest that some of the courses which you wish to take may be offered by Texas Southern University here in Houston." Interestingly, in all the responses held by the U.H. Archives, the black applicants were extremely apologetic for their attempts at admission. A response from a Merdis L.B. Holyfield read, "I am very sorry that my letter went to the wrony [sic] school.... I would'nt [sic] think of attending an all White school there. Please pardon me." Letter from Merdis L.B. Holyfield to University of Houston, President's Office Records, Courtesy of Special Collections, University of Houston Libraries. Letter from Alfred Neumann to Merdis Holyfield, President's Office Records, Courtesy of Special Collections, University of Houston Libraries.

4. A significant number of black applications came through the Admissions Office due to mis-communication, and applicants almost always apologized for their misdirected applications.

5. TSU was formed in 1947 as the separate but equal facility for the University of Texas Law School following the filing of the *Sweatt v. Painter* case. The Thurgood Marshal School of Law, located on the TSU campus, was not considered equal by the courts and black law students were allowed to enter the UT Law School.

6. The local press, particularly the *Houston Chronicle*, had been poking into the matter since early March 1956. A.D. Bruce to the Members of the Board of Regents, President's Office Records, Courtesy of Special Collections, University of Houston Libraries.

7. It should be noted that Williams, who would become university president while Bruce was chancellor, was in a heated struggle for power with Bruce. The conflict ended when Williams was forced to resign. Nicholson, *In Time.*

8. The three African American candidates seeking admission were unquestionably qualified to attend the University as one applicant held a Doctorate of Optometry, one was in a Ph.D. program at another institution, and the third possessed an M.A. degree from Texas Southern. The response was as follows: Deseg-

regation Report from Clanton Williams to A.D. Bruce, President's Office Records, Courtesy of Special Collections, University of Houston Libraries.

9. Integration Report from Clanton Williams to A.D. Bruce, President's Office Records, Courtesy of Special Collections, University of Houston Libraries.

10. The University did receive certain funds designated for junior colleges, however, this money was technically granted to particular students rather than to the University itself. Therefore, the school was not receiving outside funds during these years.

11. Memo to Bruce from J.E. Williamson, President's Office Records, Courtesy of Special Collections, University of Houston Libraries.

12. The committee did not conduct any surveys or interviews of the faculty, and therefore its ability to draw such a conclusion is questionable.

13. Strict instructions were given to those in attendance that all comments made were to keep absolutely confidential. It is also interesting that Bruce held the report for over two months before announcing a course of action. This might have been a stall tactic intended to remove the threat of legal action from the three black applicants seeking admission. Memo from A.D. Bruce to Dr. Clanton Williams, President's Office Records, Courtesy of Special Collections, University of Houston Libraries.

14. Recommendation Re: Integration at the University of Houston by A.D. Bruce, Courtesy of Special Collections, University of Houston Libraries.

15. Ibid.

16. A.D. Bruce, "Recommendation Re Integration at the University of Houston," President's Office Records, Courtesy of Special Collections, University of Houston Libraries.

17. Excerpt from the Minutes of the Executive Session of the Board of Regents, Courtesy of Special Collections, University of Houston Libraries.

18. Clanton Williams to A.D. Bruce, President's Office Records, Courtesy of Special Collections, University of Houston Libraries.

19. Ibid.

20. The University of Houston did agree to provide the professor for the course as T.S.U. had no faculty member available that semester. The two students, pleased with the

resolution of the matter, agreed not to push the issue further through the involvement of the local NAACP.

21. The Board was advised by Reagan Cartwright, its legal council, that all of these stopgaps would not protect against lawsuits. Clanton Williams to A.D. Bruce, President's Office Records, Courtesy of Special Collections, University of Houston Libraries.

22. Cullen was known to fund the University out of his personal finances whenever needed. His gifts totaled between $50 and $60 million dollars, not including funds gained from the Cullen Foundation which was formed to make the Texas Medical Center and the University of Houston (centers of world distinction." Wizig, *Cougars.*

23. Patrick Nicholson to A.D. Bruce, President's Office Records, Courtesy of Special Collections, University of Houston Libraries.

24. Hoffman was not new to the University as he had been handling the majority of the day to day operations since his arrival on 10 June 1957. Nicholson, *In Time.*

25. Dr. Nicholson sent Dr. Hoffman the editorial along with a message which read, "Little rumbling from a situation that I assume you will want to look into quietly sometime in the next month." Patrick Nicholson to Philip Hoffman, President's Office Records, Courtesy of Special Collections, University of Houston Libraries.

26. Unsigned, "Absence of Freedom at University of Houston," *Dallas Express*, 18 November 1961.

27. In addition to comments on the naturalized African American population, it also suggested a further study on the inclusion of non-citizen blacks and the cultural accommodations they would require.

28. The report from Ramon Vitulli, the registrar who was also on the integration committees in 1956, also reiterated that integration should occur immediately to avoid legal involvement and to gain public support. To made the process even more attractive, he suggested the possibility of an academic study on the academic capabilities of blacks and the affect of their presence on campus. Ramon Vitulli to Philip G. Hoffman, President's Office Records, Courtesy of Special Collections, University of Houston Libraries.

29. A different U.S. Office of Education program, Counseling and Guidance Training Institute, also provided fifty thousand dollars per year bringing the total annual potential

revenue loss to $100,000 dollars. Philip G. Hoffman, "Integration at the University of Houston," President's Office Records, Courtesy of Special Collections, University of Houston Libraries.

30. Minutes of the Executive Committee Meeting, President's Office Records, Courtesy of Special Collections, University of Houston Libraries.

31. He went on to say, "I believe we must be prepared to recognize that sooner or later we will have only one Law School." Hoffman, "Remarks on Integration."

32. Ibid.

33. Unsigned, "Hoffman Reminisces About His Presidency at UH," *UH Today*, 18 October 2005.

34. This attitude toward the necessity of quiet racial change prevailed in the city of Houston. The same process occurred when the city itself desegregated as community leader ensured that no riotous behavior would accompany the integration. See Cole, *No Color is My Kind* (Austin: University of Texas Press, 1997).

35. The first black student was a college music professor who sought an advanced music degree.

36. It was also noted that the black students performed better academically than the average white student. Bill Daniel to Philip G. Hoffman, President's Office Records, Courtesy of Special Collections, University of Houston Libraries.

37. Patrick J. Nicholson to Philip Hoffman, President's Office Records, Courtesy of Special Collections, University of Houston Libraries.

38. The University was not completely immune to racial unrest as the late 1960s did see disturbances but nothing no common to campus across the nation. The Afro-Americans for Black Liberation (AABL) presented the University a list of demands which Hoffman assessed and tried to meet.

39. Patrick J. Nicholson to Philip G. Hoffman, President's Office Records, Courtesy of Special Collections, University of Houston Libraries.

40. There is some uncertainty as to the first public presentation of the school's policy. Although a confidential document was signed off on by Hoffman in 1966, the 1969 press release was referred to as the first official statement. Philip G. Hoffman, Summary Statement RE Desegregating the University of Houston, President's Office Records, Courtesy of Special Collections, University of Houston Libraries.

41. It also addressed the status of black faculty members and hiring practices stating that the school had trouble recruiting qualified black staff members. Ibid.

42. African American students could, however, use other facilities such as dining halls. Philip G. Hoffman to Bill Daniel, President's Office Records, Courtesy of Special Collections, University of Houston Libraries.

43. By 1969, the only other colleges with more or equal students, San Antonio College, Dallas Junior College, and Lamar State Junior College of Technology, were all community colleges. It should be noted that Texas A&M and the University of Texas did not provide figures for the study. Negro Student Survey, President's Office Records, Courtesy of Special Collections, University of Houston Libraries.

44. Unsigned, "Hoffman Reminisces About His Presidency at UH," *UH Today*, 18 October 2005.

45. He remarked almost 40 years later that in retrospect, this was one of the proudest moments in his career at UH. Ibid.

Chapter 2

1. Jerry Wizig, *Eat 'Em Up Cougars* (Huntsville: Strode Publishers, 1977), 52.

2. Jack Valenti later became a personal confidant of Lyndon Johnson during his presidency. He passed away in 2007.

3. Corbin Robertson, the son-in-law of Hugh Cullen, contributed his time and finances to the athletic vision of his father-in-law, and the Cougars' on-campus stadium is named in his honor.

4. John R. Bender, a former football coach at Washington State University, selected the Cougar mascot because of his ties to the WSU Cougar football program.

5. Ellington Air force Base, located in Houston, currently houses the Texas Air National Guard.

6. Cougars, 55.

7. Harry Fouke, Report to the Board of Governors of the University of Houston, Courtesy of Special Collections, University of Houston Libraries.

8. It is interesting that of the schools in that conference, almost all of them currently

participate in Division II athletics. The decision by Fouke to move forward seems exceedingly wise in light of that situation.

9. Harry Fouke, Report to the Board of Governors of the University of Houston, Board of Regents Minutes, Courtesy of Special Collections, University of Houston Libraries.

10. Ibid.

11. The editorial continued, "We take exception to this attitude, and hope that it is not final. If it is, then the community as a whole is bound to suffer ... and respect for Rice cannot help but suffer with it." KHOU Editorial Broadcast Editorial #183, "Rice vs. U. of H.," Wednesday, 6 May 1964, 6:28 P.M.

12. As recounted by President Philip Hoffman, Rice officials "told me there was a great deal of opinion within our sister institution ... to the effect that Rice University would sponsor the University of Houston.... I was specifically asked not to allow any other Southwest Conference institution to sponsor the University of Houston until Rice had been given to give full consideration to this matter.... I have been informed today that Rice does not anticipate placing our name in nomination at the meeting of this week.... It is obviously too late for any other institution, however well disposed, to take the necessary steps to act as our sponsor." Philip G. Hoffman Statement, President's Office Records, Courtesy of Special Collections, University of Houston Libraries.

13. KHOU Editorial Broadcast Editorial #183, "Rice vs. U. of H.," Wednesday 6 May 1964, 6:28 P.M.

14. Eddie Einhorn and Ron Rappoport, *How March Became Madness* (Chicago: Triumph Books, 2006) 85.

15. This link between sport and white domination would not fully disappear until the all-white teams consistently lost to their integrated counterparts.

16. "Those two schools were not considered on par with the Southwest Conference or the University of Houston." Ted Nance, interview by author, tape recording, Corpus Christi, TX, 12 October 2006.

17. "The Negro Athlete Is Invited Home," *Sports Illustrated*, 14 June 1965, 26.

Chapter 3

1. William Yeoman, interview by author, tape recording, Houston, TX, 12 September 2006.

2. Ibid.

3. Ibid.

4. He scored 19 points in the 62–35 season opening victory over North Texas State University on January 10, 1946.

5. His last losing seasons came during the last years in the Missouri Valley Conference.

6. Latin was part of the famous 1968 NCAA Texas Western University Championship team who played against Adolph Rupp's Kentucky squad. Guy V. Lewis, interview by author, tape recording, Houston, TX, 28 August, 2006.

7. "Elvin: Houston Cager Battles Alcindor," *Ebony*, vol. XXIII, no. 5.

8. Ted Nance, interview by author, tape recording, Corpus Christi, TX, 12 October 2006.

9. William Yeoman, interview by author, tape recording, Houston, TX, 12 September 2006.

10. *Sports Illustrated* made the same argument about the motivations behind integration. It wrote, "The motives of the men involved in lifting the last barrier to Negro participation in college athletics may be purely pragmatic: they want their schools to be winners. But the results are nonetheless beneficial." Frank Deford, "The Negro Athlete is Invited Home," *Sports Illustrated*, 14 June 1965, pg 26–27 vol. 22 no. 24.

11. Ibid.

12. Thus far, no record as to the conversation between Fouke and Hoffman has been discovered.

13. Guy V. Lewis, interview by author, tape recording, Houston, TX, 28 August 2006.

14. 'William Gildea, "U. of Houston Enjoys Top Billing," *Washington Post*, 21 January 1968, sec. 4C.

15. David Llorens, "No Back Seat for Elvin," *Ebony*, March 1968, 125.

16. William Yeoman, interview by author, tape recording, Houston, TX, 12 September 2006.

17. Mease was also heavily involved in the integration of the city of Houston, directing many of the sit-ins and student protest movements. The Harris County Hospital District has a hospital named in his honor recognizing the efforts he made to improve the health of the African-American community.

18. William Yeoman, interview by author, tape recording, Houston, TX, 12 September 2006.

19. William Yeoman, interview by author, tape recording, Houston, TX, 12 September 2006.

20. Ibid.

21. Jerry Wizig, "44 Comes First," *Houston Chronicle*, 18 December 1993, sec. 1B.

22. Although tremendously successful at the high school level, press coverage did not proliferate because the two played at segregated black schools and the white schools received the lion's share of the attention.

23. "Say Hayes," *Time*, 26 January 1968, 65.

24. Mickey Herskowitz, "Warren McVea Goes Thisaway and Thataway," *Sports Illustrated*, 9 November 1964, p.49.

25. Guy V. Lewis, interview by author, tape recording, Houston, TX, 28 August 2006.

26. Hayes was intending on attending Grambling State University while Chaney had determined to attend Loyola University. During that time however, athletes could not sign official acceptance letters until the conclusion of the high school season. So, the two were able to change their choice of school without any repercussions.

27. Guy V. Lewis, interview by author, tape recording, Houston, TX, 28 August 2006.

28. Although the article did raise the possibility of Hayes breaking the existing freshmen scoring records set by current varsity team member Leary Lentz, it did not communicate any tone of instigation. John Walter, "Lewis-Pate Recruit Top Players from Louisiana," *Daily Cougar*, 8 September, 1964, p. 19.

29. That level of production, amounting to 10.4 yards per carry, was not isolated to his last high school year as his sophomore and junior seasons he scored 128 and 148 points respectively. The ballot for the Texas all-state first team included the instructions to vote for "McVea and 10 others." John Hollis, "Warren McVea is Signed by Cougars," *Houston Post*, 12 July 1964, sec. 4 p. 1.

30. The number of offers varies in each report however the majority report the number as seventy-five or greater.

31. William Yeoman, interview by author, tape recording, Houston, TX, 12 September 2006.

32. McVea returned home early from several recruiting trips because being away from his home bothered him so much.

33. The authenticity of this quote was questioned at the time of its printing. An editorial in the *Daily Cougar* said of it, "A final quotation from Coach Yeoman to McVea ... has a less than authentic tone." Tim Fleck "Magazine Write-Up on McVea Sarcastic," 13 October 1967, p. 6. Original quote in Dan Jenkins, " You've Got to Have Some 'O,'" *Sports Illustrated*, 16 October 1967, 42.

34. Dan Cook, "McVea Signs with U. Of Houston," *San Antonio Express and News*, 12 July 1964, sec. B1.

35. The only response McVea's camp (his family) would pass on was that McVea "'said he doesn't like cold weather' that would seem to eliminate any school very far north." Bob Seaman, "McVea is Star in New Mystery," *San Antonio Express* 11 June 1964, sec. D1. State newspapers also reported on McVea's summer knee injury received during a pick-up basketball game.

36. Ibid

37. Dick Peebles, "McVea en Route," *Houston Chronicle*, 13 July 1963, sec. 2, p. 1.

38. "McVea is Here — Cougs Got 'Em," *The Informer*, 18 July 1963, p. 10.

39. "McKibben on Sports," *The Informer*, 22 August 1964, p. 11.

40. Ned Sweet, "Big 8 'Blackball' of McVea Told," *San Antonio Light*, 13 July 1964, p. 17.

41. The Big Eight became the Big Twelve following the collapse of the Southwest Conference when the University of Texas, Texas A&M, Baylor, and Texas Tech joined. While simply speculation, it is curious that when the Southwest Conference disbanded Houston was the only major institution left out of the newly formed Big 12 Conference.

42. Ibid.

43. Ibid.

44. Johnny Janes, "'Don't Quote Me,'" *San Antonio Express*, 14 July 1964, sec. D1.

45. The message read, "McVea might announce his choice of colleges today. Appreciate close watch please and thanks." Ibid.

46. John Hollis, "UH, McVea in the middle of Newspaper Feud," *The Houston Post*, 15 July 1964, sec. 4, p. 1.

47. Ned Sweet, "Sports Chat," *San Antonio Light*, 13 July 1964, sec. A17. The column also had a mug-shotesque picture of McVea looking defiant and aggressive.

48. The issue of schools removing themselves from the Cougars' schedule did arise. Texas A&M University, despite dominating Houston on the fields and courts, ended its agree-

ment with Houston following the 1965 season.

49. Dan Jenkins, "You've Got to Have Some O," *Sports Illustrated,* 16 October 1967, 41.

50. Johnny Janes, "'Don't Quote Me,'" *San Antonio Express,* 14 July 1964, sec. D1.

51. His age was misprinted as 18 in this article. At the time of his signing, McVea was a little less than three weeks away from his 18th birthday. John Hollis, "UH, McVea in the middle of Newspaper Feud," *The Houston Post,* 15 July 1964, sec. 4, p.1.

52. Ibid.

53. Alex Durley, "McVea is for Real," *The Houston Informer,* 19 July 1964, p.10.

54. Johnny Janes, "Sooner Coach denies 'blackball' of McVea," *San Antonio Express,* 15 July 1964, sec. B1.

55. Ibid.

56. Jerry Wizig, "UH Cougars sign Grid Star McVea," *Houston Chronicle,* 12 July 1964. sec. 7, p. 1.

57. John Hollis, "UH, McVea in the Middle of Newspaper Feud," *The Houston Post,* 15 July 1964, sec. 4, p.1.

58. Letter from Arthur J. Bergstrom (NCAA Committee on Infractions, Secretary) to Harry Fouke, President's Office Records, Courtesy of Special Collections, University of Houston Libraries.

59. Comments of the University of Houston to the Confidential Report No. 42, President's Office Records, Courtesy of Special Collections, University of Houston Libraries.

60. Comments of the University of Houston to the Confidential Report No. 42, President's Office Records, Courtesy of Special Collections, University of Houston Libraries; Confidential Report No. 42 by the NCAA Committee on Infractions, President's Office Records, Courtesy of Special Collections, University of Houston Libraries.

61. He later withdrew the statement and offered to issue an apology for his statements. Mickey Herskowitz, "Mickey Herskowitz," *Houston Post,* 2 February 1966, sec. 4, p. 1; Jerry Wizig, "McVea Not Cause of UH Probation," *Houston Chronicle,* 11 January 1966, sec. 2, p. 1.

62. Auburn University received a five year probation from all sports and Indiana University received a four year sentence. None of these probations would compare with the death penalty placed on Southern Methodist University in 1987. "Citing penalties intended to 'eliminate a program that was built on a legacy of wrongdoing, deceit and rule violations,' the NCAA Committee on Infractions for the first time barred a school from playing football for an entire season." David McNabb, "SMU Football Canceled for 1987," *Dallas Morning News,* 26 February 1987, sec. A1.

63. Tim Fleck, "Same Old Question," *The Daily Cougar,* 27 September 1967, p. 2.

Chapter 4

1. It is interesting to note that the town known for its intense discrimination has now developed into a primarily black city. The 2000 U.S. Census shows that 67.3 percent of the population is African American, a drastic change in racial makeup.

2. The Civil Rights Act of 1964, the first landmark civil rights legislation, was signed into law on 2 July 1964 — just ten days before McVea signed with Houston. While conditions within the south did not improve dramatically overnight, Lyndon Johnson's signature marked the beginning of the end of the system of segregation.

3. Elvin Hayes, *They Call Me the "Big E,"* (Englewood Cliffs, NJ: Prentice Hall, 1978), 8.

4. Chris Hayes, Elvin's father, died of a heart attack when Hayes was in the 9th grade.

5. Jack Olson, "The Black Athlete: A Shameful Story, Pt.1," *Sports Illustrated,* 1 July 1968, 21.

6. By the end of 2007, Hayes will have completed training to become a peace officer. From a youth living in fear of the local police, he has become the only current Hall of Fame athlete to be a member of the law enforcement. The transformation shows that Hayes has overcome the past that dominated his perceptions of race for so many years.

7. Howard Lorch, interview by author, digital recording, Houston, TX, 1 July 2006.

8. Jerry Wizig, "44 Comes First," *Houston Chronicle,* 18 December 1993, sec. B1.

9. Ibid, 6.

10. Hayes, *Big E,* 6.

11. Ibid, 17.

12. Hayes received little attention in Louisiana until he began producing substantial wins at Houston. As he found continued success with Houston, the white press began covering his career. In January of 1968, he was named as the Louisiana amateur athlete of the

year, the first African American athlete to receive the honor.

13. Hayes longed to attend the University of Wisconsin because his sister had received her Ph.D. from that institution.

14. Fran Blinebury, "Lewis Suffering 'Great Injustice," *Houston Chronicle*, 18 December 1993, sec. B1.

15. The Texas Southern coach helped the University of Houston recruiting process because he knew that if Houston did not sign Hayes, TSU would have to face him in competition. That fear drove him to assist his third ward neighbors.

16. Katherine Lopez, "Two Paths to Greatness," *The Houston Review of History and Culture* 3, no. 1 (2005): 44–47.

17. Jerry Wizig, "44 Comes First," *Houston Chronicle*, 18 December 1993, sec.1.

18. Ibid.

19. Jack Olson, "The Black Athlete: A Shameful Story, Pt.1," *Sports Illustrated,* 1 July 1968, 21.

20. Edward Walsh, "The Long Road From His Backyard is Just a Part of Elvin's Dream," *Houston Chronicle,* 28 January 1968, sec. 2, p.1.

21. Most likely, his response communicates the influence of his mother and her emphasis on education. Elvin Hayes, Athletic Questionnaire, University of Houston Athletic Department Records.

22. Bill Bradley was a stellar basketball athlete at Princeton (1961–1965).

23. Lorch took the peril faced by his parents to heart and drew from their experiences. He saw the most extreme consequences of racism and therefore treated all people equally without differentiation between the races.

24. Howard Lorch, interview by author, digital recording, Houston, TX, 1 July 2006.

25. Ibid.

26. Einhorn, *Madness, 82.*

27. John Tracy, interview by author, tape recording, Los Angeles, CA, 15 November 2006.

28. Einhorn, *Madness,* 81.

29. Chaney remembered that "Guy had the gift of gab. I'll tell you that. And wherever he went, he always rented a red convertible... and his clothes were always perfectly tailored so they would fit just right. He was really something." Ibid.

30. Ibid.

31. Thomas Bonk, "True Colors Don Chaney and John Tracy Broke a Barrier at Houston," *Los Angeles Times,* 20 April 1993, sec. C1.

32. Einhorn, *Madness.*

33. John Tracy, interview by author, tape recording, Los Angeles, CA, 15 November 2006.

34. Bill Russell, a native of Monroe, LA, and others like him had long been escaping the South through athletic scholarships. The black community recognized that sports provided the easiest way out for those with the talent to be noticed.

35. Thomas Bonk, "True Colors Don Chaney and John Tracy Broke a Barrier at Houston," *Los Angeles Times,* 20 April 1993, sec. C1.

36. See Robert A. Goldberg "Racial Change on the Southern Periphery: The Case of San Antonio, Texas, 1960–1965," *The Journal of Southern History,* vol. 49, no. 3. (Aug. 1983): 349–374.

37. Interestingly, he, along with Linus Baer of Lee High School, integrated the all-star game in 1964. Unsigned, "Coaching School Game May Draw Record Crowd," *San Antonio Light,* 3 July 1964, sec. A10.

38. Warren McVea, interview by author, tape recording, Houston, TX, 15 September 2006.

39. Ibid.

40. Ibid.

41. Like Lewis and Pate, Yeoman concentrated his sales pitch on McVea's parents. Apparently, they all realized the key to gaining the boys signatures was convincing their parents that Houston was the best place for them. Ibid.

42. Ibid.

43. Tom Beer Questionnaire.

44. Richard Pennington, *Breaking the Ice* (Jefferson: McFarland, 1987).

45. Warren McVea, interview by author, tape recording, Houston, TX, 15 September 2006.

46. Pennington, *Breaking.*

47. Warren McVea, interview by author, tape recording, Houston, TX, 15 September 2006.

48. Ibid.

49. Ibid.

Chapter 5

1. In high school athletics, the school's population determines the level of play it par-

ticipates on; 5A high schools are the largest programs while 1A schools are the smallest. Lopez, "Greatness."

2. Ibid.

3. Elvin Hayes, *They Call Me the "Big E"* (Englewood Cliffs, NJ: Prentice Hall, 1978), 33.

4. Arthur Hayes remained in Houston for a four month period.

5. Howard Lorch, interview by author, digital recording, Houston, TX, 1 July 2006.

6. Jack Olson, "The Black Athlete: A Shameful Story, Pt. 1," *Sports Illustrated,* 1 July 1968, 23.

7. Eddie Einhorn, *How March Became Madness* (Chicago: Triumph Books, 2006), 82.

8. Thomas Bonk, "True Colors Don Chaney and John Tracy Broke a Barrier at Houston," *Los Angeles Times,* 20 April 1993, sec. C1.

9. Lorch, who by his own admission was obsessively neat, most often clashed with Hayes over trivial things such as the organization of their dorm room.

10. Howard Lorch, interview by author, digital recording, Houston, TX, 1 July 2006.

11. Jerry Wizig, "44 Comes First," *Houston Chronicle,* 18 December 1993, sec. B1.

12. Lopez, "Greatness."

13. Wizig, "44."

14. Hayes, *Big E,* 41.

15. Wizig, "44." Even the black press would come to recognize the pioneering efforts of Lewis and praise his role. See Artis Vaughn, "About the Cougars Head Man ... Guy," *Forward Times,* 20 January 1968, p.62.

16. John Tracy, interview by author, tape recording, Los Angeles, CA, 15 November 2006.

17. John Tracy hypothesized, "In thinking back, I thought maybe Coach Lewis never asked him because he'd never show up. That might have frightened him so they never said anything till he arrived." Ibid.

18. Ibid.

19. Ibid.

20. The quote continues, "I would come in when he wasn't there to see if he was going through my things. There was no trust at all. It was almost as if an alien had come down." Thomas Bonk, "True Colors Don Chaney and John Tracy Broke a Barrier at Houston," *Los Angeles Times,* 20 April 1993, sec. C1.

21. John Tracy, interview by author, tape recording, Los Angeles, CA, 15 November 2006.

22. One of the most humorous anecdotes involved Tracy promising to stop using Chaney's toothpaste, which he thought responsible for Chaney's jumping ability.

23. John Tracy, interview by author, tape recording, Los Angeles, CA., 15 November 2006.

24. Thomas Bonk, "True Colors Don Chaney and John Tracy Broke a Barrier at Houston," *Los Angeles Times,* 20 April 1993, sec. C1.

25. Eddie Einhorn, *How March Became Madness* (Chicago: Triumph Books, 2006), 82.

26. One athlete made claimed "the minority players were not dealt with the same discipline for fear of alienating the black community." Since no other evidence seconds this claim, we cannot say with any certainty that such preferential treatment existed.

27. Richard Lapchick, *Broken Promises* (New York: St. Martins, 1984), 178.

28. Hayes, *Big E,* 37.

29. David Fink, "Era of Greatness," *Houston Post,* 10 March 1968, sec. 10, p 12.

30. Howard Lorch, interview by author, digital recording, Houston, TX, 1 July 2006.

31. John Tracy, interview by author, tape recording, Los Angeles, CA, 15 November 2006.

32. Ibid.

33. It is not certain what leverage the athletic department had with these segregated facilities, however, it was, in fact, able to gain admittance for all the athletes regardless of color. Ibid.

34. Lopez, "Greatness."

35. Gary Grider to Katherine Lopez, Desegregation Questionnaire, Summer 2006, author's collection.

36. Lee Leary Lentz to Katherine Lopez, Desegregation Questionnaire, Summer 2006, author's collection.

37. Grider Questionnaire.

38. Hayes, *Big E,* 38.

39. Howard Lorch, interview by author, digital recording, Houston, TX, 1 July 2006.

40. David Fink, "Sideline," *Daily Cougar,* 4 December 1964, p. 4.

41. Guy V. Lewis, interview by author, tape recording, Houston, TX, 28 August 2006.

42. The records were as follows: 512 total points scored, 24.4 points averaged per game, 23.8 rebounds per game, 43 point single game total, 40 rebounds in a single game.

43. Hayes received his nickname from John Hollis, sports writer for the *Houston Chronicle*, who compared Hayes to the U.S. Battleship named "the Big E."

44. David Fink, "First Three Negro Athletes at UH Started an Era of Greatness," *Houston Post*, 10 March 1968, sec. 10, p. 12.

45. While in high school, accusations arose against McVea's relationship with a white teenager. Football boosters and city leaders made those charges go away as to not harm the young star. While it does not appear as though any facts substantiated the claims, the issue was nevertheless hushed. Richard Pennington, *Breaking the Ice* (Jefferson: McFarland, 1987).

46. Unlike the others, McVea would have a room to himself and would not have to deal with the roommate issue. It does not appear as though the living arrangements were due to objections from teammates or supporters of the program. That is not to say McVea lived in seclusion away from the other athletes. The coaching staff always assigned members of the team to be McVea's quasi-roommate. They would make certain he kept up with his studies, that he did not miss class, and that he was doing okay in the Houston system. In reading of the arrangement, it should not be assumed that McVea was excluded or coddled by Houston. He was simply an athlete living without a roommate. The same environment would have existed if McVea were a white athlete living alone.

47. Dick Woodall, interview by author, digital recording, Houston, TX, 10 August 2006.

48. Michael Tracy to Katherine Lopez, Desegregation Questionnaire, Summer 2006, author's collection.

49. Kenneth Hebert to Katherine Lopez, Desegregation Questionnaire, Summer 2006, author's collection.

50. Warren McVea, interview by author, tape recording, Houston, TX, 15 September 2006.

51. Ibid.

52. Ibid.

53. William Yeoman, interview by author, tape recording, Houston, TX, 12 September 2006.

54. Michael Barbour to Katherine Lopez, Desegregation Questionnaire, Summer 2006, author's collection.

55. Warren McVea, interview by author, tape recording, Houston, TX, 15 September 2006.

56. Richard Stotter to Katherine Lopez, Desegregation Questionnaire, Summer 2006, author's collection.

57. Warren McVea, interview by author, tape recording, Houston, TX, 15 September 2006.

58. Ibid.

59. Houston police were notorious for their mistreatment of African Americans. Their improper treatment of a black driver helped spark the civil rights movement within the city.

60. Mickey Herskowitz, "Warren McVea Goes Thisaway and Thataway," *Sports Illustrated*, 9 November 1964, p. 49.

61. "Fans Disappointed; McVea Didn't Play ... They Bolted," *The Houston Informer*, 26 September 1964, p. 11.

62. Mickey Herskowitz, "Warren McVea Goes Thisaway and Thataway," *Sports Illustrated*, 9 November 1964, p. 49.

63. "McVea's Feats in AF Game to be Televised," *The Houston Informer*, 31 October 1964, p. 11.

64. Mickey Herskowitz, "Warren McVea Goes Thisaway and Thataway," *Sports Illustrated*, 9 November 1964, p. 49.

65. Hayes, *Big E,* 38.

66. Ibid, 38.

Chapter 6

1. Sonny Yates, "'65 Coog Outlook-Color it Improved," *The Daily Cougar*, 8 September 1965, p. 16.

2. Johnny Janes, "'Don't Quote Me,'" *San Antonio Express*, 7 September 1965, sec. D1.

3. Some media pointed to the lack of a sold out crowd as a disinterest on the part of the fans. They claimed that the seven thousand empty seats meant that McVea was not as good or as popular as the school had insisted. Sam Blair, "Tulsa Trips Houston, McVea, 14–0," *Dallas Morning News*, 12 September 1965, sec. B1.

4. Dick Peebles, "Coogs' Bid on Line," *Houston Chronicle*, 10 September 1965, sec. 2, p. 1.

5. Ibid.

6. Johnny Janes, "'Don't Quote Me,'" *San Antonio Express,* 2 September 1965, sec. D1.

7. Jerry Wizig, "'Pressure' is now on Says Cougars' McVea," *Houston Chronicle*, 8 September 1965, sec. 8, p. 2.

8. John Hollis, "Post—Number 1 or Bust," *Houston Post,* 7 September 1965, sec. 4, p. 4.

9. Jerry Wizig, "Cougar Machine Tops but Spare Parts are Few," *Houston Chronicle,* 8 September 1965, sec. 8, p. 1.

10. Richard Stotter to Katherine Lopez, desegregation questionnaire, summer 2006.

11. Michael Spratt to Katherine Lopez, desegregation questionnaire, summer 2006.

12. Pat Pryor to Katherine Lopez, email, 21 March 2007.

13. Tom Beer to Katherine Lopez, Desegregation Questionnaire, summer 2006, author's collection.

14. Pat Pryor to Katherine Lopez, email, 21 March 2007, author's collection.

15. Dick Woodall, interview by author, digital recording, Houston, TX, 10 August 2006.

16. Other collegiate integration efforts did not proceed so smoothly. For example, Calvin Patterson, the first black football player at Florida State University, committed suicide during what would have been his senior season. Unable to keep up with his studies, he failed out of school and was removed from the team. Unable to cope with losing his position on the team, he took his life. See Alexander Wolff, "Ground Breakers," *Sports Illustrated,* 7 November 2005, 58–67.

17. Dick Peebles, "McVea Loses Ball 4 Times in Sad Debut," *Houston Chronicle,* 12 September 1965, sec. 6, pg. 1; Frank Boggs, "McVea Turns Flat as Houston Falls," *Dallas Times Herald,* 12 September 1965, sec. C1.

18. John Hollis, "Miami Massacres Helpless UH, 44–12," *Houston Post,* 17 October 1965, sec. 5, p. 1.

19. Frank Boggs, "McVea Turns Flat as Houston Falls," *Dallas Times Herald,* 12 September 1965, sec. C1. The use of the word entertainer to describe McVea is interesting as seems to reference the minstrel shows where the only purpose of blacks was to entertain. It did not matter that McVea was young or that the game was a team effort. If he failed to perform according to the white standard of entertainment, he was useless.

20. Dan Cook, "Frustrating Debut for Cougars' McVea," *San Antonio Express,* 12 September 1965, sec. D1.

21. Johnny Janes, "'Don't Quote Me,'" *San Antonio Express,* 14 September 1965, sec. B1.

22. Johnny Williams, "McVea on the Bench for Cincy Game," *San Antonio Express,* 24 September 1965, sec. C2; Dan Cook, "McVea Makes Large Gain," *San Antonio Express,* 19 September 1965, sec. B1.

23. Sam Blair, "Tulsa Trips Houston, McVea, 14–0," *Dallas Morning News,* 12 September 1965, sec. B1.

24. Johnny Williams, "Houston U. Finally Wins," *San Antonio Express,* 25 September 1965, sec. B2.

25. Jerry Wizig, "Cougars Don't Blame Hard Field for Loss," *Houston Chronicle,* 12 September 1965, sec. 6, p. 6; Jerry Wizig, "Yeoman Says UH 'Not That Bad in Loss,'" *Houston Chronicle,* 13 September 1965, sec. 2 p. 4.

26. John Hollis, "Glum McVea 'Just Couldn't Believe It,'" *Houston Post,* 12 September 1965, sec. 5, p. 4; Unsigned, "Yeoman Can't Figure UH Loss," *Houston Chronicle,* 20 September 1965, sec. 3, p. 3.

27. Express News Service, "'Like Nightmare,' Comments McVea," *San Antonio Express,* 12 September 1965, sec. D4; Jerry Wizig, "McVea Baffled Over Turn (And Drop) of Events," *Houston Chronicle,* 12 September 1965, sec. 6, p. 6; Frank Schultz, Jr., "Frankly Speaking," *Daily Cougar,* 28 October 1965, p. 6.

28. Frank Schultz, Jr., "Frankly Speaking," *Daily Cougar,* 28 October 1965, p. 6.

29. Warren McVea, interview by author, tape recording, Houston, TX, 15 September 2006.

30. Jerry Wizig, "Cougars Dispel Worry About Mental Letdown," *Houston Chronicle,* 14 September 1965, sec. 3, p. 2.

31. Clark Nealon, "Post Time," *Houston Post,* 9 November 1965, sec. 4, p. 1.

32. "Yeoman Denies Rumors," *San Antonio Light,* 23 September 1965; Jerry Wizig, "UH Catches Cincinnati Tonight," *Houston Chronicle,* 24 September 1965, sec. 6, p. 1.

33. John Hollis, "UH Prexy, AD Deny Yeoman 'Bought Up,'" *Houston Post,* 22 September 1965, sec. 4, p. 1.

34. Jerry Wizig, "UH Leaders Repeat Support of Bill Yeoman," *Houston Chronicle,* 23 September 1965, sec. 2, p. 2.

35. Frank Schultz, Jr., "Frankly Speaking," *The Daily Cougar,* p. 7; John S. Daigle, "Unknown Persons 'Hang' UH Coach," *The Daily Cougar,* 27 October 1965, p. 1.

36. Dave McNeely, "There're No Longer Tears, Jeers Over Cougarland," *Houston Chronicle,* 26 September 1965, sec. 3, p. 2. Yeoman responded to the situation with a

degree of levity, saying, "I don't mind [it] as long as it isn't the real thing. At least it shows they are interested in what is going on." John S. Daigle, "Unknown Persons 'Hang' UH Coach," *The Daily Cougar*, 27 October 1965, p. 1.

37. Hollis, "Prexy."

38. William Yeoman, interview by author, tape recording, Houston, TX, 12 September 2006.

39. The schedule included Ole Miss, Kentucky, Florida State, and Tennessee-Chattanooga.

40. John Hollis, "UH Finally Comes Alive, Rips Cincy, 21–6," *Houston Post*, 25 September 1965, sec. 4, p. 1.

41. Rich Burk, "Cougars Whoop It Up After Big Win," *The Daily Cougar*, 16 November 1965, p. 8.

42. Dave McNeely, "Jeers."

43. Mickey Herskowitz, "Movies are Better Than Ever, Says Yeoman of Cougar Win Over Rebels," *Houston Post*, 12 November 1965, sec. 4, p. 2.

44. Clark Nealon, "Post Time: Cougars Breaking All Attendance Records with Rallying Finish," *Houston Post*, 10 November 1965, sec. 4, p, 1; "Film of UH-Ole Miss Game at Cougar Club," *Houston Chronicle*, 9 November 1965, sec. 2, p. 3.

45. Dick Woodall, interview by author, digital recording, Houston, TX, 10 August 2006.

46. Justice, "Mother."

47. Dick Peebles, "A Royal Shock," *Houston Chronicle*, 27 September 1965, sec. 2, p. 3.

48. Paul Justice, "Warren's Mother Feels Better Now," *Houston Post*, 7 November 1965, sec. 4, p. 1.

49. "McVea's Mother Missed Seeing Warren Have His Best Night," *Houston Chronicle*, 7 November 1965, sec. 6, p. 8.

50. He continued, "The game or any team sport does not lend itself to jealousy or bigotry. Football is sufficiently physically and mentally demanding that to accomplish one's assignment, one is not afforded the luxury of donating mental or physical energy to bigotry.... Sure there were jealousies about playing time, squabbles over whether the Chiefs could beat the Packers in the Super Bowl but I know of no racially based problems, ever." Pat Pryor to Katherine Lopez, email, 21 March 2007.

51. Jerry Wizig, "What's New? UH, That's Who," *Houston Chronicle*, 14 November 1965, sec. 6, p. 1; Frank Schultz, Jr., "Cougars Bury Kentucky Hopes," *The Daily Cougar*, 16 November 1965, p. 1.

52. Jerry Wizig, "Cougars Beat Ole Miss at Last, 17–3," *Houston Chronicle*, 7 November 1965, sec. 6, p. 1.

53. John Hollis, "McVea-Led Cougars Stun Ole Miss, 17–3," *Houston Post*, 7 November 1965, sec. 1, p. 1; David Fink, "'We Knew He'd Get Loose Sometime — but Why Tonight?'" *Houston Post,* 7 November 1965, sec. 4, p. 8.

54. The southern states so identified football as part of their cultural heritage that the Alabama Governor Lurleen Wallace, wife of George Wallace, decreed in 1967 that the "Confederate flag will wave again and the bands will play "Dixie" at college football games in Alabama." "'Bama Football Adorned by 3 Flags, 3 Anthems," 16 September 1967.

55. Tom Beer to Katherine Lopez, Desegregation Questionnaire, summer 2006, author's collection; Pat Pryor to Katherine Lopez, 21 March 2007, author's collection.

56. Yeoman recalled the incident, saying, "I told the little girl at the [hotel] desk to leave the phones turned off there until after 10 o'clock. She left the phones with our black kids open and they were called up by the KKK." William Yeoman, interview by author, tape recording, Houston, TX, 12 September 2006.

57. Dick Woodall, interview by author, digital recording, Houston, TX, 10 August 2006.

58. Tom Beer to Katherine Lopez, letter, Summer 2006, author's collection.

59. William Yeoman, interview by author, tape recording, Houston, TX, 12 September 2006.

60. Michael Spratt to Katherine Lopez, Desegregation Questionnaire, Summer 2006, author's collection.

61. Nick Curran, "The Game Breaker," *The Football News*, 30 September 1967, p. 10.

62. After one particularly bad game, the white fans embraced the star white athlete and said to the surrounding press, "'Here's our McVea.'" Unsigned, "No Trouble with Footing in Dome," *Houston Chronicle*, 19 September 1965, sec. 7, p. 8.

63. Jerry Wizig, "Cougars Tie Fla. State," *Houston Chronicle*, 21 November 1965, sec. 6, p. 1.

64. Jerry Wizig, "Cougars Meat Ole Miss

At Last, 17–3," *Houston Chronicle*, 7 November 1965, sec. 6, p. 1.

65. In addition to playing teams such as Ole Miss, Kentucky, and Mississippi State at home, McVea had to play on the road against Tennessee. He became the first African American athlete to play on any field in the Southeastern Conference.

66. R. Curtis Newberry II, "As a Matter of Fact," *The Daily Cougar*, 18 November 1965, p. 7.

67. Frank Schultz, Jr., "Frankly Speaking," *The Daily Cougar*, 9 December 1965, p. 6.

68. John Hollis, "Bigger Feet in UH Basketball Shoes," *Houston Post*, 21 November 1965, sec. 4, p. 8.

69. Rich Burk, "Cage Opener Nears," *Daily Cougar*, 23 November 1965, p. 8.

70. Jerry Wizig, "Cougar Cagers Set for Drills," *Houston Chronicle*, 11 October 1965, sec.2, p. 3.

71 John Hollis, "Lewis Home for 1st Cage Drill," *Houston Post*, 13 October 1965, sec.4, p. 2.

72. Jack Agness, "UH, Rice Cage on KPRC," *Houston Post*, 30 November 1965, sec.4, p. 2.

73. John Hollis, "UH Cagers Open in San Francisco," *Houston Post*, 29 November 1965, sec. 4, p. 6.

74. John Hollis, "Bigger Feet in UH Basketball Shoes," *Houston Post*, 21 November 1965, sec. 4, p. 8.

75. Bill Russell played basketball at the University of San Francisco and went on to great success in the NBA. His two memoirs, *Second Wind* and *Go Up for Glory*, recount his collegiate and professional experiences and the race issues he encountered.

76. John Hollis, "Lewis Sees Some Sunshine in UH Loss to SF," *Houston Post*, 3 December 1965, sec. 4.

77. John Hollis, "Bruised Cougars Head for Home," *Houston Post*, 6 December 1965, sec. 4, p. 3.

78. John Hollis, "UH Planning Big Changes," *Houston Post*, 8 December 1965, sec. 4, p. 5.

79. Jerry Wizig, "Aggies Rally to Top Coogs," *Houston Chronicle*, 10 December 1965, sec.6, p. 2.

80. John Hollis, "Bruised Cougars Head for Home," *Houston Post*, 6 December 1965, sec. 4, p. 3.

81. Jerry Wizig, "Lewis Aims Cougars on

Positive Approach," *Houston Chronicle*, 7 December 1965, sec. 4, p. 5.

82. John Hollis, "Home Sweet Home for UH Against Wisconsin," *Houston Post*, 11 December 1965, sec. 4, p. 1.

83. Historians have argued that the mental discipline required to succeed in sports prepared these pioneering athletes for the hostile situations they encountered in society. Hayes, *Big E*, 29. See Patrick B. Miller and David K. Wiggins, eds., *Sport and the Color Line: Black Athletes and Race Relations in 20th Century America* (New York: Routledge, 2004).

84. David Fink, "First 3 Negro Athletes at UH Started an Era of Greatness," *Houston Post*, 10 March 1968, sec. 10, p. 12.

85. "UH Fall, 75–67," *Houston Chronicle*, 2 December 1965, sec. 4, p. 2.

86. Frank Schultz, Jr., "Cagers Seek Initial Road Victory," *The Daily Cougar*, 3 December 1965, p. 3.

87. Guy V. Lewis, interview by author, tape recording, Houston, TX, 28 August, 2006.

88. John Hollis, "UH Gets First Win, Outshoots Wisconsin," *Houston Post*, 12 December 1965, sec. 6, p. 1.

89. Jerry Wizig, "Cougars Rip Wisconsin," *Houston Chronicle*, 12 December 1965, sec. 7, p. 1.

90. Frank Schultz, Jr., "UH Beats Badgers," *Daily Cougar*, 12 December 1965, p. 6.

91. John Hollis, "Boom-Boom Cougars Explode, Friars Fall," *Houston Post*, 21 December 1965, sec. 4, p. 1.

92. Rich Burk, "Hayes Leads Cagers to Easy Win," *Daily Cougar*, 15 February 1966, p. 7.

93. Jane Whitaker, ed., *Houstonian '66*, vol. 32, p. 164.

94. John Hollis, "UH Gets First Win, Outshoots Wisconsin," *Houston Post*, 12 December 1965, sec. 6, p. 1.

95. Jerry Wizig, "Christmas Comes Early at UH," *Houston Chronicle*, 21 December 1965, sec. 3 p. 1.

96. Curry Kirkpatrick, "Elvin, Melvin, and the Duck," *Sports Illustrated*, 2 January 1967, 42–43.

97. Even in this point, the author inaccurately identified the origins of Hayes's nickname. It did not, in fact, stem from Robertson's nickname but was assigned by a member of the Houston press after a famed Texas battleship. Ibid.

98. Rich Burk, "All in the Game," *Daily Cougar*, 17 February 1966, p. 6.

99. There was one report of a set to between Hayes and a member of the press but as the source is questionable, the event has not been included in the main text. As the report stated, Hayes responded to reporter who called him boy: "Boy's on Tarzan. Boy Plays on Tarzan. I'm no boy. I'm 22 years old. I worked hard to become a man. I don't call you boy." Jack Olson, "The Black Athlete: A Shameful Story, Pt. 1," *Sports Illustrated,* 1 July 1968, 20.

100. Frank Fitzpatrick, *And the Walls Came Tumbling Down: the Basketball Game that Changed American Sports* (Lincoln: University of Nebraska Press, 2000).

101. Other desegregated programs would encounter similar situations while traveling through the South and, in some instances, white players would refuse to visit segregated establishments. Patrick B. Miller and David K. Wiggins, eds. *Sport and the Color Line* (New York: Routledge, 2004).

102. Guy V. Lewis, interview by author, tape recording, Houston, TX, 28 August 2006.

103. Howard Lorch, interview by author, digital recording, Houston, TX, 1 July 2006.

104. See Patrick B. Miller and David K. Wiggins, eds., *Sport and the Color Line* (New York: Routledge, 2004).

105. David Fink, "First 3 Negro Athletes at UH Started an Era of Greatness," *Houston Post,* 10 March 1968, sec. 10, p. 12.

106. The Cougar ball club despite being treated as a lesser program defeated A&M in the Bluebonnet Classic 90–85 and TCU 132–102 that same season.

107. Alexander Wolff, "Ground Breakers," *Sports Illustrated,* 7 November 2005, p. 60.

108. Fred Sanner, "The Double Take," *The Austin American,* 1 February 1966, p. 23.

109. The article also insulted Texas Western, which went on to win the NCAA title that year with five black starters, saying, "If Houston is an outlaw, [it] is even lower on the scholastic scale. There are those who have claimed that some of the scoring averages at [the school] are higher than their respective intelligence quotients." Fred Sanner, "The Double Take," *The Austin American,* 1 February 1966, p. 23.

110. John Hollis, "UH on Last Trek to A&M," *Houston Post,* 9 December 1965, sec. 7, p. 1; Jerry Wizig, "No Santa at Sugar Bowl Meet, Lewis Warns Coogs," *Houston Chronicle,* 23 December 1965, sec. 4, p. 1.

111. Mike Ferguson, "No UH Comment on Cash," *Houston Post,* 3 February 1966, sec. 6, p. 1.

112. Hayes, *Big E,* 47.

113. Ibid, 47.

114. Other college campuses, including Texas Western University, did experience racial protests led by athletes. See David K. Wiggins, *Glory Bound* (Syracuse: Syracuse University Press, 1997).

115. Edward Walsh, "The Long Road From His Backyard is Just a Part of Elvin's Dream," *Houston Chronicle,* 28 January 1968, sec. 2, p.1.

116. Hayes and wife Erna, also a student at the university, married and had a son, Elvin Hayes, Jr.

Chapter 7

1. Tim Fleck, "Grid Predictions Sour for Cougars," *Daily Cougar,* 7 September 1967, p. 20.

2. The Playboy College Bureau had high praise for the Cougar star: "We can't begin to tell you how impressed we all were with Warren. He certainly is a real gentleman and handled himself with a great deal of poise throughout his entire stay. We would appreciate it if you could tell Coach Yeoman that he can be very proud of Warren." Letter from Brice Draper to Ted Nance, 18 May 1967, Warren McVea folder, University of Houston Athletic Archives, University of Houston Sports Information Department.

3. Tim Fleck, "Gipson, McVea Lead UH to 33–13 Win Over FSU," *Daily Cougar,* 19 September 1967, p. 6.

4. "Cougar Dressing Room Jubilant Following Win," *Daily Cougar,* 7 November 1967, p. 8.

5. Jeff Young, "Coog Fans Cry 'We're No. One,'" *Daily Cougar,* 27 September 1967, p. 7; "Sweet Taste of Victory," *Daily Cougar,* 26 September 1967, p. 2.

6. Jesse Miller, "Cougars Reap the Spoils," *Houston Chronicle,* 26 September 1967, sec. 6, p. 1.

7. Tim Fleck, "Extra Points," *Daily Cougar,* 29 September 1967, p. 6.

8. "Press Honors Heaped upon UH Gridders," *Daily Cougar,* 28 September 1967, p. 6. Tim Fleck, "Extra Points," *Daily Cougar,* 28 September 1967, p. 7.

9. "Houston Heads New Look on College Football Front," *San Antonio Light,* 25

September 1967, p. 14; Tim Fleck, "UH Stuns Third-Ranked MSU, 37–7," *Daily Cougar*, 26 September 1967, p. 6; "Houston Humbles Spartans, 37–7," *San Antonio Light*, 24 September 1967, sec. B1.

10. Dan Jenkins, "The Spartans Get Stabbed by Mac the Knife," *Sports Illustrated*, 2 October 1967. See also Dick Peebles, "New Grid Season," *Houston Chronicle*, 14 September 1967, sec. 3, p. 1; Dick Peebles, "Cougars Lash Michigan State in 37–7 Upset," *Houston Chronicle*, 24 September 1967, sec. 1, p. 1; Dan Cook, "Cougars Aiming for Top Against MSU," *San Antonio Express*, 23 September 1967, sec. C1; Johnny Janes, "'Don't Quote Me,'" *San Antonio Express*, 29 September 1967, sec. B1.

11. The entire quote read, "The Cougars have our boy, Warren McVea, on their side and ... that adds up to nothing but trouble for [opponents]." Johnny Janes, "'Don't Quote Me,'" *San Antonio Express*, 15 September 1967, sec. F1.

12. Dan Cook, "McVea Paces Cougar Upset," *San Antonio Express*, 24 September 1967, sec. S1.

13. Tim Fleck, "Extra Points," *Daily Cougar*, 30 November 1967, p. 6.

14. Tim Fleck, "Extra Points," *Daily Cougar*, 28 September 1967, p. 7.

15. Tim Fleck, "Extra Points," *Daily Cougar*, 22 September 1967, p. 6.

16. "McVea Goal May Mean U of H Success," *San Antonio Light*, 8 September 1967, sec. A15.

17. David Fink, "McVea is on Spot Saturday," 20 September 1967, sec. 4, p. 1.

18. This seems like a strange point to emphasize since the most powerful fear regarding black men was their sexuality. Dan Jenkins, "The Spartans Get Stabbed," Jerry Wizig, "Spartans 'Blew' a Chance," *Houston Chronicle*, 25 September 1965, sec. 2, p. 1.

19. "Warren McVea Lives as He Runs-Fast," *San Antonio Light*, 28 September 1967, p. 26.

20. Jerry Wizig, "Tiniest Cougar Wanted Beaumont Championship," *Houston Chronicle*, 24 September 1967, sec. 6, p. 1.

21. Nick Curran, "The Game Breaker," *Football News*, 30 September 1967, p. 10.

22. John Hollis, "Two TD's and Tension Turned to Elation," *Houston Post*, 16 September 1967, sec. 4, p. 4.

23. Jerry Wizig, "Tiniest Cougar Wanted Beaumont Championship," *Houston Chronicle*, 24 September 1967, sec. 6, p. 1.

24. "Lofty Poll Rating Thrills Cougars," *San Antonio Light*, 26 September 1967, p. 23.

25. Warren McVea, interview by author, tape recording, Houston, TX, 15 September 2006.

26. "Hebert, Woodall Pace Houston Romp," *San Antonio Light*, 30 September 1967, sec. A9; Tim Fleck, "Sparks Fly as Cougars Blast Deacons, 50–6," *Daily Cougar*, 3 October 1967, p. 6.

27. Warren McVea, interview by author, tape recording, Houston, TX, 15 September 2006.

28. Jerry Wizig, "Coogs Revise Five Records," *Houston Chronicle*, 30 September 1967, sec. 1, p. 6; John Hollis, "Near Fight Shocked Fans," *Houston Post*, 30 September 1967, sec. 4, p. 4.

29. Mickey Herskowitz, "Mickey Herskowitz," *Houston Post*, 1 October 1967, sec. 2, p. 6.

30. John Hollis, "Near Fight Shocked Fans," *Houston Post*, 30 September 1967, sec. 4, p. 4.

31. The article went well beyond an overview of McVea as it also insinuated that Houston had paid McVea to join the program and his primary role on the team, and that of other black athletes, was only to entertain. It said of teams without African American athletes, "The team which does not have the brilliant Negro runner is about as exciting to watch as a clumsy baton twirler." Dan Jenkins, "You've Got to Have Some 'O,'" *Sports Illustrated*, 16 October 1967, p. 41–49.

32. Dick Peebles, "Cougars Chew Up Wake Forest, 50–6," *Houston Chronicle*, 30 September 1967, sec. 1, p. 6.

33. Dan Jenkins, "Football's Way Out Season," *Sports Illustrated*, 25 December 1967, vol. 27, no. 26, p 45.

34. The Cougars and NC State would go on to have a storied relationship. In what many consider the greatest upset in basketball history, NC State defeated the heavily favored Phi Slama Jama Cougar basketball team, which included Clyde Drexler and Hakeem Olajuwon, on a last second shot in the NCAA title game in 1983 and winning by a score of 54–52.

35. Tim Fleck, "Extra Points," *Daily Cougar*, 9 November 1967, p. 7.

36. Ken Gibson, "Letter to the Editor," *Daily Cougar*, 5 October 1967, p. 2.

37. The insult directed toward the school is still thrown around to this day. Tim Fleck,

"Extra Points," *Daily Cougar*, 27 October 1967, p. 6.

38. Tim Fleck, "Extra Points," *Daily Cougar*, 9 November 1967, p. 7.

39. Tim Fleck, "Extra Points," *Daily Cougar*, 27 October 1967, p. 6.

40. Tim Fleck, "Cougars Ready for Bulldogs," *Daily Cougar*, 3 November 1967, p. 6.

41. Tim Fleck, "Dressing Room Reflects Post-Game Disbelief," *Daily Cougar*, 10 October 1967, p. 7.

42. Jerry Wizig, "Cougars Test Bounce," *Houston Chronicle*, 20 October 1967, sec. 8, p. 1; Nell Little, "From Just Outside the Locker Room: The Girl Who Came to Dinner," *Daily Cougar*, 27 September 1967, p. 6; Nell Little, "From Just Outside the Locker Room," *Daily Cougar*, 1 November 1967, p. 7.

43. Benaye Bryant, "Letter to the Editor," *Daily Cougar*, 8 November 1967, p. 2.

44. Tim Fleck, "Extra Points," *Daily Cougar*, 9 November 1967, p. 7.

45. "Articles Praise Coog Gridders," *Daily Cougar*, 6 October 1967, p. 12. Tim Fleck, "Magazine Write-Up On McVea Sarcastic," *Daily Cougar*, 13 October 1967, p. 6.

46. James Dunne, "Letter to the Editor," *Daily Cougar*, 4 October 1967, p. 2. This demand for McVea was viewed as inappropriate by some, "I have nothing against Warren McVea, in fact, I think he is a great football player, but after all, it's a coach's job to make decisions to win the game as he sees fit." Steve Clark, "Letter to the Editor," *Daily Cougar*, 10 November 1967, p. 2.

47. Bart Bueker, "Letter to the Editor," *Daily Cougar*, 8 November 1967, p. 2.

48. Dwight Allen, Jr., "Letter to the Editor," *Daily Cougar*, 1 November 1967, p. 2.

49. Harry Edwards led the Olympic Boycott in 1968 and encouraged all black athletes to skip out on the event. UH's athletes, including Elvin Hayes, refused to participate in the event.

50. Yeoman made an interesting comment about traveling into Mississippi in 1967. He pointed out that the integrated Cougar teams were starting to chip away at segregated athletics: "Several coaches made a point of telling us last week when we were there scouting that they were glad we were bringing over Negro players." Jerry Wizig, "State's D.D. 'Double Dynamite'?" *Houston Chronicle*, 19 October 1967, sec. 6, p. 2.

51. Tim Fleck, "Extra Points," *Daily Cougar*, 26 October 1967, p. 11; Wally Lewis, "Cougar-Bulldog Clash Marred by Incidents," *Daily Cougar*, 24 October 1967, p. 6.

52. Wally Lewis, "Cougar-Bulldog Clash Marred by Incidents," *Daily Cougar*, 24 October 1967, p. 6; Wallace Lewis, "Lewis Replies," *Daily Cougar*, 8 November 1967, p. 2; Little Nell, "From Just Outside the Locker Room," *Daily Cougar*, 25 October 1967, p. 6.

53. Tim Fleck, "Extra Points," *Daily Cougar*, 20 October 1967, p. 7.

54. Tim Fleck, "Cougar Power Converts MSU in 43–6 Rout," *Daily Cougar*, 24 October 1967, p. 1.

55. Tim Fleck, "Extra Points," *Daily Cougar*, 20 October 1967, p. 7.

56. The game was ultimately moved to Jackson, TN, where the Cougars lost to Ole Miss 40–7. That would not be the only time a game with Ole Miss was relocated as in 1966 the game took place in Memphis. McVea said the racial taunts he endured during that game were worse than any other he had endured. Interestingly, he told reporters that he received letters of apology from Ole Miss co-eds for the insults hurled at him. Dan Jenkins, "You've Got to Have Some 'O,'" *Sports Illustrated*, 16 October 1967, p. 49.

57. "Let's Miss Ole Miss," *Daily Cougar*, 2 October 1962, p. 5.

58. Preston Ivens, "Letters to the Editor," *Daily Cougar*, 9 October 1962, p. 2; Steve Kaura, ""Letters to the Editor," *Daily Cougar*, 9 October 1962, p. 2.

59. Hamp Mabry, "Letter to the Editor," *Daily Cougar*, 4 October 1962, pg 5. Bettye Laurer, "Letters to the Editor," *Daily Cougar*, 9 October 1962, p. 2.

60. Tim Fleck, "Extra Points," *Daily Cougar*, 26 October 1967, p. 11.

61. William Yeoman, interview by author, tape recording, Houston, TX, 12 September 2006.

62. "Florida State Commemorates 40th Anniversary of Racial Integration," 30 January 2004.

63. FSU integrated its football team in the fall of 1968 with Calvin Patterson. His career there ended disastrously as flunked off the team and committed suicide in the spring of 1972 during what would have been his senior year.

64. Pat Pryor to Katherine Lopez, email, 21 March 2007.

65. "Seniors Jubilant After Last Win," *Daily Cougar*, 21 November 1967, p. 7.

66. Dick Woodall, interview by author, digital recording, Houston, TX, 10 August 2006.

67. The American Football League was the rival league to the current National Football League. The two merged in 1970.

68. University of Houston Sports News Service From Ted Nance, Warren McVea folder, University of Houston Athletic Archives, University of Houston Sports Information Department.

Chapter 8

1. By 1967–68, Hayes had become the focal point of the team, and Chaney became one of the supporting cast rather than the star athlete. Although it would seem that such a situation would lead to resentment from a player so heralded coming out of high school, he did not vocalize any such sentiments. He once said of the situation, "Playing with Elvin forced me to make adjustments to my game that really helped me later in the NBA. He was our big scorer, so I made a commitment to play defense.... We were very effective." Eddie Einhorn, *How March Became Madness* (Chicago: Triumph Books, 2006), 82.

2. Oddly enough, that perception of the Cougars has returned to a degree. Guy Lewis, despite his incredible achievements with the team and the impressive number of NCAA appearances he has accumulated, is not considered in the same league as the greats such as Wooten and Rupp. He has yet to receive an induction into the basketball Hall of Fame as year after year he is overlooked by the selection committee.

3. Texas Western had defeated the University of Kentucky in 1966 but that win did not have the same impact as Houston's rise to ascendancy for two reasons. One, El Paso is not really considered part of the South but of the West. Two, the school did not establish a lasting reputation among the basketball culture. The team won and then faded away and no one had to deal with the racial challenges it brought with it. Houston, on the other hand, did not leave the scene. The Cougars challenged the racial standard and forced other institutions to deal with it.

4. A baseball has a circumference of 9" while a NCAA basketball has a 30" circumference.

5. CBS televised the game and network affiliates as far away as Anchorage, Alaska carried the game.

6. William Gildea, "Alcindor Leads UCLA in Showdown Tonight," *Washington Post*, 20 January 1968, sec. D1. David Fink, "55,000 Due to See What Lew Can Do," *Houston Post*, 20 January 1968, sec. 4, p. 1.

7. "Cougars-Bruins Ready for Dome Showdown," *The Informer and Texas Freeman*, 20 January 1968, p. 11; Mack Smith, "Is UCLA Unbeatable?" *The Daily Cougar*, 12 January 1968, p. 7.

8. *Time*, 12 January 1968, 26.

9. In another article, St. John misidentified Hayes's hometown and wrote that he had trouble with Houston's system of basketball despite Hayes's proven ability to lead the team even when it struggled during the first varsity season. Bob St. John, "It's Big E vs. Lew Tonight," Dallas *Morning News*, 20 January 1968, sec. B1. Bob St. John, "Easy Come Easy Go," Dallas *Morning News*, 20 January 1968, sec. B2.

10. Jerry Wizig, "Is It 'The Game of the Century'?" *Houston Chronicle*, 19 January 1968, sec. 7, p. 1.

11. Karl O'Quinn, "Morning Line," *San Antonio Express*, 20 January 1968, sec. D1.

12. Fans remarked of the view from the upper seats, "It looks like you're up in an airplane.... The court looks like you can hold it in your hand, but I can follow the action well with field glasses. Without the glasses, the players look like ants." "Players Look like Ants without Field Glasses," *UPI report*, 20 January 1968. Joe Jares, "A Dandy in the Dome," *Sports Illustrated*, 29 January 1968, 16.

13. The State Department had taken the Cougars on a tour through South American during the summer of 1967, and the team was treated like celebrities. The Information Agency distributes information on American culture and life to promote understanding between the US and other nations. Hayes said following the South American tour, "You would have thought we were the Beatles." William Gildea, "U. of Houston Enjoys Top Billing," *Washington Post*, 21 January 1968, sec.C4.

14. The UPI report wrote of the scene, "The crowd went wild at the end, mobbing the Cougar team on the floor of the $31 million arena at the game's end and chanting 'We're Number 1.'" *Unsigned*, "'We're Number 1, We're Number 1.,'" *Houston Post*, 21 January 1968, sec. 1, p. 1. "Wow! Coogs Beat UCLA," *UPI report*, 21 January 1968, p. 9.

15. The broadcasting booth was dug down into the ground as to not obstruct the spectators' views. Eddie Einhorn, *How March Became Madness* (Chicago: Triumph Books, 2006).

16. Joe Jares, "A Dandy in the Dome," *Sports Illustrated*, 29 January 1968, 16.

17. Wells Twombly, "Gorgeous Revenge," *Houston Chronicle*, 21 January 1968, sec. 6, p. 5; *Houston Post* Headline, 21 January 1968, sec 1; Mickey Herskowitz, "Who's No. 1? Hayes, Houston, That's Who!," *Houston Post,* 21 January 1968, sec. 3.

18. David Fink, "Cougars Too Tired to Smile or Talk," *Houston Post,* 21 January 1968, sec 3; Gordon S. White, "Houston Won, but Issue is: Who's Really One?" *New York Times*, 22 January 1968, p. 39.

19. Tim Fleck, "Cougars Stand Alone at the Peak," *Daily Cougar*, 7 February 1968, p. 7.

20. Mickey Hershowitz, "Who's No. 1? Hayes, Houston, That's Who!," *Houston Post*, 21 January 1968, sec. 3, p. 1.

21. Ibid.

22. Little Nell, "From Just Outside the Locker Room," *Daily Cougar*, 8 February 1968, p. 7.

23. Joe McLaughlin, " 'Just Take It To 'em and Pray — Lewis,'" *Houston Chronicle,* 21 January 1968, sec. 6 p.6.

24. Wells Twombly, "Gorgeous Revenge," *Houston Chronicle*, 21 January 1968, sec. 6, p. 5; Mickey Herskowitz, "Who's No. 1? Hayes, Houston, That's Who!," *Houston Post,* 21 January 1968, sec. 3.

25. See David K. Wiggins, "Great Speed but Little Stamina," in *New American Sport History*, ed. S.W. Pope (Urbana: University of Illinois, 1997); Martin Kane, "An Assessment of Black Is Best," *Sports Illustrated*, 18 January 1971, pp. 72–83; Michael Govan, "The Emergence of the Black Athlete in America," *The Black Scholar*, November 1971, pp. 16–28; Harry Edwards, "The Sources of the Black Athlete's Superiority," *The Black Scholar*, November 1971, pp. 32–41.

26. Tim Fleck, "Cougars Stand Alone at the Peak," *Daily Cougar*, 7 February 1968, p. 7.

27. John Hollis, "Hayes' Mates Not Chokers," *Houston Post*, 21 January 1968, sec. 3, p. 3.

28. Spain had a tremendous career at Houston and played on the 1968 U.S. Olympic Basketball team which won the gold medal as well as with the American Basketball Association. Sadly, he passed away in 1990 of cancer. Joe McLaughlin, " 'Just Take It To 'em and Pray — Lewis,'" *Houston Chronicle,* 21 January 1968, sec. 6, p. 6.

29. Joe McLaughlin, "'Just Take It to 'em and Pray — Lewis,'" *Houston Chronicle,* 21 January 1968, sec. 6, p. 6.

30. David Fink, "Too Tired to Smile or Talk," *Houston Post,* 21 January 1968, sec. 3, p. 2; Bob St. John, "Hayes Leads UH Past Uclans, 71–69," *Dallas Morning News,* 21 January 1968, sec. B1.

31. Ibid.

32. Clark Nealon, "Post Time," *Houston Post*, 23 January 1968, sec. 4, p. 1.

33. "UH-UCLA Tilt Setting Unlike Any Other Game," *Daily Cougar,* 7 February 1968, p. 8.

34. Mickey Herskowitz, "Ken Spain: Setting 'em Up for Elvin," *Houston Post*, 10 March 1968, sec. 6, p. 2.

35. Jerry Wizig, "Cougars' Hayes Has 39 Points," *Houston Chronicle*, 21 January 1968, sec. 1, p. 1.

36. Article Vaughn, "Super Sports," *Forward Times,* 27 January 1968, p. 64.

37. "Tan Basketball Aces Changing Image and Tradition of Game," *The New Courier*, 3 February 1968, p. 15.

38. Article Vaughn, "Super Sports," *Forward Times*, 27 January 1968, p. 64.

39. "About the Cougars Head Man ... Guy," *Forward Times,* 20 January 1968, p. 62.

40. "Hayes Destroys Bruins, Gets 39 Points in 71–69 Win," *Dallas Express*, 27 January 1968, p. 11.

41. Patrick Miller and David Wiggins, *Sport and the Color Line* (New York: Routledge, 2004), 104.

42. Not everyone within the black community reacted so pleasantly to the rise of Chaney, Hayes, and their fellow black team mates. Ric Roberts, "Temporarily 'White,'" *The New Courier*, 20 January 1968, p. 15.

43. David Fink, "Era of Greatness," *Houston Post*, 10 March 1968, sec. 20, p. 12.

44. Ibid.

45. Chaney's roommate John Tracy reflected on the situation later and supposed that the black athletes were simply not cognizant of the tenseness of the situation they were in. He said, "When you're in your coming of age years .... [You] don't realize how pressurized or frightening the consequences ... could have been." John Tracy, interview by

author, tape recording, Los Angeles, CA, 15 November 2006.

46. In this editorial, Houston's reputation as an "independent operator" surfaced. As many within the Houston administration feared, the athletic world saw UH as an illegal program. In a strange twist, however, Houston no longer cared about others opinion because they were more significant than any other state programs. Mickey Herskowitz, "Editorial," *Houston Post*, 22 January 1968, sec. 4, p. 1.

47. Joe Drape, "Changing the Face of Texas Football," *New York Times*, 23 December 2005, D1.

48. Pat Pryor to Katherine Lopez, email, 21 March 2007.

49. Lou Maysel, "Top O' Morn," Austin *American Statesman*, 21 January 1968, sec. D1.

50. The Southeastern Conference integrated in 1966 when the University of Kentucky brought in Greg Page. The Southwest Conference desegregated when Southern Methodist University signed Jerry Levias in 1965, and Atlantic Conference schools switched over when Florida State, a frequent competitor of Houston, brought on Calvin Patterson in 1968.

51. An article in the *Times Picayune* read, "While Elvin Hayes could probably get elected mayor of Houston today if he wanted, he'll have to settle for outstanding amateur athlete of the year laurels in his home state of Louisiana." Unsigned, "Hayes Chosen Top Amateur in La.," *Times Picayune*, 22 January 1968, sec. 2, p. 8.

52. Sports writers also questioned the minimal level of press attention black athletes had received in the past. One wrote, "It makes you wonder how Houston found him (how did they even find Rayville?) and why more school's hadn't sought him." Karl O'Quinn, "Morning Line," *San Antonio Express*, 22 January 1968, sec. D1.

53. Edward Walsh, "The Long Road From His Backyard Is Just a Part of Elvin's Dream," *Houston Chronicle*, 28 January 1968, sec. 2, p. 1.

54. Hayes became the first Cougar athlete to have his jersey number retired in 1993.

55. David Fink, "Hayes, Chaney Make Final Home Appearance for UH," *Houston Post*, 2 March 1968, sec. 4, p. 1.

56. Linda Callaway, ed., *The Houstonian* vol. 34 (1968); 186.

57. "Say Hayes," *Time* 91, no. 4 (1968): 64.

58. Karl O'Quinn, "Morning Line," *San Antonio Express*, 25 September 1967, sec. D1. Another wrote following the Cougar's victory over Michigan State, "greybeards, wearing black armbands, are trying to remember when the [SWC] had its prestige so badly smeared as it did this past weekend." Dick Peebles, "Voice of the Peebles: Gentlemen's Agreement," *Houston Chronicle*, 25 September 1967, sec. 2, p. 1.

59. Associate Press, "Cougars Eye SWC Berth," *San Antonio Light*, 27 September 1967, p. 34.

Chapter 9

1. The '68 Olympic boycott did not happen as Harry Edwards and other black leaders had hoped. They still managed to make a statement, however, with the metal stand display of John Carlos and Tommie Smith.

2. Jack Olson, "The Black Athlete: A Shameful Story, Pt. 1," *Sports Illustrated*, 1 July 1968, p. 12.

3. The other three parts dealt with non–Houston related issues including the injustices within professional ranks, the educational inequalities at UTEP, and the impact of racism on team unity.

4. Jack Olson, "The Black Athlete: A Shameful Story, Pt. 1," *Sports Illustrated*, 1 July 1968, p. 20.

5. Ibid, 15.

6. Ibid, 15.

7. Hayes, *Big E*, 5.

8. Eddie Einhorn, *How March Became Madness* (Chicago: Triumph Books, 2006), 82. Lynn Eusan, a well-known black activist on the UH campus, was crowned homecoming queen in the fall of 1968. Sadly, she was murdered three years later under circumstances still uncertain. A park on campus is named in her honor.

9. Hayes's wife Erna Livingston Hayes graduated at the same time as her husband.

10. Hayes, *Big E*, p. 32.

11. Hal Lundgren, "The Outspoken Mr. Hayes," *Houston Chronicle*, 27 May 1971, sec. 4, p. 12.

12. Warren McVea, interview by author, tape recording, Houston, TX, 15 September 2006.

13. Ibid.

14. Jack Olson, "The Black Athlete: A Shameful Story, Pt. 2," *Sports Illustrated*, 8 July 1968, 29.

15. One reader referenced Hayes's desire to spend time with those with poor language skills in his letter to editor saying sarcastically, "[Whites] warned the black people of Rayville, LA, that there would be trouble if they tried to speak the language like their cultured, white neighbors. Yes, we did all that and now we feel guilty as [heck] about it." George White, "19th Hole: The Readers Take Over," *Sports Illustrated*, 15 July 1968, p 94.

16. Jack Olson, "The Black Athlete: A Shameful Story, Pt. 1," *Sports Illustrated*, 1 July 1968, 19.

17. Ibid, 27.

18. Ibid, 26.

19. Ibid, 26.

20. The rest of quote read, "He didn't want me to come in my uniform or in my jersey or anything like that, but just as an ordinary person that came over and sat at his table. I was really touched by that." Ibid, 26.

21. Ibid.

22. Dick Woodall, interview by author, digital recording, Houston, TX, 10 August 2006.

23. Jack Olson, "The Black Athlete: A Shameful Story, Pt. 1," *Sports Illustrated*, 8 July 1968, 23.

24. Ibid.

25. In one of my meetings with Hayes, he remarked that had it been 1964 he and I could not be socializing in such a manner without stares and comments from others.

26. Jack Olson, "The Black Athlete: A Shameful Story, Pt. 2," *Sports Illustrated*, 8 July 1968, 28.

27. Ibid, 26.

28. Fran Blinebury, "Lewis Suffering 'Great Injustice,'" *Houston Chronicle*, 18 December 1993, sec. B1.

29. Einhorn, *Madness*, 81.

30. David Fink, "First 3 Negro Athletes at UH Started an Era of Greatness," *Houston Post*, 10 March 1968, sec. 10, p. 10.

31. Warren McVea, interview by author, tape recording, Houston, TX, 15 September 2006.

32. The two men speak at least once a week and the only way to contact McVea is through Yeoman. Whenever the athletic department needs to speak with him, Yeoman acts as the go-between.

33. Jack Olson, "The Black Athlete: A Shameful Story, Pt. 1," *Sports Illustrated*, 1 July 1968, 23.

34. Jack Olson, "The Black Athlete: A Shameful Story, Pt. 2," *Sports Illustrated*, 8 July 1968, 29.

35. Jack Olson, "The Black Athlete: A Shameful Story, Pt. 1," *Sports Illustrated*, July 1968, 29.

36. Ibid, 27.

37. Pat Pryor also pointed out that these men, changed by their lives at Houston, took those progressive attitudes back home with them. He said, "Many of our players were from small towns in Deep East Texas ... where racial intolerance was preached from their pulpits. Four years of Coach Yeoman's discipline plus real up close and personal contact with persons of color had to soften those attitudes which were then returned to those same hamlets of hatred. Over time, hopefully, those tiny but geometric injections of reality had an impact outside of the field of sports." Pat Pryor to Katherine Lopez, email, 21 March 2007, author's collection.

38. A few of the letters sent to the magazine did criticize the journalism expressing frustration that the white population had once again been portrayed as the "Almighty White Man" at that the racial strides had been downgraded in such a manner. One wrote, "We must overcome 100 years or more of horrible neglect. Give us a chance, we can't make progress through this type of negative sensationalism." Al Rinaldi, "19th Hole: The Readers Take Over," *Sports Illustrated*, 22 July 1968, 72.

39. Brent Musberger, "19th Hole: The Readers Take Over," *Sports Illustrated*, 15 July 1968, 94.

40. Nathan El Lamm, "19th Hole: The Readers Take Over," *Sports Illustrated*, 22 July 1968, 71. Charles Bronz, "19th Hole: The Readers Take Over," *Sports Illustrated*, 15 July 1968, 94.

41. Neil Cohen, "19th Hole: The Readers Take Over," *Sports Illustrated*, 22 July 1968, 71.

42. Ibid., 72.

43. Don Haskins, *Glory Road* (New York: Hyperion, 2006), 196.

44. Jesse Owens was extremely vocal about his opposition to the mixing of the athletics and politics. He stated, "Politics shouldn't enter into the field of athletics, especially in the amateurs." George Minot, Jr., "Owens Fires Barb at New York AC," *The Washington Post*, 20 January 1968, sec. D3.

45. Among the areas of unrest were Grambling State where eighteen students were expelled from the university for pointing out

that "a poor black woman ... overweighs 60 footballers who have made the pros," and Cal State, where athletes called for the firing of three coaches for "an inability or unwillingness to relate to black athletes." Unsigned, "Campus Upheaval Blamed on them," *The New Courier*, 20 January 1968, p. 2; Dick Edwards, "Sports in the Amsterdam News," *New York Amsterdam News*, 20 January 1968, p. 29; Associated Press Report, "Cal Negroes May Boycott," 24 January 1968.

46. William Yeoman, interview by author, tape recording, Houston, TX, 12 September 2006.

47. The Committee was concerned that athletes would not complain out of fear of retaliation and took extreme measures to assure the athletes they would not suffer any repercussions for speaking their minds. Section Two-Committee Observations Committee to Study Special Problems of the Black Athletes at the University of Houston, 1969, President's Office Records, Courtesy of Special Collections, University of Houston Libraries.

48. Afro-American Demands Administrative Meeting, 1969, President's Office Records, Courtesy of Special Collections, University of Houston Libraries.

49. Michael Spratt, a member of the 1965 football team, agreed that financial gains and integration were linked. Michael Spratt to Katherine Lopez, Desegregation Questionnaire, Summer 2006, author's collection.

50. Even with the progress demonstrated at Houston, some southern institutions could not relinquish their white supremacy. For instance, the University of Texas boasted that it was the last all-white team to win a national championship in NCAA football in 1971. Although the squad had an African American athlete on the junior varsity team, the varsity squad remained all white until the 1972 season.

51. Sheryl Taylor, "A Conversation with Gene Locke," *The University of Houston Magazine*, spring 2007, 17.

52. Tom Beer to Katherine Lopez, letter, Summer 2006, author's collection.

Conclusion

1. Jeff D'Alessio, "Phi Slama Jama Part of Lewis' Legend," *The Sporting News*, available online at http://www.sportingnews.com/

archives/ncaa/lewis.html. Accessed January 12, 2007.

2. Only five other coaches have more appearances than Lewis: John Wooden (12), Dean Smith (10), Mike Krzyzewski (8), Adolph Rupp (6), Denny Crum (6).

3. In 2007, Lewis was a member of the inaugural class of the NCAA Collegiate Hall of Fame. The snub from the Basketball Hall of Fame continues. See, Mickey Herskowitz, "A Call From Hall Overdue for Lewis," *Houston Chronicle*, 22 March 2001, sec. 3, p. 1.

4. He was inducted to the UH Hall of Honor the same year as Sports Information Director Ted Nance.

5. Josh Gajewski, "The Changing Face of Cougar Football," *Daily Cougar*, 18 January 2000.

6. "UH at a Glance," http://uh.edu/uh_ glance/index.php?page=info, (accessed 1 March, 2007).

7. Tom Beer to Katherine Lopez, desegregation questionnaire, summer 2006, author's collection.

8. The Cougars did suffer a slight down turn in 1989 as they were once again placed on probation for a three year period under Coach Jack Pardee but that did not stop Houston from excelling as Andre Ware won the Heisman Trophy, the award given to the top athlete in the nation, in 1989.

9. The athlete enters the game only when a win is certain. The fans let the coach know when they feel confident that the game is won by chanting his name.

10. On the 2006 Cougar Football team 57.9 percent were African American, 36.8 percent were white, and 5.3 percent were of other origins. Author's statistics.

11. The program keeps former athletes under the control of the Athletic Department because the department sees these men and women as "a really important group of student athletes.... We still consider them our peers, our family." Chris Elliott, "Crossing the Finish Line," *The Daily Cougar*, 5 March 2007, p. 1.

12. At a game during the 2006 season, a white girlfriend of a black athlete was harassed by opposing fans because of the bi-racial relationship. The group of students taunted the girlfriend mercilessly until finally being escorted from the stadium.

13. In September of 2007, McNabb told the press that he, as a black quarterback, was held to tougher standards than his white counterparts.

14. In the past, some have argued that excessively highlighting the contributions of these three men would unfairly overshadow the contributions of all the other athletes that came through the doors of the athletic department. When the new UH basketball arena was completed in 1969, many fans and students wanted it to be named after Elvin Hayes as they believed it was "The House Elvin Built." Ultimately, the pro-Hayes contingency lost out, and the area was named after Judge Roy Hofheinz, an alum who devoted a significant amount to the fundraising campaign. As one alumnus described the decision to honor a donor rather than Hayes, "While not lessening [Hayes's] impact I do wonder about the appropriateness of concentrating in him all the honors due each and every Cougar athlete since 1946." Letter from Theodore Hendricks to Wally Lewis, *Daily Cougar Editor*, President's Office Records, Courtesy of Special Collections, University of Houston Libraries.

15. The only facility currently named after an athlete is the Carl Lewis Outdoor Track Facility. The Guy V. Lewis Court and the Bill Yeoman Indoor Field House celebrate the commitment of these coaches to the program.

Bibliography

Archival Collections

Athletic Archives, Sports Information Collection, University of Houston, Houston, TX.
Board of Regents Minutes, Special Collections, University of Houston, Houston, TX.
Patrick Nicholson Papers, Special Collections, University of Houston, Houston, TX.
President's Office Records, Special Collections, University of Houston, Houston, TX.

Oral History Interviews

Beer, Thomas (August 2006)
Grider, Gary (August 2006)
Hebert, Kenneth (August 2006)
Lentz, Leary Lee (August 2006)
Lewis, Guy V. (August 2006)
Lorch, Howard (July 2006)
McVea, Warren (September 2006)
Nance, Ted (October 2006)
Pryor, Pat (March 2007)
Spratt, Michael (August 2006)
Stotter, Richard (August 2006)
Tracy, John (November 2006)
West, Ronald (August 2006)
Woodall, Dick (August 2006)
Yeoman, William (September 2006)

Newspapers and Periodicals

Austin-American Statesman
Brownsville Herald
Chicago Tribune
Daily Cougar
Dallas Express
Dallas Morning News
Dallas Post
Ebony Magazine
Football News

Bibliography

Football Weekly
Galveston Daily News
Houston Chronicle
Houston Forward Times
Houston Informer
Houston Post
Los Angeles Times
New York Times
Pittsburgh Courier
San Antonio Light
San Antonio Express
Sports Illustrated
Time Magazine
Times Picayune
University of Houston Magazine
Washington Post

Books

Abdul-Jabbar, Kareem, and Peter Knobler. *Giant Steps.* New York: Bantam Books, 1983.

Adelson, Bruce. *Brushing Back Jim Crow: The Integration of Minor League Baseball in the American South.* Charlottesville: University Press of Virginia, 1999.

Ashe, Arthur, and Arnold Rampersad. *Days of Grace: A Memoir.* New York: Knopf, 1993.

_____, and _____. *Hard Road to Glory: A History of the African-American Athlete.* New York: Warner Books, 1988.

Baker, William. *Jesse Owens: An American Life.* New York: Free Press, 1986.

Barry, John. *Power Plays: Politics, Football, and Other Blood Sports.* Jackson: University Press of Mississippi, 2001.

Bass, Amy, ed. *In the Game: Race, Identity, and Sports in the 20th Century.* New York: Palgrave Macmillan, 2005.

_____. *Not the Triumph but the Struggle: The 1968 Olympics and the Making of the Black Athlete.* Minneapolis: University of Minnesota Press, 2002.

Behee, John. *Hail to the Victors! Black Athletes at the University of Michigan.* Michigan: Swenk-Tuttle Press, Inc., 1974.

Bloom, John, and Michael Willard. *Sports Matters: Race, Recreation, and Culture.* New York: New York University Press, 2002.

Bontemps, Arna. *Famous Negro Athletes.* New York: Dodd, Mead & Company, 1964.

Cady, Edwin. *The Big Game: College Sports and American Life.* Knoxville: University of Tennessee Press, 1978.

Carroll, John. *Fritz Pollard: Pioneer in Racial Advancement.* Urbana: University of Illinois Press, 1992.

_____. *The Struggle of the African American Athlete in the Early 20th Century.* Beaumont: Lamar University, 1990.

Chalk, Oceania. *Black College Sport.* New York: Dodd, Mead, 1976.

_____. *Pioneer of Black Sport: The Early Days of the Black Professional Athlete in Baseball, Basketball, Boxing, Football.* New York: Dodd, Mead, 1975.

Coakley, Jay. *Sport in Society.* St. Louis: Mosby, 1978.

Cohodas, Nadine. *The Band Played Dixie.* New York: Free Press, 1997.

Cole, Thomas. *No Color Is My Kind.* Austin: University of Texas Press, 1997.

Dunning, Eric. *Sport Histories: Figurational Studies in the Development of Modern Sport.* New York: Routledge, 2004.

Bibliography

Edwards, Harry. *The Revolt of the Black Athlete.* New York: Free Press, 1969.
_____. *The Sociology of Sport.* Homewood: Dorsey Press, 1973.
_____. *The Struggle That Must Be: An Autobiography.* New York: Macmillan, 1980.
Einhorn, Eddie. *How March Became Madness.* Chicago: Triumph Books, 2006.
Eisen, George, and David K. Wiggins, eds. *Ethnicity and Sport in North American History and Culture.* Westport: Greenwood Press, 1994.
Faulker, David. *Great Time Coming.* New York: Simon & Schuster, 1995.
Fitzpatrick, Frank. *And the Walls Came Tumbling Down.* Lincoln: University of Nebraska Press, 2000.
Foreman, Thomas. *Discrimination Against the Negro in American Athletics.* San Francisco: R and E Research Associates, 1975.
Gems, Gerald. *For Pride, Profit, and Patriarchy: Football and the Incorporation of American Cultural Values.* Lanham: Scarecrow Press, 2000.
George, Nelson. *Elevating the Game.* New York: Harper Collins, 1992.
Gilmore, Al-Tony. *Bad Nigger: The National Impact of Jack Johnson.* Port Washington: Kenniket Press, 1975.
Hayes, Elvin. *They Call Me the "Big E."* Englewood Cliffs, NJ: Prentice-Hall, 1978.
Henderson, E.B. *The Black Athlete: Emergence and Arrival.* International library of Negro life and history. New York: Publishers Company, 1968.
_____. *The Negro in Sports.* Washington: ASNLH, 1939.
Herskowitz, Mickey. *The Mickey Herskowitz Collection.* Dallas: Taylor Publishers, 1989.
Hoberman, John. *Darwin's Athletes: How Sport Has Damaged Black America and Preserved the Myth of Race.* Boston: Houghton Mifflin, 1997.
Hoose, Philip. *Necessities: Racial Barriers in American Sports.* New York: Random House, 1989.
Isaacs, Neil. *All the Moves: A History of College Basketball.* New York: Harper & Row, 1984.
Jarvie, Grant, ed. *Sport, Racism, and Ethnicity.* London: Falmer Press, 1991.
Jay, Kathryn. *More Than Just a Game: Sports in American Life Since 1945.* New York: Columbia University Press, 2004.
King, Richard, and Charles Springwood. *Beyond the Cheers: Race as Spectacle in College Sport.* Albany: State University of New York Press, 2001.
Kyle, Donald, and Gary Stark, ed. *Essays on Sport History and Sport Mythology.* College Station: University of Texas A&M Press, 1990.
Lamb, Chris. *Blackout: The Untold Story of Jackie Robinson's First Spring Training.* Lincoln: University of Nebraska Press, 2004.
Lapchick, Richard. *Broken Promises: Racism in American Sports.* New York: St. Martin's, 1984.
_____. *Smashing Barriers: Race and Sport in the New Millennium.* Lanham: Madison Books, 2001.
_____, ed. *Sport in Society: Equal Opportunity or Business as Usual?* Thousand Oaks: Sage Publications, 1996.
Levy, Alan. *Tackling Jim Crow: Racial Segregation in Professional Football.* Jefferson: McFarland, 2003.
McRae, Donald. *Heroes Without a Country: America's Betrayal of Joe Louis and Jesse Owens.* New York: ECCO, 2002.
Mead, Chris. *Champion: Joe Louis, Black Hero in White America.* New York: Charles Scribner's Sons, 1985.
Miller, Patrick, ed. *The Sporting World of the Modern South.* Urbana: University of Illinois Press, 2002.

Miller, Patrick, and David Wiggins. *Sport and the Color Line.* New York: Routledge, 2004.

_____. *The Unlevel Playing Field: A Documentary History of the African-American Experience in Sport.* Urbana: University of Illinois Press, 2003.

Moore, Robert III, ed. *The Quality and Quantity of Contact.* Lanham: University Press of America, 2002.

Nicholson, Patrick. *In Time.* Houston: Pacesetter Press, 1977.

Orr, Jack. *The Black Athlete.* New York: Lion Press, 1969.

Pennington, Richard. *Breaking the Ice.* Jefferson: McFarland, 1987.

Phillips, Murray, ed. *Deconstructing Sport History: A Postmodern Analysis.* Albany: State University of New York Press, 2006.

Preston, Morgan. *The Edge of Campus.* Fayetteville: University of Arkansas Press, 1990.

Roberts, Randy. *Jack Dempsey: The Manassa Mauler.* Baton Rouge: Louisiana State University Press, 1979.

_____. *Papa Jack: Jack Johnson and the Era of White Hopes.* New York: Free Press, 1983.

Roberts, Randy, and James Olson. *Winning Is the Only Thing.* Baltimore: Johns Hopkins University Press, 1989.

Ross, Charles, ed. *Outside the Lines: African Americans and the Integration of the National Football League.* New York: New York University Press, 1999.

_____. *Race and Sport: The Struggle for Equality On and Off the Field.* Jackson: University Press of Mississippi, 2004.

Ruck, Rob. *Sandlot Seasons: Sport in Black Pittsburgh.* Urbana: University of Illinois Press, 1987.

Russell, Bill, and Taylor Branch. *Second Wind.* New York: Random House, 1979.

_____, and _____. *Go Up for Glory.* New York: Coward, 1980.

Sailes, Gary, ed. *African Americans in Sport: Contemporary Themes.* New Brunswick: Transaction Publishers, 1998.

Sayle, Watterson. *College Football: History, Spectacle, Controversy.* Baltimore: Johns Hopkins University Press, 2000.

Scambler, Graham. *Sport and Society: History, Power, and Culture.* Maidenhead: Open University Press, 2005.

Scott, Simon. *Jackie Robinson and the Integration of Baseball.* Hoboken: Wiley & Sons, 2002.

Shropshire, Kenneth. *In Black and White.* New York: New York University Press, 1996.

Spence, Christopher. *The Skin I'm In: Racism, Sports, and Education.* Halifax: Fernwood Publishers, 2000.

Thomas, Ron. *They Cleared the Lane: The NBA's Black Pioneers.* Lincoln: University of Nebraska Press, 2002.

Thompson, Richard. *Race as Sport.* London: Oxford University Press, 1964.

Tygiel, Jules. *Baseball's Great Experiment: Jackie Robinson and His Legacy.* New York: Oxford University Press, 1983.

White, G. Edward. *Creating the National Pastime: Baseball Transforms Itself.* Princeton: Princeton University Press, 1996.

White, Terry, ed. *Blacks and Whites Meeting in America.* Jefferson: McFarland, 2003.

Wiggins, David. *Glory Bound.* Syracuse: Syracuse University Press, 1997.

Wizig, Jerry. *Eat 'Em Up Cougars.* Huntsville: Strode Press, 1977.

Bibliography

Articles

Davis, Timothy. "The Myth of Superspade: The Persistence of Racism in College Athletics." In *Sports and Inequality*, edited by Michael J. Cozzillo and Robert L. Hayman, Jr., 276–286. Durham: Carolina Academic Press, 2005.

Edwards, Harry. "The Sources of the Black Athlete's Superiority." *Black Scholar* (November 1971): 32–41.

Goldberg, Robert. "Racial Change on the Southern Periphery: The Case of San Antonio, Texas, 1960–1965." *Journal of Southern History* 49 (August 1983): 349–374.

Govan, Michael. "The Emergence of the Black Athlete in America." *Black Scholar* (November 1971): 16–28.

Grundy, Pamela. "A Special Type of Discipline." In *Sport and the Color Line*, edited by Patrick B. Miller and David K. Wiggins, 101–125. New York: Routledge, 2004.

Grundman, Adolph. "The Image of Intercollegiate Sports." In *Fractured Focus*, edited by Richard Lapchick, 77–84. Lexington: Lexington Books, 1986.

Lamb, Chris. "'I Never Want to Take Another Trip Like This One': Jackie Robinson's Journey to Integrate Baseball." *Journal of Sport History* 24 (Summer 1997): 177–188.

Lopez, Katherine. "Two Paths to Greatness." *The Houston Review of History and Culture* 3, no.1 (2005): 44–47

Marcello, Ronald. "The Integration of Intercollegiate Athletics in Texas: North Texas State College as a Test Case, 1956." *Journal of Sports History* 14 (Winter 1987): 255–281.

Martin, Charles. "Integrating New Year's Day: The Racial Politics of College Bowl Games in the American South." *Journal of Sports History* 24 (Fall 1997): 358–377.

_____. "Jim Crow in the Gymnasium." In *Sport and the Color Line*, edited by Patrick B. Miller and David K. Wiggins, 233–250. New York: Routledge, 2004.

Miller, Patrick. "The Manly, the Moral, and the Proficient: College Sport in the New South." In *The Sporting World of the Modern South*, edited by Patrick B. Miller, 17–51. Urbana: University of Illinois Press, 2002.

Sammons, Jeffery. "'Race' and Sport: A Critical, Historical Examination." *Journal of Sports History* 21 (Fall 1994): 203–278.

Schollaert, Paul, and Donald Hugh Smith. "Team Racial Composition and Sports Attendance." *The Sociological Quarterly*, 28 (1987): 71–87.

Smith, Thomas. "Civil Rights on the Gridiron: The Kennedy Administration and the Desegregation of the Washington Redskins." *Journal of Sports History* 14 (Summer 1987): 189–208.

Spivey, Donald. "The Black Athlete in Big-Time Intercollegiate Sports, 1941." *Phylon* 44 (Second Quarter): 116–125.

Wiggins, David. "Edwin Bancroft Henderson, African-American Athletes, and the Writing of Sports History." In *Sport and the Color Line*, edited by Patrick B. Miller and David K. Wiggins, 271–288. New York: Routledge Press, 2004.

_____. "From Plantation to Playing Field: Historical Writing of the Black Athlete in American Sport." *Research Quarterly for Exercise and Sport* 57 (1986): 105–106.

_____. "Great Speed but Little Stamina." In *New American Sport History*, edited by S.W. Pope, 158–185. Urbana: University of Illinois Press, 1997.

_____. "Prized Performers, But Frequently Overlooked Students: The Involvement of Black Athletes in Intercollegiate Sports on Predominately White University Campuses 1890–1972." *Research Quarterly for Exercise and Sport* 9 (June 1991): 164–177.

_____. "The Year of Awakenings: Black Athletes, Racial Unrest, and the Civil Rights Movement of 1968." *The International Journal of the History of Sport* 9 (August 1992).

Index